Single Malt

SPEYSIDE

LE MALT SCOTCH WHISKY

AIGELLACHIE DISTILLERY

IN CASK

ATURE **23**⅕ SINGLE MALT

23

itting stubbornly atop a rock in Speyside, our distillery
ses rare **WORM TUB** condensers to impart unusually
trong, *sulphury flavours* to its spirit.

₀: **67·KA23**

AGED YEARS

8145512010

ALEXANDER EDWARD   PETER J MACKIE

.ED AND BOTTLED IN SCOTLAND BY

RAIGELLACHIE DISTILLERY COMPANY

750ml

Single Malt

A Guide to the Whiskies of Scotland

Clay Risen

A Scott & Nix Edition

NEW YORK • LONDON

To Dad

Quercus

New York • London

© 2018 by Clay Risen and Scott & Nix, Inc.

Photography by Nathan Sayers.

First published in the United States by Quercus in 2018

ISBN 978-1-68144-107-8

Produced by
Scott & Nix, Inc.
150 West 28th Street, Suite 1900
New York, NY 10001
www.scottandnix.com
whisky@scottandnix.com

Distributed in the United States and Canada by
Hachette Book Group
1290 Avenue of the Americas
New York, NY 10104

Manufactured in China

10 9 8 7 6 5 4 3 2 1

www.quercus.com

Contents

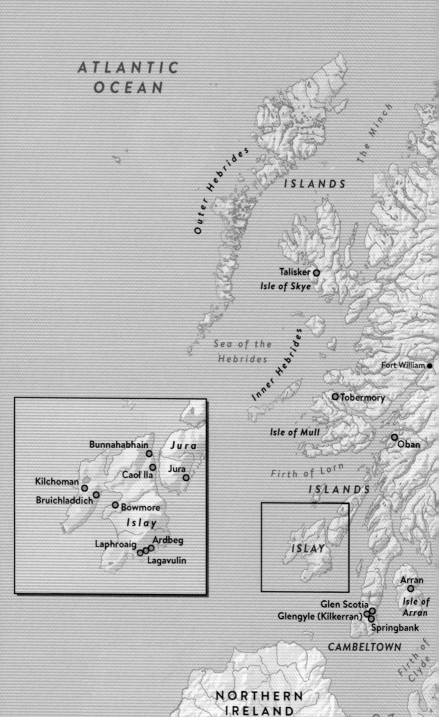

Malt Distilleries of Scotland

ATLANTIC
OCEAN

Outer Hebrides

ISLANDS

Talisker

Isle of Skye

The Minch

Sea of the Hebrides

Inner Hebrides

Fort William

Tobermory

Isle of Mull

Oban

Firth of Lorn

ISLANDS

Bunnahabhain

Jura

Caol Ila

Jura

Kilchoman

Bruichladdich

Bowmore

Islay

ISLAY

Laphroaig

Ardbeg

Lagavulin

Arran

Isle of Arran

Glen Scotia

Glengyle (Kilkerran)

Springbank

Firth of Clyde

CAMBELTOWN

NORTHERN
IRELAND

North Channel

ESTD 1846

BY APPOINTMENT TO HER MAJESTY QUEEN ELIZABETH II
SCOTCH WHISKY DISTILLERS JOHN DEWAR & SONS LTD
PERTH, SCOTLAND

ABERFELDY

HIGHLAND SINGLE MALT
SCOTCH WHISKY

GUARANTEED · **12** · YEARS IN OAK

Introduction

It is never a mistake to begin a book on spirits with a quotation from Kingsley Amis, the novelist and renowned boozehound, but it seems mandatory when the book's subject is whisky. For a man noted for his retrograde attitudes about women, class, and English politics, Amis was ahead of the curve in his love for single malt scotch. In the early 1980s, almost no one drank single malts; about 98 percent of all malt whisky produced in Scotland was mixed with lighter grain whisky to produce blended scotch. The world was in love with blends, but not Amis. "Only the finest French brandy, a Cognac or an Armagnac, could surpass" single malt scotch, he wrote in his 1983 book *Everyday Drinking*. "As far as I know, no formal comparison or competition has ever been undertaken, but from my experience, the malt is the winner."

Things certainly have changed in the decades since. Today the scotch business is booming, and while blends still account for the bulk of its sales by volume, virtually all the growth is in single malts—that is, the whiskies that are made by a single distillery, using only malted barley, yeast, and water, in a pot still. And while Scotland is the home of single malt scotch—and where, by British law and international agreement, it has to be made—global demand is so high that 80 percent of it is exported. Single malts can be found on bar shelves from Melbourne to Moscow, and not just the bestsellers like Glenfiddich and Glenlivet, but everything from Aberfeldy to Wolfburn. There is not, as of publication of this guide, a distillery beginning with the letter Z, but give it time.

And yet the scotch we know today is a relatively recent development; until the early nineteenth century, it was simply "whisky," and it was confined more or less to the northern and lower-class confines of Scotland. Heavily taxed, distillers produced most of their whisky using illegal stills. It was rarely barrel-aged, at least on purpose, and it was very often flavored with herbs and berries to soften its harsh edges. While exceptions abounded, it was only with a set of reforms in the 1820s, and the emergence of the blending industry in the mid-nineteenth century, that scotch emerged—first as a popular drink for "clubmen" in Edinburgh and London, and then as a major export to the far-flung corners of the British empire. Blending, to produce a smoother and lighter drink, was a necessary step to winning over brandy and claret drinkers, and later bourbon and rye drinkers, but it often robbed the spirit of its aggressive nobility. The clubmen of London had little interest in a challenging dram.

It took a century and a half for distillers and consumers to turn to the single malts that make up most of the component parts of a blend. Though "single" whiskies had been available in small quantities in Scotland, it was not until 1963 that Glenfiddich launched the first "single malt"—a whisky made entirely from malted barley, in a pot still, at a single distillery, and bottled and marketed as such. By the time Amis wrote his paean to single malts, many of today's leading brands—Glen Grant, Glenlivet, Macallan—had their own expressions and were selling globally. Glenlivet got in early on the American market, and today holds the number-one single malt title. Glen Grant took over Italy, and still dominates. Cardhu was and remains the most popular single malt in Spain.

Available today (in somewhat limited quantities) is a "replica" expression from Glenfiddich intended to mimic the profile of its original single malt from 1963—the very first official "single malt" on the market offered outiside of Scotland.

Yet for all its popularity, single malt scotch is a drink of contradictions. It is one of the world's most popular spirits, yet it is often derided as the drink of the elite. It is the definition of sophistication, yet its roots are with the half-wild Highlanders of northern Scotland. It is made from grain, water, and yeast, yet most of its flavor and all of its color come from a fourth source a drinker never sees: the cask. It is a straightforward, if not simple, spirit, yet its marketing and cachet have obscured its forthrightness and made it appear more intimidating than it should be.

The goal of this book is both to dispel the myths around single malt scotch and to provide a useful guide to new and experienced drinkers. While I hope readers worldwide will find it helpful, it is aimed at an American audience—the first single malt guide to do so. That means tasting notes that make sense to an American palate, and a focus on the whiskies available in the United States. While there are some expensive whiskies in this book, I have shied away from the truly exorbitant—if you are considering The Macallan 25 Year Old (average price $2,000), you either know enough to appreciate it, in which case you probably don't need my advice, or you have enough money that it doesn't matter, in which case you don't need my advice either.

This book, then, is for the rest of you. Which is to say, almost everyone.

Single Malt Scotch:
The Guide for the Perplexed

Simply put, scotch is whisky made in Scotland. By British law, in order to be called scotch, it has to be made from grain, water, and yeast and aged in an oak cask in Scotland for at least three years. Trace amounts of caramel can be added for color, but never flavor. "Scotch-style" whisky is the default for whisky distillation in most of the world; Japanese, Swedish, Australian, South African, and many other whiskies are all typically made according to similar basic principles (Irish, Canadian, and various American whisky styles are exceptions).

There are several subcategories of scotch. Malt whisky is made from malted barley alone; if any other grain is used, in combination with malted barley or not, it is called grain whisky. If you blend together malt whiskies from different distilleries, the result is blended malt whisky, or, in the case of grain, blended grain whisky. If you combine the two—malt whisky and grain whisky—you have blended whisky, the category that accounts for about 90 percent by volume of all whisky made in Scotland today.

If a whisky is made at a single distillery, it is known as either a single grain or a single malt. In short, a single malt scotch has to meet three primary rules:

- It must be made exclusively with malted barley, yeast, and water.

- It must be aged at least three years in an oak cask in Scotland.

- It must be made at a single distillery in Scotland.

There's one more rule worth noting, and that's the type of still used to make the spirit. Whisky made from corn, wheat, or other grains is usually made using a column still to distill a low-alcohol, fermented mash—beer, essentially—into high-alcohol liquor. The result is a lighter, if less flavorful, spirit. Malted barley is almost always distilled using a pot still, which is less efficient but produces more intense flavors. By law, single malt scotch has to be made in pot stills, but in practice distilleries don't need the legal pressure: Column stills don't work very well with pure malt. There are distilleries in every corner of Scotland, and on many of its islands, but they all adhere to the same basic rules—indeed, it's one of the beauties of scotch that out of these fairly strict standards, such a broad spectrum of flavors and aromas emerge.

Until the mid-twentieth century, almost all single malt scotch was made with barley that had been dried over a peat fire, since peat—semi-decomposed plant matter, cut into bricks and dried—is plentiful across Scotland, and traditionally was used as a domestic heat source. The drying grains absorb the peat smoke, so much so that some of its qualities remain even after mashing, distillation, and aging. Today peat isn't necessary, or especially efficient, but it has stuck around as a desirable, if divisive, source of aroma and flavor—depending on where the peat came from, described as smoky, "Band-Aid-y," meaty, rubbery, or brackish. Whiskies from Islay, an island off the southwest coast of Scotland, are prized for their "peat reek," but these days distilleries across the country produce peated expressions to take advantage of the escalating demand for smoky scotch.

Scotch was also traditionally aged in used sherry casks, the result of an influx during the nineteenth century of endless rivers of sherry from Spain for the British market. Since the casks were only used for shipping, importers had to find something to do with them. Fortunately, a used sherry cask, in which most of the intense wood notes have been pulled out, is the perfect vessel for long-term whisky aging. Over time, the residual sherry locked up in the cask would intermingle with the scotch, creating luscious notes of raisins, figs, and dark chocolate. Sherry was such a popular influence on scotch that as it lost favor among British drinkers through the twentieth century, distilleries got creative—today many buy their own casks and "lend" them to sherry makers, who fill them with sherry for a few years before emptying them and sending them back. And while about 90 percent of the casks in Scotland once held American whisky, today most distillers offer expressions that have been "finished"—that is, given an additional, shorter maturation period—in a cask that once contained sherry or another wine.

Aging

While all scotch has to sit in a cask for at least three years, the typical age is at least twelve years or so, and some are much older. Not all whisky is capable of supernumerary growth; every cask is a little different and sits in a slightly different part of the warehouse; these and many other factors influence whether a whisky is "ready" at ten years or can age for much longer (distillery staff check casks constantly, trying to decide if they are at their peak). Too young, and it will taste superficial and grainy; too old, and it will taste like wood chips. There is no right age for scotch, and older scotches aren't necessarily better, whatever your father-in-law tells you.

These days, even people with a passing familiarity with scotch will have heard of "non-age-statement" whisky. It is what it sounds like—rather than a 12 year old, or a 25 year old, it is given a fanciful name, like Speyburn Bradan Orach or Wolfburn Aurora. British law says that if you put an age statement on a whisky, the age has to reflect the youngest whisky in the bottle. So even if a distillery uses just a few drops from a 5-year-old cask in a batch dominated by 30-year-old casks, the whisky has to be labeled as a 5-year-old scotch. As distillery stocks get pressed by global demand, managers are looking for new ways to stretch what they have. Ditching age statements, which allows them to use younger whiskies without having to admit it on the label, is one answer.

Is this a good or a bad thing? Dropping age statements allows a distillery more room to play with their whiskies; in practice, it often means that distilleries are finding clever marketing strategies for selling spirits that would otherwise be rejected by consumers as too young. But it is certainly true that scotch drinkers have developed an unhealthy obsession with age; while a 12 year old will almost always be better than a 5 year old, I've had many 12 year olds that beat the same distillery's 16 year old, and many a 16 year old that beats a 20 year old. Helping drinkers move away from the assumption that age equals quality is a welcome step, whether a distillery benefits or not.

How Scotch Is Made

At its heart, scotch is distilled beer that's been left in an oak barrel for a few years. All the rest, as they say, is commentary—or, rather, details.

Let's begin with a common question: What is malted barley, anyway? Barley, of course, is a grain grown nearly everywhere in the world and used for a wide variety of foods, from breads to soups. At some point, people realized that dried and ground barley could be left to ferment in water, producing alcohol. Sometime later, inquisitive farmers also realized that they could get more, and more flavorful, alcohol out of a batch of barley if it were allowed to germinate slightly before being dried and ground up—in other words, if it were malted.

Over time, they developed a fairly standard method for malting barley. First, they would soak it with water, bringing the moisture content up to about 45 percent, and then spread it over a floor, where it would sit for a few days or more. Within a day or two, the barley would begin to sprout—tiny shoots at first, but growing by the day. At regular points, a distillery worker would come by and turn the bed of malting barley, to give every seed an equal chance to sprout. It took biochemists, centuries later, to explain what these early alcohol pioneers understood intuitively: Germination allows a barley seed to develop the enzymes it needs to convert its starch into glucose, maltose, and other sugars that yeast will later feed on to produce alcohol. Though the science behind malting only emerged in the 1800s, the process in its fundamentals has not changed for centuries.

The critical step, then and now, is to arrest the germination before a full-blown plant emerges and the starch is rapidly consumed by the growing shoot. The easiest way to do this is to dry it over a heat source. Today, this is usually done with indirect, natural-gas-fired kilns, though traditionally in Scotland, it was done over peat. The goal is to convert the plump, moist barley seeds into desiccated, chalky husks as quickly as possible; as one distiller told the writer R.J.S. McDowall, "When you can write your name on the wall with it, it's ready."

Today most malting, whether with peat or not, is carried out at separate, specialized malting houses, but until the mid-twentieth century, each distillery did its own. To ventilate the constant heat and fumes, distilleries had large, distinctive chimneys placed over their kilns. The characteristic "pagoda" design is still found across Scotland, even if these days they're almost always for show.

A Note (or Two, or Three) About Peat

If you've been to Scotland, you know that for all its forested beauty, it's also a country of vast treeless stretches, inhospitable to anyone looking to build a log fire. What it does have in abundance are thousands of square miles of peat bogs. Peat is composed of organic material (mostly plants) that has fallen into a wet, oxygen-deprived environment—a swamp or bog, usually—and as a result has decayed slowly, over hundreds of years. Some of Scotland's peat bogs are seven thousand years old and twenty-three feet deep. (Despite Scotland's long identification with peat, the stuff appears on every continent—the largest peat bog in the world is in the Hudson Bay Lowlands of Canada, covering some 27.4 million acres.)

Shown above is a selection of eight single malt whiskies known for their serious peatiness. This smoky, rubbery, kerosene, iodine-like quality comes from the malting process prior to distillation—before it fully germinates, barley is dried out with smoky fires fueled by blocks of peat. Many areas of Scotland are covered in large peat bogs with very little, if any, timber, and cut peat has been a source of fire for heating, cooking, and whisky-making for a very long time. Either you love it or you hate it, but it's hard to beat a peaty dram as an accompaniment to smoked fish and strong cheeses, or simply as a way to warm up a cold evening.

Peat is harvested in bricks with a small set of traditional tools, like the flaughter, a spade used to remove the top layer of soil, and the rutter, to measure and separate the bricks. (The whiskies in anCnoc's peated series on pages 70–72 take their names from these tools.) The top twenty inches or so of the soil, called the acrotelm, is what distillers are looking for. While there is occasionally some concern about overharvesting, estimates hold that at current rates, Scotland has enough peat for a few hundred years—and that's without the conservation efforts currently being put in place by responsible distillers and bog managers.

Because peat is composed of whatever plant matter fell into a bog, it is defined by its local ecology. Most of it is sphagnum, a large genus of mosses. Other components vary from region to region. On Islay, the peat is heavy with bog myrtle, lending it a sweet and bitter note. In the Orkney Islands, the peat has a lot of heather in it, giving it a lighter quality. This variation, even from bog to bog, creates an intriguing variable for distillers and source of *terroir*—the influence of local land, water, and climate—for their whiskies.

The peat character of a whisky is described as its phenolic content—phenolics being the group of compounds, like phenol and cresol, that give it that smoky, rubbery, dank smell and taste. Distilleries and single malt fans will often refer to a whisky's "ppm," or phenol parts per million, a rough measurement of its peatiness. But beware: Ppm is measured in the malted barley, not in the distilled spirit, and certainly not in the final product. Along the way, through distillation and barreling, phenolics are lost, whether through evaporation, absorption into the wood, or decomposition during the decade or more that a whisky sits in a barrel. While a high ppm level usually guarantees a smoky aged whisky, it's not a one-to-one relationship, and two distilleries that use the same ppm level in their malt, even from the same maltster, will—through their different distilling and aging programs—produce two whiskies with different levels of smokiness.

Whisky Is Born as Beer

Once the grain is malted, it is sifted through a filter to remove the loose, dried shoots, called culm, as well as any stray items like small stones or sticks that might have come through. It is then milled, with each batch split into three levels of fineness: husks, middles (i.e., roughly ground), and flour, at a ratio of about 70/20/10. The mix is important: If it's all ground to fine flour, adding water will turn it into dough; if it's left as husks, a distiller will have a hard time getting much alcohol out of it. (Malt mills, by the way, are often beautiful and astoundingly dependable pieces of industrial equipment that distilleries use for decades, if not a century; one company, Porteus, made such dependable, long-lasting mills that it drove itself out of business.)

There's one final step before fermentation: mashing, by which a distiller induces the enzymes developed during malting to convert the starches into sugar, and to dissolve the sugars into water. The grain mix is thrown into what's called a mash tun; water is then added in three increasingly hotter iterations (called "first water," "second water," and "third water"). Each temperature brings out different sugars. Distillers will often take the last water and add it to the next batch of malt, as a way of jumpstarting the process (similar, by analogy, to the "sour mash" process used to make American whisky).

The sugar-rich water from the mash tun, called "wort," is then pumped into another large vessel, the washback. The solids left over in the tun are removed and often used as animal feed. Traditionally, washbacks are made from wood, often larch or Oregon pine, though today most of them are stainless steel (if you want to get a distiller talking, ask which is better, wood or metal washbacks).

Along the way the wort is cooled to a temperature more amenable to yeast propagation. In Scotland, distillers don't spend much time thinking about yeast, and even the old and large distilleries will use commercially available brewer's and distiller's yeast (to geek out: *Saccharomyces cerevisiae,* usually the so-called M strains). If you've spent a lot of time around bourbon distillers, this will strike you as strange; among American whisky makers, their yeast strains are often their most prized, most secretly guarded possessions, which they consider the source of a large amount of their flavor. In Scotland, yeast is simply about which strain can produce the most alcohol the fastest.

Once the yeast is added, it's time to wait while the single-celled microbes go about their business, eating the sugars and excreting alcohol. Yeast may be small, but it's not quiet; at its peak, fermentation produces both heat and gas bubbles, meaning that distillers (or, these days, electronic sensors) have to monitor it closely. Many washbacks are equipped with giant fans that cut through bubbles building up above the mash.

The length of fermentation varies by distiller, and scotch makers consider it a key variable in the production of their whisky: A shorter fermentation, up to fifty hours or so, will create a spirit with a nutty, earthy flavor; a longer fermentation, between seventy and one hundred hours, will produce fruity notes; somewhere in the middle yields grassy elements.

If you added hops to the resulting liquid, called wash, which will have an alcohol content somewhere in the high single digits, you'd have something like beer. To make whisky, though, there are a few more steps.

Distillation

Again, this is a fairly basic process, built around a basic idea. Water and alcohol evaporate at different temperatures; therefore, boiling the wash will release both, along with trace compounds called congeners, but at different times. An attentive distiller can collect both at different points in the process with the alcohol being, essentially, unaged whisky.

In Scotland, this is done using a traditional device known as a pot still. Though today's pot still is high-tech and extremely safe, a distiller from 150 years ago would recognize it, and could probably use it. It is basically a pot, placed over a heat source, with a conical top and a spout running out of it. The entire item is sealed tightly, save for various openings for loading and closing. As the wash boils, the vapor rises up the copper spout, called a neck, and then down toward a condenser, where it is converted back into liquid. Pot stills are overwhelmingly made of copper, in part because of its malleability and strength, and because copper interacts with and essentially absorbs most of the undesirable congeners and other impurities.

Though all pot stills work in this basic manner, each is a little different, and each can be used a little differently. Every distiller is following the same basic procedure, but each uses minute changes in the still to create a different spirit, in the same way that different guitarists will use the same basic musical instrument to create widely varied sounds. Some distillers will even swear by impurities or wear and tear on their stills; legends tell of distillers who have ordered new stills but demanded that the manufacturer re-create the old still's various dents and bulges, believing—probably not incorrectly—that these influence the flavor of their spirit. And every still will have a shape that reflects the sort of spirit a distiller wants to produce, going by evocative names like "plain," "ball," and "lamp glass."

Small variations, like the length of a still's neck, can have a great influence on a spirit, because they affect how much of the vapor interacts with copper. The more copper, the lighter the spirit, because the copper pulls out elements like sulfur that would otherwise give a spirit a meaty, creamy, oily character (not necessarily a bad thing, and several distilleries, like Macallan, Glenmorangie, and Mortlach, seek it out). Another variable is the condenser element: Traditionally, a "lyne arm" extending from the neck would hook into a spiral tube called a worm, which was then submerged in a pool or tub of water. In the past, that was a necessity; today, distillers can also use a heat exchanger called a "shell and tube," in which the vapor is passed through up to one hundred tubes that are in turn submerged in water. Sixteen distilleries, including Talisker, Springbank, and Mortlach, still use worm tub condensers, and not surprisingly also produce whiskies that bear evidence of strikingly little exposure to copper. Mortlach goes a step further and sprays cold water on its lyne arms, the better to speed up condensation even further and limit exposure to copper—not for nothing is the resulting meaty, sulfury whisky known as "the Beast of Dufftown."

Pot still distillation is actually a two-part process, usually with two different stills, the larger wash still and the smaller spirit still; some distilleries will set them in trios, one wash still for every two spirit stills. The first is a blunt tool, a first pass, designed to strip out obvious impurities and bring up the alcohol volume of the wash. The spirit still is then used to fine-tune the liquid, to give it the elegance and alcohol strength needed to spend three years or more in casks.

Distillation is a process of concentration, but it is also a process of elimination. A distiller does not want to use everything that comes off a still; some of it, like methanol and other alcohols, is toxic. Roughly speaking, a distiller only wants the "heart" of a batch, or run—the first third or so, called the heads, and the last third, the tails, will go back into the still for redistillation. Once the distiller has enough of the hearts, it's time to put it into casks.

Barreling

Scotch, whether single malt or not, must be aged for three years in an oak cask. The cask can be of any size, of any type of oak, and it can be new or used. Casks are almost always toasted—a flame is placed inside to soften the wood for shaping and to pull flavorful compounds to the surface. Today most of the wood for the casks, no matter their source or previous use, comes from American white oak, though Spanish and French oak are used, and even occasionally oak sourced from Hungary or Russia.

Casks come in various sizes, all of which have names and different uses:

Quarter Cask: 80 liters / 21 gallons

American Barrel: 195 liters / 52 gallons

Hogshead: 250 liters / 66 gallons

Port Pipe: 500 liters / 132 gallons

Sherry Butt: 500 liters /132 gallons

Hogsheads, pipes, and butts are traditionally used to age wine, sherry, Cognac, and other continental spirits; a pipe, though it holds the same volume as a butt, is rounder and squatter.

Until the early nineteenth century, cask aging was far from standard, and most Scots drank their whisky unaged. But cask aging tends to "sand down" the rough, fiery edges of new-make spirit, and as the scotch industry expanded, it became a necessary step to get into markets where softer spirits, like brandy, had dominated. Cask aging also adds complexity: The wood not only removes harsh chemical elements, but imparts its own compounds into the spirit, which add flavor on their own or combine in the spirit to generate entirely new flavors and aromas. Distillers will tell you off the top of their heads that cask aging imparts about two-thirds of a whisky's aroma and flavor; whether or not that's accurate, there's no doubt it's true in, well, spirit. The important thing is that most distilleries will produce just one kind of distillate, or new make; their portfolios will depend on varying the age and cask type to produce different flavor profiles and, thus, expressions of whisky.

Historically, because oak, and wood generally, were in relatively short supply in Scotland, distillers relied on casks brought from abroad. Early on, this meant casks used to bring in a variety of continental spirits and wines—Cognac, Armagnac, claret, port, sherry. But after the phylloxera bug decimated French vineyards in the mid-nineteenth century, sherry, from southern Spain, became the dominant spirit in Britain. The sherry arrived in Britain not in aging casks, but in shipping casks—the former were used repeatedly, and had little flavor to give to a new spirit, while the latter were usually freshly made, and so even in the short period of time spent in transit, the wood had a significant impact on the sherry, and absorbed a fair amount of it as well. When the sherry was dumped out and scotch dumped in, the result was a whisky redolent with sherry notes, in particular dried fruits and molasses.

Offered with no age statement, the Signet expression from Glenmorangie is a superb example of the distiller's art—made from rich "chocolate" malted barley and aged in both ex-bourbon and virgin oak casks.

But sherry is a wine whose time has long passed, and through the twentieth century, fewer sherry casks arrived on Britain's shores. Then, in the early 1980s, Spanish and European law changed to effectively ban the shipment of sherry in bulk, which rendered the shipping cask more or less extinct. So scotch distillers came up with an ingenious solution: Buy new casks, then "lend" them to sherry makers, know as "bodegas," for a few years. The bodegas would use the casks to store their sherry, then send the empty casks back to Scotland. (The aged sherry can't be sold as-is after that, having taken on too many strong wood flavors; it is often distilled into brandy or made into vinegar.)

The long-term decline of sherry also meant that drinkers were less accustomed to the thick, sweet flavor that a sherry barrel imparted to a whisky. And so, without making much of a fuss, scotch distillers after World War II began aging their whisky in used American bourbon barrels as well. It was a perfect match: According to post-Prohibition laws, most American whisky had to be aged in new oak barrels, which meant that the bourbon industry was suddenly throwing off thousands of used, but still useful, barrels. At the same time, scotch distillers understood that used barrels were perfect for their purposes: Malted barley is a gentle, subtle grain, one that new oak would overpower—but take a barrel that has been used once and, like a reused teabag, it will struggle to assert much influence over the spirit contained therein. That way, even after ten or twenty years, the spirit inside will retain its sharpness and nuance, and not be overtaken by aggressive oak notes from the used barrel.

Today, with the global renaissance in American-born brown spirits, scotch makers are less reticent about their reliance on American barrels (which is a good thing, since about 90 percent of barrels used to age scotch these days are ex-bourbon). In fact, many labels have, in recent years, begun touting "bourbon barrel-aged" as a key selling point— as if it were an innovation, instead of a decades-old practice. And, unlike in the United States, there is no legal limit on how often a scotch distillery can use a cask. According to the accepted terminology, a cask that has previously held, say, bourbon or sherry but never scotch is called a "first-fill;" if it has been used once or more for aging scotch, it's called a "refill." Once a cask has been used a few times and its flavors have been largely used up, distillers will occasionally "recondition" it, which is to say, re-toast and/or re-char the inside, to reinvigorate it. Still, re-charred casks are good for just one more use, maybe two—and even then, the better distilleries will avoid the practice altogether because, as Richard Paterson, the master distiller at Dalmore, says, re-charred casks "are like sad old men who have been fitted with pacemakers."

Once the whisky is in the cask, it is set in a warehouse to age. This can be a dunnage warehouse, in which everything is on one level, or a multistory rackhouse. Each has its advantages—in a dunnage warehouse, the casks mature at about the same rate, and in the same way; in a rackhouse, temperatures can fluctuate dramatically between low and high floors, which over many years produces whiskies that, even if made in the same way on the same day, will taste dramatically different.

Whether in a dunnage warehouse or a rackhouse, there the cask will sit—by law for at least three years, by practice for at least ten to twelve, and often significantly longer. The cask plays a three-part role: It absorbs compounds from the spirit, it imparts compounds into the spirit, and the various chemicals in both the liquid and the wood interact slowly over time to create new compounds. In the summer, the cask expands, soaking in the spirit; in the winter it contracts, squeezing it back out. One of the wonderful things about scotch is that this intricate chemical dance is still not entirely understood; it is, for now, alchemy.

When a distiller fills a cask, he or she has no idea when it will reach maturity; because both the wood and the liquid are organic products, each unique in subtle ways, only time will be able to tell when the whisky in a given cask is at its peak.

Cask management—the constant checking and adjustment of potentially thousands of casks—is one of the unsung skills of whisky making. Not all whiskies make it to ten years old; those that don't are usually added to blends or sold as non-age-statement single malts.

Finishing Touches

Despite the strict production guidelines to which they must adhere, single malts are still diverse. Some undergo a further aging known as "finishing"—having spent a decade or more in an ex-bourbon barrel, they'll spend an additional few months, or a few years, in a cask of a different type, say, one that once held Pedro Ximénez sherry or port or Bordeaux. Distillers are becoming more adventurous with their finishes; some have even begun to lend barrels to breweries for aging, taking them back afterward to put their whiskies through a "beer barrel finish."

Although single malts are supposed to be produced using only water, malted barley, and yeast, one other ingredient is allowed in trace amounts: spirit caramel, which is typically added to "color correct" a standard whisky from batch to batch (though it can be used to make a whisky darker, a quality many consumers believe indicates a richer flavor). The caramel is said to have no aroma or flavor and is used only for cosmetic purposes. Distillers also often chill filter their spirits—in other words, they drop the temperature rapidly, forcing solids suspended in the spirit to condense, which are then filtered out. Otherwise, if a whisky is below 92 proof or so, adding an ice cube or a dash of cold water will give it a cloudy appearance, which is, in the eyes of some drinkers, unappealing. (Until 1982, distillers were also allowed to add paxarette, a thick, sweet reduction of sherry and wine that was said to mimic the influence of sherry-barrel finishing.) Neither the use of caramel nor chill filtration have to be disclosed on a whisky's label, except in Germany.

Since at least the late nineteenth century, scotch whiskies, whether blends or single malts, have been released with age statements. Unlike a vintage date, which tells in which year something is produced, an age statement says how long a spirit sat in a cask. And unlike wine, once a spirit like whisky is removed from the cask, it stops aging and becomes more or less inert. It can be stored in a stainless-steel container or placed directly into a bottle for sale. Either way, all things being equal (a constant temperature and humidity, and limited direct light), a whisky will taste the same whether it's been in the bottle forty years or four days. It is, effectively, frozen in time, which is why collecting and sampling antique bottles can be so fun—they are snapshots of how a whisky tasted forty, sixty, or a hundred years ago.

Blending

Technically speaking, every cask of malt whisky produced by a distillery is a potential single malt; in practice, 90 percent of the whisky produced in Scotland goes into blends. Most distilleries produce single malts, but few of those produce only single malts—and that fact shapes the sorts of whiskies produced. A perfectly delicious blend may be composed of less-than-delicious components; as the whisky writer Dave Broom put it, "I've been in enough labs to know that malts which you wouldn't wish on your worst enemy—the insanely heavily sherried one which has been left to overcook, or that silky smoky sample from a refill cask—have been deliberately crafted in this way because that's the character that the blend needs."

Some scotch fans ignore them completely—and to be sure there are many, many bad blends (though there are also many, many blends, period—more than three thousand, according to one count). They agree with George Saintsbury, a turn-of-the-century *bon vivant* who wrote in his classic *Notes on a Cellar-Book* that "I have never cared, and do not to this day care, much for the advertised blends, which, for this or that reason the public likes, or thinks it likes." A few decades later, R.J.S. McDowall derided blends as the lowest common denominator in the drinking world, the Red Bull and vodka of its day. He wrote, "An industrial spirit, out of molasses or sawdust, detained for three years in a sherry cask, reduced to 30 under proof, poured into a glass and frothed up with soda water, makes as smooth a drink as the heart of a clubman desires."

The truth is that while there are many terrible blends, there are also many wonderful blends. Blending is an art; the ability to keep a final flavor profile in mind, and to work backward to select as many as several dozen component whiskies to make that profile, is nothing short of genius. And blenders aren't the only ones who blend; any master distiller with a large enough warehouse will inevitably mix and match barrels or various ages and flavor profiles from inside his warehouse, dumping them together to create a consistent product. Blenders do the same, just with whiskies from different distillers. This book is unconcerned with blends, but not because they aren't worth discussing—there are, simply put, too many of them to do the category justice.

A Brief History of Scotch

While the history of Scottish whisky making reaches into the distant past, scotch as we know it today is a recent invention—no older than bourbon or Canadian whisky, and younger than Irish whisky. The great spirits journalist Alfred Barnard, writing in the 1890s, speculated that the very word *whisky* had been invented within the preceding one hundred years, and that "it is within the last sixty years that this enormous home industry has existed as such."

Indeed, though many a Scotsman is loath to admit it, distilling came to Scotland via Ireland. How it got to Ireland is only broadly understood. Distillation emerged in China, and then the Middle East, at least two millennia ago, long before people knew anything about why it worked the way it did. By the ninth century AD Egyptian Arabs were using a predecessor of the alembic, a form of a pot still, to distill alcohol for medicinal purposes. The word alembic itself derives from the Greek word *ambix,* which means a vase with a small opening; the word changed into *al ambiq* in Arabic.

As Muslims extended their political control into Europe, their cultural and technological prowess came with them; as their power receded, they left behind, like flotsam on the beach, things like the alembic pot still. Some posit that St. Patrick brought distilling to Ireland in the fifth century AD, though given that Patrick was a holy figure in Britain but distilling remained unknown in England and Scotland for several hundred more years, it's not clear from where he might have gained this impressive skill. What is clear is that the Irish were distilling fermented grain long before the Scots, and that it was only in the late medieval period that the technology began to seep across the North Channel of the Irish Sea to the Kintyre Peninsula (later home of the Campbeltown whisky region) and the nearby island of Islay.

It's unknown when the Scots began distilling grains, but the earliest written evidence is from a 1495 mention in the royal finance records, known as the exchequer rolls, which noted "eight bolls of malt to Friar John Cor wherewith to make *aqua vitae*." The good friar's *aqua vitae*, made at Lindores Abbey, translates from Latin to "water of life." Across Europe, many of the local terms for a distilled alcoholic liquid reflect its similarity to water, whether it's vodka ("little water" in Russian) or *uisge beatha* ("water of life" in Celtic). *Uisge beatha* eventually transmuted into the word *whisky*, though it wasn't until much later that Scottish distillers began to age the liquid regularly in casks. (Some argue that "whisky" in fact comes from the old Irish words "ai" and "iske," which combined mean "water of waters"—an equally poetic description of the distilling process and its results.) In any event, the term *whisky*, applied uniformly to distillations of fermented grains, only emerged in the late eighteenth century. It was around then that Samuel Johnson wrote his famous dictionary, in which he noted, "'Usquebaugh' is an Irish and Erse word, which signifies the water of life. It is a compounded distilled spirit, being drawn on aromaticks, and the Irish sort is particularly distinguished for its pleasant and malt flavor. The highland sort is somewhat hotter, and by corruption in Scots English they call it Whisky."

For most Scottish drinkers, though, *uisge beatha* was unlike anything we'd consider whisky today. For one thing, it was unaged; the very concept of systematic aging in a wooden cask (or any other sort of cask) was foreign to them. Instead, they would mask the rough flavors and aromas of their drink with fruit juices and herbs (some people would refer to unflavored spirits as "plain malt"). Many historians consider *uisge beatha* a separate drink from whisky, even though the latter clearly evolved from the former.

Whatever one called it, and whatever the details of its consumption, whisky became a core part of Scottish identity. On the night before the Battle of Culloden, the climactic engagement of Prince Charles's eighteenth-century Jacobite Rising in Scotland, an Episcopal priest administered the Eucharist to the men with whisky and oat cakes.

Whisky was taxed early and often in its history. The first levy was imposed in 1644, to fund a royalist army against rebellious Highlanders. Levies were used as revenue sources, as a method to keep down excessive drinking, and—after Scotland and England joined in the Acts of Union of 1707 and the English put down the Jacobite Rising—as a tool to combat expressions of Scottish nationalism.

Taxes on whisky and regulations on distilling became so onerous, in fact, that most distillation occurred illegally. The regulations were intended merely to push whisky distillation by all but the largest distilleries north of the Highland Line, which to the English of the eighteenth century constituted the edge of civilization itself.

Up to the nineteenth century, whisky was likely high-octane moonshine. It was rarely consumed outside the Highlands, let alone Scotland. True, Robert Burns sang its praises in his poetry, but as Aeneas MacDonald noted, Burns was a drunkard of peasant stock, more likely to be enthralled with its effect, not its taste. In his memoirs, Winston Churchill wrote that "My father could never have drunk whisky except when shooting on a moor or in some very dull chilly place."

Whisky's status—indeed, the very meaning of "whisky"—began to change in 1823, with a set of laws designed to bring distillation into the open. Distilling was simply a way of life; like farmers everywhere, the Scottish made whisky in part because it was the most cost-efficient way to store their grain, at a time when poor transportation and rough terrain meant that a crop could go to rot before it got to market. Still, until 1823, distilling was banned on anything smaller than a 500-gallon still, an almost unobtainable level of output for all but the largest distilleries. The law eliminated that requirement and declared that distilling would henceforth be legal, as long as the owners paid a licensing fee.

George Smith, an enterprising distiller and businessman, was one of the first to buy a license for his distilling operation. He wasn't just trying to get the law off his back; he dreamed that scotch whisky consumption could break out of the

Highlands and challenge "civilized" tipples like claret and brandy. Smith and his distillery, which he called Glenlivet, were already well regarded, and known for producing a fine aged spirit—in 1822, King George IV paid a state visit to Scotland and sampled a glass of Smith's whisky.

At first, Smith's license generated animosity among his fellow distillers, who saw him as a sellout; it's said that Smith carried two loaded pistols with him at all times. But it didn't take long for others to see the wisdom of his move: In 1817 there were 108 licensed distilling operations in Scotland; eight years later there were 329 (though the count dropped to 243 by 1833). Many of the centers of illicit distilling before 1823, like the region around Glenlivet, became the early centers of the booming legal industry as well.

The modern scotch industry would not have taken off were it not for two mid-century innovations. The first was the perfection, in 1830, of the continuous still by a former excise tax officer named Aeneas Coffey. A graduate of Trinity College in Dublin, Coffey often faced violence while enforcing the tax law, receiving a fractured skull and a bayonet wound for his trouble. He stuck with the job until 1824, when he quit to open his own distillery. He also began to tinker with the traditional still design. A pot still necessarily works with batches; it is in that sense inefficient and, at the time, when stills were heated directly, quite dangerous. Coffey realized that a still that used steam to separate the alcohol in the wash from the water, with the wash poured into the top of a column and the steam rising from below, could solve both those problems—the steam could be produced away from the wash, making it safer, and the whole thing could operate continuously. Coffey wasn't the only person working on a continuous still design—by one count, he had six contemporaries working separately—but he perfected it, which is why, today, the device is alternately called the Coffey still (though others call it a patent or column still).

The Coffey still works especially well with corn, and corn was just then beginning to pour into Britain from the vast and growing breadbasket of the American plains. The resulting whisky was lighter, sweeter, and gentler than a Highland malt, and if it passed through a still a few times it became, essentially, pure ethanol—with vast industrial applications. (It also provided a popular base for gin.)

Almost immediately, cheap grain whisky from Coffey's stills began flooding the British and European markets ("grain" meaning whisky made from anything other than malted barley). Distilleries sprang up around the Lowlands to feed demand for this new style of drink. They were amazingly efficient: In 1850, 119 pot stills across Scotland made 18 million liters of whisky, while just thirteen patent stills produced 28 million liters annually. And they were huge: One still at Port Dundas was seventy feet tall and could churn out 2,270 liters a minute.

Then, in the late 1850s, a number of grocers, whisky brokers, and others with access to both Highland pot still malt whisky and Lowland column still grain whisky realized that by combining the two, they could produce a spirit with the advantages of both: the flavor and character of pot still whisky, combined with the lightness and smoothness of grain whisky. And it offered immediate, easy variety—a blender could buy a range of malt whiskies, then vary their percentages within a given blend to achieve different flavor profiles for different markets, and at different price points. (This is still the way things work; think of the wide variety of Johnnie Walker expressions.)

Blending was nothing short of a revolution. Within a few decades a new class of business tycoon, the whisky blender, had emerged—men like John Walker, John Dewar, and James Logan Mackie (who created White Horse). But overproduction, and the severe highs and lows it created for the industry's financial health, led to efforts to control it through coordination and, eventually, consolidation. In 1877, six Lowland grain distilleries representing 75 percent of all grain whisky distilling capacity came together to form the

Distilling Company, Ltd. (DCL)—a giant in its day, and still one now, in its descendant form as Diageo plc.

Even after DCL emerged on the scene, the market continued to expand rapidly. And the demand was there, for a while. In the 1860s and 1870s, the phylloxera aphid, which devours grape vines, nearly wiped out the French wine industry, cutting off the steady flow to Britain of brandy and claret, a nineteenth-century Englishman's two favorite drinks. Blended scotch was there to step into the hole; marketers at the time consciously positioned it as a replacement for brandy, and even for red wine when the whisky was aged in used sherry or port barrels.

The global market opened up as well. The second half of the nineteenth century was the peak of the British Empire, and South Asia, South Africa, Australia, and other colonial holdings became the recipients of millions of gallons of whisky (not coincidentally, many of these modern nations, like India, Australia, and South Africa, now produce their own homegrown single malts and blends). The United States was a much smaller market, but even then, records show that wealthy Americans in particular liked to have a few cases of scotch in their cellars. An 1883 liquor store ad in the *Boston Globe* offered "fifteen year old scotch whiskey." In 1891, Andrew Carnegie, a Scottish immigrant, sent a case of scotch to President Benjamin Harrison. In 1895, the *Washington Post* commented on the growing popularity of "Glenlivet and Apollinaris," or sparkling water: "Bon vivants who knew the merit of our best American rye and bourbon whiskies, and disliked the 'smoky-peaty' flavor of the scotch whiskies, began to try them with various natural mineral and aerated waters as a substitute and now they are the fashionable drinks, not only at the clubs, but at many private tables." And in an 1898 slice-of-life report, the *Atlanta Constitution* wrote about a female doctor, Catherine Elliott, who walked into a bar and ordered a scotch, neat—"something which was too *fin de siècle* for the up-to-date men present."

Distillery owners struggled to keep pace. In 1894 DCL, which until then had made exclusively grain whisky, began producing single malt at its new Knockdhu distillery. Malt distilleries were typically self-contained, worlds unto themselves—not only did they malt their own grain, cooper their own casks, and maintain their own equipment, but they housed their workers and even sometimes provided on-site education for their children. And there were a lot of them: 161 distilleries dotted Scotland in 1898.

Almost everything these distilleries made went into blends; a few aficionados aside, drinking single malt whisky was practically unheard of, and distillers thought of themselves as strictly part of the supply chain, feeding the blending houses. Blenders, in turn, spent an increasing amount of their money on marketing; with so many blends, it was nearly impossible to distinguish one from another by quality or taste profile, so blenders invested in advertising. One house, Pattisons', trained 500 African grey parrots to shout its brand name, then gave the birds to retailers.

Eventually the crash came, and it hit hard. Blenders had overextended themselves, taking out enormously risky credit lines in the expectation that demand would continue to grow at unsustainable rates. The Pattison brothers were the first to collapse, and eventually went to jail for fraud. But they were only the most obvious culprits; the entire industry had, like in any bubble, convinced itself that the good times would last forever, and that even better times were ahead.

Everyone suffered, but the malt distilleries especially. In 1897, Balvenie Distillery used 25,000 bushels of barley in its production; in 1899, just 5,000. Charles Doig, perhaps the greatest distillery architect of the nineteenth century (he invented the iconic "pagoda" kiln chimney), predicted that another malt distillery wouldn't be built in Scotland for fifty years—and he was right: When it opened in 1949, Tullibardine was the first new malt distillery of the twentieth century.

Though the industry regained its balance, it faced controversy again a few years later, this time in court. In 1905 a judge in London's Islington neighborhood declared that whisky had to be made of malted barley in a pot still, to the great consternation of the blending industry—if the ruling stood, it meant they couldn't call their product "whisky." But the blenders weren't willing to accept defeat, and four years later they forced a reexamination of the issue by a royal commission. This time, the fates were more sympathetic, ruling that grain whisky was still whisky. Advocates for excluding blends from the definition bemoaned the ruling as the victory of commercialism over common sense; writing in 1930, Aeneas MacDonald said that "it is unfortunately true that the whole modern history of whisky is a record of the opening of door after door to commercial vandalism." But wise distillers knew that the ruling was a blessing, because it allowed them to sell their products to reliable blending houses and reap a steady profit.

Still, the bubble-burst was only the beginning of a long slide in the whisky industry. In 1900, even after the bubble popped, Scotland produced 37.1 million proof gallons of whisky (a proof gallon is a gallon of spirits at 100 proof); in 1932, it produced only 285,418 proof gallons. At one point in the 1930s, there were only eight distilleries operating in all of Scotland. Within that span there were fluctuations—in 1908, Scottish distilleries produced 24.4 million gallons— but the downward trend was undeniable.

What brought whisky so low? Prohibition, a global as well as an American phenomenon, played a part. Particularly in the English-speaking, whisky-drinking world, in the late nineteenth century governments at all levels began to restrict who could drink alcohol, where and when they would drink it, and above all how much they'd pay for it. In Britain the charge was led by David Lloyd George. First as chancellor of the Exchequer—the equivalent of the secretary of the Treasury in the United States—and then as prime minister, he proposed and won a series of tax increases and regulations on spirits that were significantly higher than those on beer and wine. Things became even more onerous during World War I, when Lloyd George claimed whisky was a threat to national security—the risk that workers in munitions plants would drink on the job—to impose even more restrictions, some of which remain today: regulating minimum proof, for example, or imposing a three-year minimum for aging whisky, under the false belief that raw spirits were toxic.

Lloyd George was the scourge of the distilling industry, but he had a point. Drinking was a problem in Britain, especially in Scotland. Higher taxes and better enforcement of public drunkenness laws had their effect: In 1913, 3,482 people were arrested for public drunkenness in Britain; in 1917, just 929 were. At the same time, by 1933, retail prices for whisky were 162 percent higher than in 1920 in real terms. In 1921, there were 143 distilleries in Scotland; in 1933, there were just fifteen (including six patent still operations).

But it wasn't just Lloyd George, or Britain. By the 1910s, the United States had become a major source of demand for scotch—and then disappeared in the fog of Prohibition. To get around the law, scotch makers exported millions of gallons to small markets like the Bahamas and the tiny French islands of St. Pierre and Miquelon, coincidentally located within a short, fast boat trip of the American coast. Still, it wasn't enough to make up for the loss of a major legal market. And then of course there were the economic tumults of the 1920s, which shook the European continent and depressed demand for imported liquor.

All of this misfortune had a happy ending, at least for the scotch industry. Lloyd George's reforms elevated the status and quality of whisky; the minimum aging requirement meant that legal whisky was a mature, rounded spirit, with complex aromas and flavors—just the sort of thing that makes for great ad copy for a company trying to take a brand upmarket. The reforms also encouraged amalgamation, so that by the end of World War II the industry was consolidated

behind a few massive companies—in 1946, DCL was
Britain's fourth-largest manufacturer. Without intending to,
Lloyd George had positioned the scotch industry for its next
phase, providing whisky for the tens of millions of people
worldwide who were digging out of a global depression and
joining the middle class.

World War II devastated Britain's population and urban
areas, but it left the distilling industry largely untouched.
Early in the conflict, Britain realized that scotch was a
national asset, worth billions; at one point, it considered
shipping much of the whisky sitting in bond to Canada for
safekeeping. Such a move would have put the scotch closer
to what was fast becoming its hottest market: Before 1920,
scotch commanded just 1 percent of American whisky
consumption; by 1942, with Prohibition long since repealed,
it was 5 percent and growing, and the United States was
the industry's biggest market, taking a third of all exports. In
January 1942, a ship carrying fifty thousand cases of scotch
to the United States was sunk by a German submarine,
making global headlines.

When the British government went scrambling for
revenue sources in the late 1940s, it turned to whisky
exports as a ready source of hard cash. In 1945, Prime
Minister Winston Churchill sent a letter to the Ministry of
Food declaring that they should "on no account reduce the
amount of barley for whisky. It takes years to mature and is
an invaluable export and dollar earner. Having regard to our
difficulties about export, it would seem improvident not to
preserve this characteristic element of British ascendency."

The industry listened. Distillation doubled from 1950
to 1960, and almost everything went overseas. The
government set an export quota of 80 percent, but it was
often exceeded. In 1949, out of 13 million gallons distilled,
only 2 million were set aside for domestic consumption; of
the 11 million gallons set for export, 7 million was destined
for the United States. To meet the new demand, thirty
distilleries opened in the few years after World War II.

Scotch had long been a part of Scotland's identity, but in the postwar years it became nearly synonymous with what it meant to be Scottish. In 1949 the film *Whisky Galore* showed a country obsessed with its national liquor, even if Scottish per-capita consumption of scotch was down significantly from its Victorian-era highs.

The American market might have been the largest, but it wasn't the only. The Italian market in particular was increasingly important in size, and for the fact that Italians loved "single whiskies"—what today we call single malts. Glen Grant became a national favorite and remains among the country's best-selling whiskies. France and Germany both developed tastes for scotch, as did parts of Latin America. What was once a fiery drink confined to the Scottish Highlands, and then later a popular spirit among Anglo-Saxon and colonial lands, became after the war a global phenomenon.

But it was the Americans who drove the industry. Imports doubled between 1950 and 1960. Scotch represented relatively affordable yet sophisticated style; it was also significantly easier to drink, at least as a blend, than bourbon or rye. As James Leith of White Horse whisky, a scotch blend, said: "Americans in all income brackets, all social levels and all geographic locations are taking to scotch whisky."

The trend continued through the 1960s: In 1963 Americans imported 16 million gallons of scotch; a year later, 18 million. Not surprisingly, the industry responded by investing enormous sums in production—new facilities, higher rates of distillation, more casks in more warehouses. The 1960s was also the period when single malts began to appear in sizable numbers outside Britain. Before then it had been possible to find "single" whiskies; in his 1920 memoir *Notes on a Cellar-Book,* George Saintsbury notes that he keeps on hand Clynelish, Glenlivet, Glen Grant, Talisker, and "one of the Islay brands—Lagavulin, Ardbeg, Caol Isla, etc." But it wasn't until 1963 that Glenfiddich launched and marketed a single malt as such; within two years it was available in the United States and other markets, under the advertising slogan, "Sit for a Glenfiddich—You May Never Stand for a Blend Again." Other single malts soon began making a similar push, among them Cardhu, Glenlivet, and Glen Grant.

The next decade opened with a milestone: In 1970, scotch finally outsold bourbon in the United States, with 32 million cases versus 29 million. But the signs of excess, retrenchment, and shock were already appearing. The millions of gallons of whisky aging across Scotland led observers to imagine it all in one giant pond, the so-called whisky loch. The peak of overproduction came early in the decade, just as a series of external and internal shocks rattled the industry and sent it on a downward spiral. The energy crisis put the availability of ready electricity in doubt; war in the Middle East and domestic social tensions made exports harder and put consumption at home in doubt.

Scotch's hold on the American consumer continued to tighten; by 1977 its market share was up to 15 percent. The problem was that people were simply drinking less spirits generally, and fewer brown spirits in particular—in 1969, vodka was the fourth best-selling liquor in America; by 1979, it was number one. Meanwhile, that same year saw a 12-percent drop in scotch sales from 1974. For an industry that exported 80 percent of its products, the vast majority of it to the United States, this was a disaster.

The news grew grimmer through the early 1980s. Production cratered; distilleries stopped operating or were shut down completely. From 1981 to 1982, scotch production fell 35 percent, and exports were down 15 percent. DCL closed eleven malt distilleries in 1983 alone. Blenders tried everything—including marketing scotch to women. In 1982 the brand Bell's adopted the slogan "Perfectly Proper in Mixed Company." Nothing worked. By 1986, only two scotch brands, Johnnie Walker and J&B, were in the top ten global spirits by sales volume. That same year, Balvenie didn't fill a single cask.

Not everyone was convinced that whisky was dying off, though. In 1987, a time most people consider the nadir of the scotch industry's fortunes, an English beer writer named Michael Jackson published *The World Guide to Whisky.* The book was a revelation, providing in-depth profiles of individual distilleries and their products, something most consumers had always thought of as the component ingredients of scotch, not a drink on their own. Jackson was onto something. As early as 1972, *The Times* of London declared that "single malt is the connoisseur's choice." By the end of the decade, the secret was out: In 1980, the *Los Angeles Times* wrote, "malt whiskies of the Highlands are to scotch what château-bottled classed growths are to Bordeaux."

Single malts were only a tiny part of total scotch production; when Jackson's book appeared, they represented just $180 million of a $3 billion industry. And there weren't many options: Though there were seventy single malt brands available, just five distilleries—Glenfiddich, Glen Grant, Glenlivet, Glenmorangie, and Macallan—accounted for 75 percent of sales. In 1988 United Distillers, the successor to DCL and the forerunner of Diageo, introduced its Classic Malts range, a selection of six single malts from different regions. All of this paid off: In 1988 sales for seven of the twelve top blends dropped, but sales for every major single malt brand doubled. Overall, single malt sales were up 500 percent since 1974. And while exports to the United States were still significant, the industry had learned to diversify—in the late 1970s, half of all exports went to America; by 1989 only a third did. That fall, the *New York Times* summed up the state of scotch: "A tradition-bound industry has gone through a shakeout while learning how to market to status-seeking Americans, high-spending Japanese and neighboring Europeans."

The rest is history. While single malts still constitute a fraction of the entire scotch market—in 2017, about 10 percent—they are driving all of its growth. Between 2002 and 2016, American imports of blended Scotch dropped

11.1 percent, according to the Distilled Spirits Council, while imports of single malts were up 183 percent.

What changed? When malt distilleries were primarily concerned with providing stock for blenders, they could afford to be a bit shopworn, a bit behind the times, even if they were owned by a multinational corporation. Much of the production was by hand, and many of the production methods were unchanged since the birth of the modern industry in the 1820s. Many distilleries were still largely self-contained, with their own maltings and cooperages. Today, when even small distilleries are bottling their own single malts, the industry has gone corporate and digital. Stills are heated indirectly with steam. Malting is done elsewhere, by third-party malting houses; the same goes for cask making. All this makes for a more efficient, precise, and safer production process, but those who've tried very old single malts will tell you that the taste has changed as a result—not necessarily for the worse, but not likely for the better, either.

Whisky is also much more globally integrated. About 80 percent of scotch distilleries are owned by foreign or multinational corporations, and while some of them have a good degree of autonomy, they are also subject to corporate whims and strategies.

The scotch industry buys an enormous number of American barrels—some 90 percent of the casks used to age scotch once held American whisky—a trend that began in the 1930s, after the United States passed a law that most whisky had to be aged in new oak barrels.

And the scotch industry is more innovative than ever before. It has learned to keep ahead of trends and adapt to them, not simply to weather them. Finishing, a practice that began in the 1980s, is now ubiquitous, with whiskies finished in wine casks, port casks, beer barrels, Japanese oak barrels—the list goes on ad infinitum.

There's no way to promise that this time will be different, but for the foreseeable future, things look good for the scotch industry, and for single malts in particular.

Scotch Regions

Scotland is generally divided into three parts: The Lowlands, which go from the English border up to a line running from northwest of Glasgow on the western coast to a bit above Edinburgh in the east; the Highlands, which constitute the rest of the mainland; and the Islands, of which there are 790.

Scotch regions, however, are a little more complicated. Although, like French wine, scotch has legally defined appellations, it is harder to say what they signify. Barley, once it is fermented and distilled, arguably loses whatever mark of its native soil and climate it once had, what the French call *terroir.* On the other hand, unlike beer, there is at least a general sense that regional variations in scotch whisky do exist—if not in ingredients, then in the local culture and customs that prescribe how to make whisky, and what drinkers should expect of a whisky made in a particular region.

With wine, regions—and subregions, some of which are very specific—identify a variety of variables. These include legal requirements regarding grape varietals, differences in climate and other growing conditions, and cultural variation (i.e, how the wine is made). Scotch has no such requirements, and these days, most scotch is far from being a regionally based product. The grain often comes from somewhere else (sometimes elsewhere in Scotland, sometimes as far away as Australia); it is often malted at one of the large malting firms scattered around Scotland, which may or may not have any regional affinity with the distillery; and in the case of large distilling companies, the whisky is often aged far off-site, making it difficult to talk about the climactic influences on the spirit.

And yet, talk of regions persists—and even, in the case of Speyside, breaks down into further subregions. Part of this is marketing: Distilleries know that all other variables generally being equal, labeling one whisky an Islay and another a Speyside makes it more likely that a consumer will want to buy both. One of the early landmarks in the evolution of modern single malts was the release of Diageo's Classic Malts line, which highlights one of the company's distilleries in each of six regions.

But regionality is not only about marketing, and it's not all hype. There really is a difference between, say, the typical whisky made on Islay and the typical Speyside whisky. Generally speaking, Islay whiskies are strongly peated, imparting seaside notes of iodine, brine, and seaweed. Speysides, in contrast, tend to be unpeated, defined instead by notes of honey and flowers.

There are three important qualifiers to keep in mind in the consideration of the regionality of Scottish single malts.

First, regions are not definitions; instead, they describe what an anthropologist would call an "ideal type": Beyond a fairly general description, there may be no single whisky that meets every characteristic, and there will be nearly as many exceptions as there are examples. But if you were somehow able to plot every whisky in a region on a graph that mapped out its characteristics and drew a line through them, the line would describe a fairly accurate, coherent statement about the region. Put differently, not every Islay whisky is briny and iodic, but those are indisputably typical notes for Islay whiskies.

Second, modern supply chains and the spread of high-tech equipment, along with the mobility of skilled distillers, mean that anyone can basically make anything anywhere. Peat from Speyside could quite easily be shipped to Islay, or vice versa. A Highland distillery could, with a little practice, make a Lowland-style spirit. There are reasons they don't, and those reasons have something to do with an understanding that regions matter.

Third, traditions are subject to change. A century and a half ago, most Speyside whiskies were peated, because peat fires were the cheapest, easiest way to kiln malted barley. That's not to say they were indistinguishable from

Islay whiskies—the plant matter in the peat, for example, was very different, and that matter imparted different scents and tasting notes. The point is that what we take as a region's immutable style is, in some cases, a fairly recent innovation.

These qualifiers point to what we're really talking about when we talk about scotch regions: custom and tradition—culture, in other words. Islay distilleries don't have to make peated expressions, and, in fact, Bunnahabhain generally eschews peat. Likewise, while there is no rule that Lowland whiskies be light in body and/or triple-distilled, it's what we expect when we hear the name "Lowland single malt." And while these categories are not locked in by deep history—indeed, many are relatively recent developments—they are nonetheless treated like near-Scripture by distillers and consumers alike.

The reasons for this are, again, partly marketing—it helps consumers enormously to know what a Speyside or a Lowland whisky tastes like. And it helps lift all boats when a distillery proudly embraces a regional identity. It also helped blenders at work in the late nineteenth century to know, as a shorthand, what a whisky would be like, if all they knew was which region it came from. But it's also about tradition, however recent its development. Distillers and connoisseurs revel in the idea of regionality, of breaking down the market into component parts and then talking about each, whether they make a huge difference or not.

According to the Scotch Whisky Association, there are five regions: Campbeltown, Highlands, Islay, Lowlands, and Speyside. Each of these is worth examining further, along with a sixth, unofficial region, the Islands.

Campbeltown

Once upon a time, Campbeltown was the beating heart of the Scotch industry, located on the long, thin Kintyre Peninsula, which juts off the southwestern coast of Scotland and whose tip sits less than twenty miles from Ireland. In fact, one of the myths driving the early growth of the Campbeltown whisky industry is that it was there that Irish migrants first brought distilling technology, making Kintyre the spiritual home of scotch. Certainly by the eighteenth century, distilling was a central part of local life; in 1710, a local law was passed forbidding washing in the town water "because said water is used by the inhabitants of the Burgh for their Mean, Brewing, and other such uses and ought to be kept clean and not to be abused."

Beyond myth and tradition, other factors came into play in Campbeltown's favor: A nearby coal seam provided an easy source of power, while Glasgow and its vast blending houses were easily reachable by boat—and Campbeltown is blessed with a fine harbor (it was also, at one time, a leading port for the Scottish herring industry). At its height, there were twenty-six distilleries jammed into central Campbeltown, and most everyone who didn't work on a boat worked in a still house. In 1887 Alfred Barnard wrote, "It is said that there are nearly as many places of worship as distilleries in the town."

And for several decades, blenders and consumers wanted what Campbeltown had to sell. Its rich, oily, peaty style meant that a little malt whisky could go a long way in a blend, allowing blenders to use a higher percentage of cheaper grain whiskies without sacrificing depth and flavor. Barnard praised Campbeltown whiskies as "the Hector of the West," the deepest voice in the choir; Aeneas MacDonald wrote that "The Campbeltowns are the double basses of the whisky orchestra."

But Campbeltown got greedy. By the late nineteenth century it was churning out whisky in volume, feeding the insatiable demand of blenders with little concern for quality—and zero concern for what could happen should the industry contract. But it did, and at the wrong time: The whisky collapse of 1899 coincided with a change in taste among blenders and consumers; they increasingly preferred lighter-bodied Lowland malts and the sweet elegance of Speyside. And by the end of the nineteenth century, many of the Speyside distilleries had direct rail access, negating Campbeltown's geographic advantage.

By 1950 all but one distillery, Springbank, had closed, and it was hanging on by a fingernail, with lengthy silent periods. Even today, there are just three distilleries, none of them large: Springbank, Glen Scotia, and Glengyle. The only justification for keeping Campbeltown as a separate regional classification is tradition and history—a not-inconsiderable concern—and the hope that one day, central Campbeltown might again bustle with distilleries.

Islay

Islay (pronounced *EYE-la*) is practically synonymous with smoky scotch. Home to eight distilleries (more are in the works), Islay is best known for peaty, briny, iodine-rich whiskies, though at least two distilleries, Bruichladdich and Bunnahabhain, produce a sizable number of unpeated expressions within their portfolio. Like the Isle of Skye to the north, Islay is famed for its foul weather; it gets between forty and sixty inches of rain a year, about twice as much as London. It's the sort of weather that calls for a robust, smoky spirit, though Islay specialized early on in peated whisky for more banal, commercial purposes: Its expansive bogs made it easy to produce, and blenders demanded concentrated, highly phenolic malts to go into their blends.

Highlands

Though Campbeltown may lay claim to the origin of Scotch distilling, the Highlands are its spiritual home. For centuries prior to the emergence of the modern whisky industry in the nineteenth century, Highlanders were distilling spirit, largely for drinking at home, or for selling locally. Very little of it was aged, very little of it was considered potable by outsiders, and, as a consequence, very little of it ever made it to markets in the Lowland cities, let alone England or the rest of the world. And beginning in the eighteenth century, it was taxed heavily—both to create a source of revenue, and as a method for tamping down on Scottish traditions, lest they give rise to thoughts of rebellion. (Kilts were largely banned for the same reason.)

In a strange twist, Highland scotch, which was once considered the roughest, most near-to-barbaric drink available in the British Islands, is today considered the most sophisticated, often characterized as flowery, fruity, and honeyed. While there are great distilleries in all corners of the country, the most prized are all Highland malts: Macallan, Glenmorangie, Glenfiddich, and Dalmore, among others.

The Highlands is a large geographic region and one well-stocked with distilleries, which vary greatly in style, from the smoky coastal notes of Oban to the dried fruits of a sherried malt like Glenmorangie. Though the Scotch Whisky Association does not officially break down the vast Highlands into subregions, distinctions do emerge. Whiskies from the northern Highlands, for example, are robust, but elegant. Running from the northwestern corner of Speyside to the top of the mainland, this region produces full-bodied, richly fruited whiskies that are at the same time proudly poised, and are often, but not always, sherried.

Whiskies from the central Highlands are more eclectic. Those from the islands, which range along the western and northern coasts, deserve further discussion.

Lowlands

Like Campbeltown, the Lowlands remains an official region largely because of tradition: It is, arguably, the birthplace of the modern scotch industry, the place where the first blending houses learned how to take a portfolio of robust Highland malts, combine them with lighter, cheaper grain whisky made on a continuous still, and produce a product that could captivate domestic and foreign consumers. Today there are only three Lowland distilleries that export to the

United States: Auchentoshan, Bladnoch, and Glenkinchie (Rosebank, recently reopened, may be coming to a store near you soon). The characteristic Lowlands style—light-bodied, floral, slightly honeyed—is achieved by triple distilling, though of the Lowland whiskies currently available in the United States, only Auchentoshan uses a third distillation.

Speyside

Hanging south like a pennant from the Moray Firth, Speyside is the Napa Valley of scotch—not only the largest concentration of distilleries, but also home to some of the most renowned and best-selling whiskies. Not surprisingly, it is also one of Scotland's main tourist attractions, despite its relative remoteness (a four-hour train ride from Edinburgh). Speyside emerged as a whisky heartland in the nineteenth century. It has an excellent source of good water (drawn from tributaries to the Spey, but not the Spey itself) and is near expansive barley fields, as well as easy rail access. Varied microclimates have allowed scores of distilleries to emerge and thrive, offering a variety of expressions despite sitting cheek-by-jowl. Glenlivet was the first major distillery to operate legally in the region, and until a few decades ago, many Speyside distilleries appended its name to theirs (for example, Aberlour-Glenlivet)—even some as far as thirty miles away, leading one observer to quip that it must be "the longest glen in all of Scotland."

Islands

The Scotch Whisky Association does not separate out the many distilleries located on Scotland's many islands, except for Islay. Maybe it should: There is something uniquely Scottish about the fact that some of the most famous and desirable scotches are made in some of the country's most remote places. Until recently, only six of Scotland's 790 islands were home to whisky distilleries: Orkney, Skye, Mull,

Jura, Islay, and Arran. Since then, small distilleries have opened on Lewis, Harris, Raasay, and other islands, but it will be a few years before their products reach the United States. Broadly speaking, Island whiskies are light- to medium-peated, with strong coastal notes—think saltwater, seaweed, beach fire, and storm-weathered wood. But they can also be surprisingly sweet and juicy; Americans often leap to descriptors like barbecue sauce and pickles. Setting aside Islay, which is its own region, the Islands are:

ORKNEY   Located off the northern coast of Scotland, the Orkney Islands are sometimes said to have the same relationship to Scotland as Scotland has to England. While the islands are not about to go independent, they are increasingly assertive about their Nordic identity—and, to be fair, they were under Norse control from 874 to 1468. While there are seventy islands in the group, almost all Orcadians, as their residents are called, live on the main island of Orkney, and mostly in the main city of Kirkwall. Orkney is home to two distilleries, the well-known Highland Park and its often-overlooked gem of a neighbor, Scapa. Highland Park is the more peated and overall more typically "Island" of the two, though its broad range makes it hard to pin down.

SKYE   The second-largest Scottish island, and the largest among the Inner Hebrides, Skye is infamous for its foul weather (even by Scottish standards)—but also famous for its mountainous, breathtaking views when that foul weather occasionally clears. Skye was well-populated by small farmers in the 1800s, but oppressive clearance laws during the middle of that century consolidated control over the land in the hands of a few estates and drove most off the island. In fact, the origins of its best-known distillery, Talisker, lie in a money-making scheme by a set of landlords who—having decimated the local sheep-farming economy—needed a new source of income. In the last few years a number of small distilleries have also opened on Skye, though Talisker is the only one that currently exports to the United States.

MULL   Large but sparsely populated, Mull has nearly as many castles as people. It is also home to a single distillery, Tobermory, which produces both the Tobermory (unpeated) and Ledaig (peated) single malt lines.

JURA   Though it has a rich history highlighted by bloody clan feuds, Jura is perhaps best known for Barnhill, the remote house at its northern tip where George Orwell wrote *1984*. Not far from Barnhill, just off the coast, is one of the world's largest whirlpools, the Corryvrecken (the namesake of a whisky from Ardbeg). In 1947, while he was writing his novel, Orwell nearly drowned in the maelstrom when he was out boating without a life jacket and the craft capsized. Jura the distillery is located far to the south, a quick ferry and bus ride from Islay.

ARRAN   A squat, sparsely populated island tucked into the Firth of Clyde, between the Kintyre Peninsula and the Scottish mainland, Arran is home to a single distillery, aptly named the Isle of Arran Distillery. (Located on the north of the island in Lochranza, as of 2018, the distillery was constructing a second site on the island's southern shore.) Geologically, the island itself is split between Highland and Lowland topography, creating tourist-pleasing views and, perhaps, giving the distillery a mandate to produce its highly regarded, wide variety of whiskies.

How to Enjoy Whisky

Let's begin with what should be obvious, but often isn't: There is no right way to drink whisky. Or, rather, there is only one right way, which is however you want. This is not rocket science, or Supreme Court litigation. You drink scotch because you like it, so you should drink scotch however you like it. One of the beauties of scotch is that it shines in so many settings, and in so many combinations. A peaty Islay whisky, consumed neat, is wonderful on a cold, rainy evening; with some soda, it also works on a sunny summer afternoon. Neat, with a rock, with a dash of still water, in a highball, in a cocktail—all are fine choices. Anyone who tells you different may know a lot about scotch, but they don't know the first thing about drinking.

Of course, scotch is precisely the sort of passion that attracts the stuffy and the rules-obsessed, and the literature around scotch is replete with condemnations and commands regarding various ways of drinking it. Aeneas MacDonald, in his 1930 book *Whisky*, wrote that "no more effectual way of ruining the flavor of a good whisky could have been imagined than this one of drowning it in a fizzing solution of carbonic acid gas"—i.e., soda water. More recently, internet clickbait sites have flocked to the latest "scientific" study claiming that one or another method is the "best" way to drink scotch; in the fall of 2017, I counted nearly one hundred articles, spawned by a team of well-meaning but not particularly well-informed researchers, claiming that adding a few drops of water was the only proper way to enjoy scotch.

To be fair, there is something to that. If a whisky is above 86 proof (or 43 percent alcohol by volume, "proof" in the U.S. meaning simply twice the A.B.V.), a few drops of water tend to loosen things up and make the whisky more volatile, releasing a more effervescent nose. Generally speaking, higher-proof whiskies tend to blossom with a few drops of water, and particularly high-proof whiskies practically demand it just to be palatable. The same goes for older whiskies, which tend to be dense and settled; a few drops of water help release sleeping aromas and flavors. Water breaks up the alcohol's hold on the tasty chemical compounds in the glass. But this is very different from saying this is the "right" way to drink it.

On the flip side, there's a reason whisky can't be sold at less than 80 proof: It would be too watery. As it is, I can think of very few 80-proof whiskies that need more than a couple of drops of water, if even that. And I feel that most, though not nearly all, 80-proofers suffer from adding water: Instead of opening up, they wilt. In the Whisky Accounts section of this book, I've tried to indicate which ones hold up under the effects of water, but again, it's subjective. The only way to know how much water to add, if any, is to try it yourself.

Tasting

There's whisky drinking, and there's whisky tasting. Each has its place. You won't always have the inclination or attention span to focus on the nose and mouthfeel and finish of a whisky; sometimes you just want something that tastes good. But at other times, especially when you're encountering a new whisky, you'll want to approach it with a bit more thought.

There are four things to look for when it comes to tasting: how it smells, how it feels in your mouth, how it tastes, and how it lingers, if at all, after you've swallowed it. A good whisky will be pleasant from start to finish; a great whisky will be complex and at times challenging. In fact, you might find that the whisky you consider the most complex and well-crafted is not necessarily your favorite: An art lover can recognize Picasso's genius even if, personally, he's partial to Rockwell.

Make sure you procure the right glass. If you're out at a bar, this may not be possible, though a good bar will always have the right equipment, even if you have to ask. The important point is to get something with a wide bowl relative to the mouth: A brandy snifter is great, and a red-wine glass will do in a pinch. There are dozens of whisky-specific designs on the market, though the dominant one is the Glencairn glass. It has a squat stem, but a broad, tall bowl and narrow mouth, which allows a lot of aromas to build up within the glass. It's also the perfect size for assessing a whisky's color, allowing just enough light to push through the liquid without washing it out.

The first thing to do is give the whisky a good swirl, to release aromas into the glass. Then pass the mouth of the glass under your nose, just briefly. Even a low-proof whisky can give off heady amounts of alcohol that will singe the nostrils and prevent you from appreciating the finer points of the aroma. Treat a whisky you don't know like a dog you don't

The Glencairn style of whisky glass was developed by Glencairn Crystal, Ltd. in Scotland after the glassware used by professional whisky makers. They are ideal vehicles for sampling single malt but they are by no means mandatory—a good wine glass or brandy snifter works equally well.

know: It's probably friendly, but you don't want to stick your face right up to it without first getting a sense of its attitude.

Once you've assessed the aromatic potency, take deeper whiffs. While doing so, sort out your first impressions. What are the dominant general notes—floral, fruit, peat? Then dig deeper. What kind of floral? Is it more earthy, like geraniums, or sweet, like lilacs? Do the fruit aromas lean toward citrus, or berries? Is the peat dominated by rubber and iodine, or campfire and creosote?

I usually pour two glasses, side by side, when I'm tasting. One I'll leave neat, the other I'll dose with a few drops of water. I'll then assess each, in parallel. How are the aromas different in each? Does the water enliven the whisky, or thin it out? Do new aromas emerge with water?

Finally, it's time for a taste. A lot happens quickly as the whisky plays across the tongue. You're looking at a three-step sensation: what it tastes and feels like right as it enters your mouth, how it changes as it sits on your tongue, and what it's like as you're swallowing it. Try to pick out the most notable flavors and dissect them. If there's spice, is it more cinnamon, like an Atomic Fireball, or smoky, like a chili pepper? Or is it more like black or white pepper? Is there a wine-like flavor and, if so, is it buttery, like a chardonnay, or dark and chewy, like a Burgundy? At the same time, think about how the whisky feels in your mouth: Is it thin and oily, or thick? Give this some thought, since it's important to keep the senses apart—how a whisky feels can bias what you think of its taste, and vice versa.

Make sure the whisky washes over your entire tongue—but don't slosh it. Let it take its time. Whisky is a volatile substance, given to change at the slightest alteration in its surroundings—it shouldn't be surprising when it changes rapidly as soon as it enters the wet warmth of your mouth.

After a few seconds, let it slide down your throat. Here you'll find a whole new set of sensations. Does it burn, and in what way? Does the spice linger? Like wine, whisky can be extremely dry, leaving little behind, or it can stay with

you, leaving all sorts of residual sweet and spicy notes;
sometimes there's even a sour tone.

Just like there's no one way to enjoy whisky, there's no
set list of tasting notes—everyone's body chemistry is slightly
different, and it will have a lot of influence over what they
taste in the whisky. If the person next to you finds cherry cola
notes and you don't, it doesn't mean your taste buds
are deficient.

That said, learning to discern the flavors in a whisky is
an acquired skill; and like any skill, some pick it up quickly,
while others need practice. But almost everyone can develop
a knowledgeable palate with enough experience. While
there's a wide range of tastes to be found across the world
of whiskies, and with the caveat that everyone will find
something a little different, some flavors are more common
than others. Islay single malt whisky, for example, will have
lots of peaty, seaweed, and iodine notes, thanks to the peat
used to dry the malt, while a Speyside aged in ex-bourbon
barrels will demonstrate honeyed, candied flavors.

The chart on the next two pages offers a sample of typical
tasting aromas and flavors of single malt whisky.

Typical Tasting Aromas and Flavors

PEAT	WOOD	SPICE	CEREAL
Medicinal/iodine	Fresh-sawn wood	Cinnamon	Malt
Smoky	Sandalwood	Black pepper	Grain
(bonfire, wood	Spicy oak	White pepper	Mash
ash, char)	Pine	Chili pepper	Porridge
Moss	Cedar	Ginger	Corn
Fish	Resin/sap	Mint	Biscuit
(fresh, smoked,		Clove	
oysters)		Cumin	
Creosote			
Earthy			
Seaweed			
Seashells			

FEINTY	MEATY	CITRIC	FRESH FRUIT
Solvent	Pork	Orange	Apple
Leather	Barbecued meat	Tangerine	Pear
Plastic	Sausage	Orange zest	Peach
Rubber		Lemon zest	Apricot
(pencil eraser,		Meyer lemon	Banana
tires)		Orange peel	Strawberry
Oak dust			Raspberry
Beeswax			Cherry
Honey			
Cheese			
Yeast			
Sweaty			
Tobbaco			
(cigarette, cigar,			
ash)			
Black tea			

SULPHUR	OFF-NOTES
Brackish	Cardboard
Cabbage water	Metallic
Stagnant	Baby vomit
Marsh gas	Rancid

OIL	WINE	FLORAL	NUTTY
Linseed oil	Sherry	Geranium	Salted nuts
Buttery	Port	Cut flowers	Marzipan
	Chardonnay	Lavender	
	Applejack	Hay	
		(mown, dried)	
		Perfume	
		Fabric softener	
		Grassy	
		Coconut	
		Herbaceous	

COOKED FRUIT	DRIED FRUIT	VANILLA	CHOCOLATE
Stewed apple	Raisin	Caramel	Cream
Marmalade	Fig	Toffee	Butter
Jam	Dried apricot	Brown sugar	Milk chocolate
Barley sugar	Prune	Molasses	Cocoa
Candied fruit	Fruit cake	Maple syrup	Bitter chocolate
Glace cherries		Nougat	Chocolate
		Butterscotch	mousse
			Dark chocolate
			Fudge

Organizing a Tasting

Drinking alone is never as fun as drinking with company, and the same goes for tasting. It's a good way to explore new whiskies, or to compare well-known whiskies in different combinations. Depending on how formal you want to make a tasting, there are a few basic things to keep in mind.

Make sure everyone has the same glassware—you can order a half-dozen Glencairn-style glasses online for practically nothing. If you're going all out, give everyone two glasses for each whisky to be tasted, so they can compare them side by side—one neat, one with water. You should have at least one large glass or bucket for tasters to dump their whisky into—not everyone will want to drink more than a few sips; some will want to taste and spit. And make sure to have a bottle of filtered, room-temperature water, along with a water dropper. Eschew ice—this is about tasting, not drinking, and ice will weaken the whisky's intensity.

Food is a must. At the very least, you should provide some unsalted crackers, which help clear the palate without offending any taste buds. If you're trying new whiskies, this is probably the best way to go. If you know the whiskies well, though, you could try pairing them with different foods—chocolates, caramels, nuts, berries, citrus, smoked fish, meats, all depending on what you think complements each expression.

And while it's not necessary, a good tasting host provides each guest with a pad and pen for note-taking. Impressions come very quickly and fleetingly, so it's good to have a way to record them. Again, if you're going all out, you could print sheets with sections for nose, taste, finish, and overall impression. But make sure you know your audience—the worst thing you could do is intimidate people with what is supposed to be an enjoyable undertaking. After all, it's just whisky.

ESTᴰ 1892

SINGLE MALT SCOTCH WHISKY

Distilled at

THE BALVENIE®

Distillery, Banffshire

SCOTLAND

FINISHED IN **PORTWOOD**® PORT CASKS

AGED **21** YEARS

In the making of The Balvenie PortWood, our Malt Master
carefully selects rare reserves of Balvenie and transfers them to
port casks for a further few months of maturation.

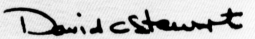

THE BALVENIE MALT MASTER

THE BALVENIE DISTILLERY COMPANY
BALVENIE MALTINGS, DUFFTOWN, BANFFSHIRE,
SCOTLAND AB55 4BB

43%

How to Read a Whisky Label

Interpreting a whisky label can be a confounding experience for anyone trying to make an informed choice of what to drink or what to give as a gift. Some bottles will display a lengthy declaration and backstory about the contents; others are terse or cryptic, while others plainly state the case. On the opposite page is an example of a whisky label—and a superb whisky at that—with a good deal of information. Below are annotations by me regarding elements on the label.

NAMES This label states that it is a "Single Malt Scotch Whisky," which means it follows the three rules:

- It must be made exclusively with malted barley, yeast, and water.

- It must be aged at least three years in an oak cask in Scotland.

- It must be made at a single distillery in Scotland.

Owned by William Grant and Sons, The Balvenie Distillery Company produces a wide range of different types, a.k.a. expressions, of spirits, including this whisky with quite a long "full name": The Balvenie Portwood Finished Aged 21 Years. (For more about Balvenie, see page 93.)

AGE STATEMENT This whisky is labeled "Aged 21 Years," which means the distilled spirit was stored in an oak cask for at least twenty-one years before it was bottled. Not all whisky carries an age statement, which does not, in all cases, reflect the quality of the drink. Older whisky tends to be more expensive for obvious reasons—it was stored for a long time and a good deal of it will have evaporated each year.

CASK TYPE The whisky in this bottle matured for at least twenty-one years in an oak barrel that once stored American bourbon and was then "finished" for a few months in an export wine cask from Portugal. This style of finishing whisky has become very popular, and Balvenie's master distiller, David C. Stewart, has led the way.

ALCOHOL BY VOLUME/PROOF By law, all whisky bottles must state the level of alcohol by volume. Often this is abbreviated as "Alc/Vol" or "ABV." This whisky is bottled at 43 percent alcohol by volume. Some bottles also include proof, which in the U.S. is simply double the alcohol by volume. Whisky is available from a minimum of 40 percent Alc/Vol (80 proof) and up.

LIQUID MEASURE By law, liquor bottles for sale in the U.S. must somewhere display the measurement of its contents in metric values. (In the case of this bottle, it is printed on the side.) Whisky is most commonly sold in bottles labeled 750 ml (milliliters), which converts to a little more than twenty-five U.S. ounces. This measurement equals one-fifth of a gallon and, thus, a "fifth" of whisky. Of course, both larger and smaller bottles of whisky are also available.

Whisky
Accounts

ABERLOUR ®

ESTD 1879

HIGHLAND SINGLE MALT
SCOTCH WHISKY

A'BUNADH

means 'of the origin'
a respectful toast to
nder James Fleming,
day is produced in the
of 19th century malts

Matured exclusivel
Aberlour a'bunadh
strength and withou
chill-filtering meth
luxurious and rich

MATURED IN SPANISH OLOROSO SHERRY BUTTS

ED STRAIGHT FROM THE CASK AT 61.2% alc/vol.

HILL-FILTERED   BATCH NO. 56

G. CRUICKSHANK   MASTER D

STILLED & BOTTLED IN SCOTLAND   ABERLOUR DISTILLERY COMPANY LTD.   ABERLOUR SPEYSIDE AB3

About the Accounts

The "Whisky Accounts" section of this book is organized by maker and/or brand in alphabetical order. Included for each is background and historical information about the company that offers the whisky to consumers. Each "expression" (that is, individual offering) has its own tasting notes, separated into text regarding nose and palate (including body and finish), as well as general notes about the whisky. In the upper right corner of the entry is the alcohol by volume percentage (proof) and, when known, its age.

At the bottom center is the price with dollar signs corresponding to the following range of costs to the consumer in U.S. dollars per bottle:

$ = $50 or less
$$ = $51–90
$$$ = $91–200
$$$$ = $201 or more

I have based the dollar amounts on average prices found in my local shops and advertised on the internet for the bottles pictured. The whiskies covered in this book are sold in a standard 750 ml measure and the prices indicated are for this size of bottle. You may find bottles that cost much more or less than the range of prices I have indicated. These are strictly estimates. And like so many things in life, price is not always commensurate with value.

Rating whisky is a vastly subjective undertaking. I have included ratings as an indication of my own personal taste. My low marks for a whisky do not make it "bad." I just don't recommend it. So why include it at all? The ratings (and price ranges) are for the neophyte, curious, and adventurous drinkers out there, to give them some type of benchmark for making informed choices. When you order at the bar or buy a bottle for yourself, for a special occasion, or as a gift, I can say from personal experience that it helps to have an opinion from someone else. I would never urge drinkers not to try what many may consider subpar whisky, or a drink that receives a particularly low mark in a book, on a website, or in a magazine for that matter. Drinking unusual or daring or even unappealing whisky is a learning moment, too.

My ratings are also driven by my own desire to figure out which whiskies I value more than others, which to avoid, and why. There are so many whiskies to try and, hopefully, so much time to figure it all out. With this in mind, the ratings in this book follow this scale:

★★★★ = Phenomenal

★★★ = Excellent

★★ = Good

★ = Decent; some flaws, but drinkable.

NR = Not recommended

While not every whisky in this book will be available in every store, I have attempted to build as near-comprehensive a list of the regular-production, "core range" expressions available from distilleries on the market. That excludes most super-premium and limited-edition expressions. Several expressions have been discontinued, but I've kept them in the book because bottles are still plentiful, and I believe they're worth seeking out.

I have largely excluded whiskies that are sold by independent bottlers, often termed "IBs." These are companies that buy stocks of whisky from distilleries, then bottle and sell them under their own label. These are often sold at ages, alcohol levels, and finishes not found in the distilleries' official ranges. Many of them, though, are also bought and bottled on an as-available basis, and it's hard to review something that came out in just a few hundred bottles and will never be seen again. What I advise is that you use this book to identify brands and expressions you like, then dabble in independent bottlings. They can be a great way to deepen a whisky collection and hunting them can be a rewarding adventure. (You'll see a few IBs in the book, but they are only from bottlers who refuse to identify the source of the whisky, an arguably arbitrary but nevertheless necessary cut-off).

I've also included a number of "private label" whiskies—like Kroger-brand breakfast cereal or Walmart-brand dog food, these are whiskies that are distilled by one company, typically acquired by a middleman, and then sold to retailers who want to put their brand on them. (If you thought Costco or Trader Joe's made their own single malt whisky, well, we should talk.) Several of these are worth considering—they offer a lot of quality for a low price.

Here's hoping that *Single Malt* will enhance your own exploration of what makes whisky such a fascinating and enjoyable part of life.

Aberfeldy

OWNER: JOHN DEWAR & SONS/BACARDI

FOUNDED: 1896

REGION: HIGHLANDS

PRONUNCIATION: *AB-er-fell-dee*

Aberfeldy, located near the River Tay and just east of the central Highland town of the same name, was part of the wave of late-Victorian distilleries founded by blenders to supply their booming businesses—in this case, John Dewar & Sons, which opened the distillery in 1896 (there was an earlier distillery on the site, also called Aberfeldy, which operated from 1830 to 1849). Though Dewar owns Aberfeldy today (and itself is a fully owned subsidiary of drinks giant Bacardi), for most of its life the distillery was under the ownership of DCL—Dewar sold it to the distilling behemoth in 1925, who sold it back in 1998, along with Aultmore, Craigellachie, and Royal Brackla. Aberfeldy is a medium-size distillery, pumping out 2.7 million liters per annum. It has relatively tall stills, which help it achieve its signature oily, fruity character. Along with producing the Aberfeldy single malt range, the distillery is also the "brand home" for Dewar's blended scotch, and features an impressive visitor center largely dedicated to the blend.

Aberfeldy
12 Years in Oak

If it reminds you of Dewar's 12 Year Old, that's because Aberfeldy is one of the blend's primary components. Aged in a combination of ex-bourbon and ex-sherry casks.

AGE	ALC/VOL
12 years old	**40**%

NOSE

Watermelon Now and Laters, iodine, caramel, and varnish; water opens it up, with banana, maple, wood shavings, pears, and an unplaceable sweatiness.

GENERAL

A fantastic value whisky. Light, crowd pleasing—vanilla, floral, gentle notes.

PALATE

Waxy and on the thin side of medium, with vanilla, toasted coconut, maple, and dried seaweed; water, surprisingly, mellows but doesn't kill it, and adds vanilla and orange peel. The finish is medium in length, with bakery dough, maple, and pepper notes.

PRICE	RATING
$	★ ★

Aberfeldy
16 Years in Oak

Older than the 12 year old, and finished in oloroso sherry casks.

AGE
16
years old

ALC/VOL
40%

NOSE

Waxy, floral, vanilla, Luden's cough drops, cinnamon, oak shavings, and, with time, maple candy; adding water makes it less sweet and slightly savory and smoky, with some Dr. Pepper, leather, and dill in there as well.

PALATE

A thin mouthfeel, with maple, vanilla, dill, and Swedish Fish; water brings out tobacco, raisins, sherry, and cola. The finish is short and slightly tannic, though it goes a bit longer and spicier—think hot peppers—with water.

GENERAL

A good scotch for a newbie American palate—it has the maple and cinnamon notes of a bourbon, with just a bit of smoke and leather. It's full-flavored but quite sessionable.

PRICE
$$

RATING
★★

Aberfeldy
Aged 21 Years

The distillery's oldest expression. Aged in a combination of ex-bourbon and ex-sherry casks.

AGE
21
years old

ALC/VOL
40%

NOSE

Snuffed candles, pancake batter, toast, raspberries, heather, and slight smoke; water elicits tropical fruit, vanilla, and orange peel.

GENERAL

Waxy and fruity notes, but thin and dry. There are no real flaws, but of the three Aberfeldys, this is the only one that tastes like it should be bottled at a higher proof. Don't add water, in any case.

PALATE

A thin-to-medium mouthfeel, with honey-suckle, wildflower honey, maple, cola, and a general fruitiness; water brings out grilled orange, Bit-O-Honey, and leather. The finish is thin, slightly dry, and smooth, with a lingering honey note.

PRICE
$$$

RATING
★★

Aberlour

OWNER: CHIVAS BROTHERS/PERNOD RICARD

FOUNDED: 1879

REGION: SPEYSIDE

PRONUNCIATION: *AB-er-lough-er*

Located on the southern edge of the town of Aberlour, at the foot of Ben Rinnes mountain, this seemingly quaint distillery is in fact a single malt powerhouse, producing 3.9 million liters of spirit a year—and the number-one scotch in France. Though distilling on the site goes back to 1825, the brand traces its official birth to 1879, when James Fleming, a local businessman who had worked at Dailuaine, moved back home to open his own distillery. Fleming was wildly successful, and used his resulting largesse to fund a nearby hospital and a bridge over the Spey River a few hundred yards from the distillery. He died in 1895; a fire three years later destroyed much of the site, but it was rebuilt with a design from distillery architect extraordinaire Charles Doig. Aberlour is known for its luxuriant sherried character; as Iain Banks wrote, "If Fabergé made a whisky, you suspect this is what it would taste like."

Aberlour
12 Years Old

AGE
12
years old

A marriage of whiskies aged in ex-bourbon barrels and sherry butts.

ALC/VOL
40%

NOSE

Apples, pears, ginger, sandalwood, mushrooms, dried fruit, yeasty bread, and ripe bananas; water emphasizes the sherry notes significantly.

PALATE

A thinnish mouthfeel, with stone fruits, pepper, cinnamon, fruit punch, new make spirit; water adds more chocolate, candied ginger, cloves, and cough syrup. The finish has more dark chocolate and spicy fruit.

GENERAL

The nose offers an intriguing blend of umami and sweet notes. The palate is surprisingly complex for such a low proof. A fantastic entry-level whisky, especially at its price.

PRICE
$

RATING
★★

Aberlour
16 Years Old

AGE
16
years old

Like the 12 Year Old, a marriage of whiskies aged in ex-bourbon barrels and sherry butts.

ALC/VOL
40%

NOSE

Honey, leather, new car, caramel, cheese popcorn, SweeTarts dust, and a certain sugary funkiness; water brings out more of a buttery, umami note.

PALATE

Caramel, chocolate, grilled pineapple, floral, orange zest, and a big sherry hit at the mid-palate; water brings out a bitter note, like peanut skins. The finish is dry, with orange zest and bittersweet chocolate.

GENERAL

Hotter and drier than the 12 Year Old, and noticeably less complex. Still, a solid drink.

PRICE
$$

RATING
★★

Aberlour
18 Years Old

Aged in a combination of ex-bourbon and second-fill ex-oloroso sherry casks.

AGE
18
years old

ALC/VOL
43%

NOSE

New leather, Kraft caramels, oranges, heather, salty air, old wood, honey, rancio, wood varnish, flat cola, and persimmons; water softens the nose substantially and brings out a Christmas cake note.

PALATE

A medium, rich, oily mouthfeel, with honeycomb, leather, marmalade, hard chocolate candy, lemon Jolly Rancher; the finish is long with orange peels, dark chocolate, and cake batter.

GENERAL

Despite being just twenty-four months older than the 16 Year Old, this whisky is richer, and more balanced—like the difference between a high school junior and a college freshman.

PRICE
$$$

RATING

Aberlour
A'bunadh

A non-age-statement, cask-strength version of the regular Aberlour line, *a'bunadh* is Scottish Gaelic for "the original." Its characteristics vary slightly from batch to batch.

AGE
No age statement

ALC/VOL
61.2%

NOSE

The rubber notes of an old rum, leather, coal tar, licorice, bubblegum, caramel, rum-soaked raisins; water elicits a sweeter note, with vanilla and banana bread.

PALATE

More rubber and raisin notes on the palate, along with cloves, Chinese five-spice blend, and sweet cinnamon; it starts off very tight and boozy, but opens with water. The finish is surprisingly spicy compared to the smoothness of the younger expressions.

GENERAL

An unmistakably sherried whisky, with big, bold flavors and a long, impressive finish. Not for the fainthearted, though.

PRICE
$$$

RATING

Ainsley Brae

PRIVATE LABEL

OWNER: TOTAL WINE & MORE

PRONUNCIATION: *AYNES-lee Bray*

Ainsley Brae is the house brand of Total Wine & More, a large American wine and spirits chain. The brand is supplied by Alexander Murray & Co., a California-based independent bottler that also provides the whisky for Costco's Kirkland range and Trader Joe's, among others. Neither Total Wine nor Alexander Murray will reveal Ainsley Brae's source, though the private-label range also features independent bottling of Glendullan and Royal Brackla (not reviewed here).

Ainsley Brae
Oak Cask

Aged in ex-bourbon casks.

AGE
No age statement

ALC/VOL
40%

NOSE
Cranberry juice, putty, green apple Jolly Rancher, acetone, plywood; water destroys it.

GENERAL
Showy and superficial.

PALATE
Thin and astringent, with the immature grain notes of a young bourbon, along with copper and pepper; as with the nose, water kills it. The finish is long and hot, with no real flavor.

PRICE
$

RATING
NR

Ainsley Brae
Sauternes Cask Finish

Aged in ex-bourbon casks, then finished for six to eight months in ex-Sauternes casks.

AGE
No age statement

ALC/VOL
40%

NOSE
Bananas, powdered sugar, freshly sawn wood, swimming pool, and a breeze through the trees; water lessens the sweetness and adds a floral, grassy note.

PALATE
Thick and juicy, grassy, caramel, with a big burn at the mid-palate; water adds an umami, mineral note. The finish is long, dry, and spicy.

GENERAL
The grass and sweet notes are appealing, but it's off balance.

PRICE
$

RATING
NR

Ainsley Brae
Burgundy Cask Finish

Aged in ex-bourbon casks, then finished for six to eight months in ex-Burgundy casks.

AGE
No age statement

ALC/VOL
40%

NOSE
Mushrooms, old warehouses, barley soup, sulfur, stewed cherries, maple glaze, and caramel; water thins it significantly and adds a sour note.

PALATE
Medium-to-thin mouthfeel, with notes of grape candy, grain, and bandages; water shows white pepper, raspberry candy, and caramel. The finish is a bit drying.

GENERAL
Unremarkable, inadvisable.

PRICE
$

RATING
NR

Ainsley Brae
Sherry Cask Finish

Aged in ex-bourbon casks, then finished for six to eight months in ex-sherry casks.

AGE
No age statement

ALC/VOL
40%

NOSE
Pear, pine, cinnamon, toasted nuts, gingerbread, raisins, and grain; water brings out dried ginger, white pepper, and hazelnuts.

GENERAL
A reasonable facsimile of a sherried single malt, and fine for the price, but still thin and underwhelming.

PALATE
Thin and bland, with muted notes of oak, toasted almonds, hot pepper, metal, and burnt grain; water adds a creamy streak. It turns bitter on the finish, with a dash of chocolate and grapefruit.

PRICE

RATING

anCnoc

OWNER: INVER HOUSE/INTERNATIONAL BEVERAGE COMPANY

FOUNDED: 1894

REGION: SPEYSIDE

PRONUNCIATION: *AH-knock*

AnCnoc is the whisky; Knockdhu is the distillery. Located in the eastern reaches of Speyside, Knockdhu was DCL's first malt distillery, built to supply its popular Haig blended Scotch (until then, DCL had only owned grain distilleries). United Distillers, the descendant of DCL, mothballed the distillery in 1983 and sold it to Inver House in 1988. The first release under the new owners came in 1993, this time under the anCnoc label, chosen to avoid confusion with one of United's (now Diageo's) other distilleries, Knockando. AnCnoc is known for its light, fruity character, though it has also made a big push over the last few years with a peated range as well.

anCnoc
12 Year Old

The basic anCnoc, a standout example of un-sherried Speyside whisky.

AGE

12

years old

ALC/VOL

43%

NOSE

Light on the nose, some candy apples, orange zest, and light oak.

PALATE

Orange peel, herbs, candied cherries; buttery and estery, with a finish that lingers in white wine.

GENERAL

A lovely bright nose, but the palate is a bit thin, and a few drops of water ruins it. Still, a solid entry-level expression.

PRICE

RATING

anCnoc Cutter

AGE
No age statement

ALC/VOL
46%

Named for the tool used to slice up peat bogs, Cutter clocks in at a solidly smoky 20.5 ppm. A throwback to the days when Knockdhu specialized in peated malts.

NOSE
Strongly peated, but not over-whelming—it smells like a vinegar barbecue sauce, alongside banana cream and a hint of sherry, with a meatiness coming through with water.

PALATE
Raisins, grilled meat, barbecue chicken, bit of cigar, and sweet vanilla; the finish lingers with vinegar.

GENERAL
Robust but balanced peat, but a bit one-note—like drinking barbecue sauce.

PRICE
$$

RATING
★★

---

anCnoc Flaughter

AGE
No age statement

ALC/VOL
46%

Named for the tool used to remove the top layer of peat, which is prized for being richer and earthier, Flaughter has a relatively restrained phenolic content of 14.8 ppm.

NOSE
Orange rind, grape juice, match heads, seaweed, and herbal tea; water brings out a fresh coastal note, but the peat practically vanishes.

PALATE
Grape skins, minty sweetness, char, umami, tannic toward the middle; a meaty, strawberry note emerges with a drop of water. The finish dries off quickly, leaving a slightly sweet smokiness on the tongue.

GENERAL
A captivating balance among sweet, smoky, and tannic notes. The best of the anCnoc peated range.

PRICE
$$

RATING
★★

anCnoc Rutter

AGE
No age statement

ALC/VOL
46%

Named for the spade used to carve out thicker, slower-burning peat, which produces a mellower reek. Rutter has a modest 11 ppm.

NOSE
Pipe tobacco, orange zest, spice cake, skin lotion, herbal tea, and bacon; water brings out sandalwood, pear, and rosewater.

PALATE
Sweet up front, giving way to pepper, smoked ham, citrus oil, and burnt toast; water brings on an oak and fruit-skin astringency. The finish is medium in length, with echoes of smoke and fennel seed.

GENERAL
A good example of restrained peat that allows anCnoc's signature Highland character to shine through.

PRICE
$$

RATING

anCnoc Rascan

AGE
No age statement

ALC/VOL
46%

Rascan is named for the tool used to break up the topsoil of a peat bog. It has a moderate 11.1 ppm.

NOSE
Malty and slightly sour beer, vanilla, minerality, salt, grass, dried apricot, match heads, sulfur; with water, the minerality pops up, with orange pulp, pineapple, and vanilla.

PALATE
A medium mouthfeel that opens with spicy tangerine and orange zest, then darkens into ash, dark chocolate, leather, and cigars; water adds a salty, nutty note. The finish is long, with mint and smoked nuts.

GENERAL
A restrained, crisp, and saline smokiness, well balanced between sweet, smoke, and salt. It loves water—a few drops turns it on.

PRICE
$$

RATING

anCnoc
18 Year Old

Aged in a combination of ex-oloroso and ex-bourbon barrels.

AGE
18 years old

ALC/VOL
46%

NOSE

Light sherry notes, with honey, dark berries, marzipan, oak, orange marmalade, and cola, with water bringing out honeyed pears and jasmine.

PALATE

Boiled meat, roasted coffee beans, honeydew, and a hint of sherry with a full mouthfeel; the finish is quick and dry.

GENERAL

Smells like bourbon, but underneath the sweetness is a fine balance between oak and malt. A few minutes resting in the glass is critical, though—it needs to open up.

PRICE
$$$

RATING

anCnoc
24 Year Old

Aged in a combination of ex-oloroso and ex-bourbon barrels.

AGE
24 years old

ALC/VOL
46%

NOSE

Strong sherry influence, with white pepper, cherries, melon, oaky vanilla, cheese, and an unplaceable feinty, vegetal note; water shows celery salt, cream, and cocktail sauce.

PALATE

Malty sweet up front, resolving into honey-glazed ham, roasted coffee beans, leather, and ginger; the long finish has cinnamon, mint, and herbs.

GENERAL

For 24 years and all that sherry, it still tastes sprightly and bright without losing complexity.

PRICE
$$$

RATING

anCnoc
Limited Edition

A thirty-nine year old from anCnoc, drawn from just three American and Spanish oak ex-sherry casks. Rare as hen's teeth, but worth searching for because you won't find another whisky this old for a mid-three-figures price.

AGE

39

years old

ALC/VOL

44.2%

NOSE

Rum raisin, fruitcake, toasted herbs, soap, mushrooms, Bit-O-Honey, and a bit of sulfur; diluting it brings out fruit juice, ash, and Christmas cookies.

GENERAL

For an almost forty-year-old whisky, it's an amazing deal. Bright, spicy, and vibrant. The nose alone is worth the price.

PALATE

A medium-to-thick palate with burnt sugar, beef bouillon, espresso, candied violets, pencil shavings, and sherry; water brings out a meaty, dark chocolate richness. The finish is long and slightly metallic, with lingering sherry and mint notes.

PRICE

$$$$

RATING

Ardbeg

OWNER: LVMH

FOUNDED: 1815

REGION: ISLAY

PRONUNCIATION: *ARD–beg*

Like its neighbor Bruichladdich, Ardbeg is a born-again distillery. In the nineteenth century it was a small but successful operation, producing about 500 gallons a week and sustaining a community of about 200 people around it, including a school and a bowling green. The Hay family owned Ardbeg until 1959, when it was bought by DCL and the Canadian firm Hiram Walker; twenty years later, DCL bought out Hiram Walker's shares, only to mothball the distillery in 1981. DCL restarted it in 1989 and then re-closed it in 1996, at which point it was on the verge of destruction when Glenmorangie bought it. Glenmorangie—later purchased by the luxury-goods company LVMH—poured money into Ardbeg, and production restarted in June 1997. Today Ardbeg is known for its robust, aggressively peaty style, though old-timers insist that DCL Ardbeg was even more peaty (and with a phenolic content of 20 ppm in its new make, compared to the Octomore line from Bruichladdich, which runs into the triple digits, Ardbeg is far from the peatiest of Islay whiskies).

Ardbeg
10 Year Old

Ardbeg's entry-level expression, made with grain peated at the Port Ellen maltings. The whisky is aged in ex-bourbon casks.

AGE
10
years old

ALC/VOL
46%

NOSE

Banana and cherry candy, popcorn butter, orange cream, charcoal, and bacon; water makes it significantly sweeter.

GENERAL

Despite its cult status, Ardbeg has kept its prices relatively stable, making the 10 Year Old a great value for an introductory expression from a high-end distillery. It's less smoky than one might expect from its reputation, and not especially complex, with the peat notes in harmony with the grain.

PALATE

Honey-glazed ham, wood char, Kansas City barbecue sauce, almond, grilled pineapple; water calms down the char and introduces a salty note. The finish lingers, with cigar and charred orange.

PRICE

RATING

Ardbeg
An Oa

AGE
No age statement

Pronounced *AHN-oh*, this whisky is aged in a combination of ex–Pedro Ximénez and virgin oak casks.

ALC/VOL
46.6%

NOSE

Fennel, grapeseed, citrus, cream, saltwater, a good dose of peat; it opens with water, revealing simple syrup and berries.

PALATE

Thin, with a burst of menthol and wood char up front, followed by milk chocolate, grilled meat, raisins, and sea salt; water brings out barbecue spices and Big Red chewing gum. The finish is quick, though the cinnamon lingers.

GENERAL

The sherry influence is restrained, allowing the typical fun Ardbeg notes to tumble out. But they're a bit jumbled, especially on the palate, and never quite resolve themselves.

PRICE

$$

RATING

Ardbeg
Uigeadail

AGE
No age statement

A marriage of younger whiskies aged in ex-bourbon casks with older ex-sherry casks, Uigeadail is considered the favorite among the distillery's most ardent fans. Pronounced *OOGEH-dull*.

ALC/VOL
54.2%

NOSE

Wet stone, antique leather, iodine, smoked meat, and the mustiness of an Army/Navy surplus store; water brings out rubber balloons, caramel chews, and cinnamon. There's a vague herbaceous quality as well, like fresh-cut mint.

PALATE

Full-bodied and sweet up front, then turns toward rubber and charred meat; water dampens the sweetness but brings out dark chocolate and cinnamon notes. The cinnamon continues through the lingering finish.

GENERAL

Satisfying, full, and delicious—but only if you're a serious peat head.

PRICE

$$

RATING

Ardbeg Corryvreckan

AGE
No age statement

ALC/VOL
57.1%

The Gulf of Corryvreckan, northeast of Islay (actually, off the northern tip of the adjacent island of Jura), is home to the world's second-largest whirlpool—a powerful, angry swirl of water, which makes a good name for a scotch. Aged in ex-bourbon and ex–French wine casks.

NOSE

Citrus, pine, flower basket, dark cream, brisket; water makes it smell like maple syrup over pancakes.

GENERAL

A solid representative of the Ardbeg style, though just a tad unbalanced in favor of dark, burnt notes. Still, it has its partisans.

PALATE

A deep char note, with grilled oranges, smoky cherries, potpourri, and burnt cinnamon cookies. Water reveals a slightly funky umami note, like dank mushrooms. The finish is long, woody, and chewy, with just a hint of sweetness.

PRICE

$$$

RATING

Ardbeg Perpetuum

AGE
No age statement

ALC/VOL
47.4%

A still widely available "limited-edition" whisky, released in 2015 for the distillery's 200th anniversary. According to Ardbeg, it's a blend of old and new casks, both ex-bourbon and ex-sherry.

NOSE

Soapy, floral, fresh rubber, toasted coconut, grilled orange, blue cheese, and burning hay; water brings it down a notch and adds soy sauce and smoked gouda.

GENERAL

Slightly sweeter and smoother than a typical Islay, probably thanks to the older barrels included in the vatting. A bright and gorgeous Islay dram.

PALATE

A creamy mouthfeel, with wasabi, smoked meat, rubber gasket, orange drink—but also vanilla, honey, and buttercream; water amps up the spice and peat notes. The finish is slightly dry, with grilled habaneros, smoked cheese, and barbecue sauce.

PRICE

$$$

RATING

Ardmore

OWNER: BEAM SUNTORY

FOUNDED: 1898

REGION: HIGHLANDS

Ardmore was the brainchild of Adam Teacher, the son of the blending baron William Teacher, built to provide malt whisky for the Teacher's Highland Cream blend. The distillery remains primarily a supplier for Beam Suntory's various blends; though it has a capacity of 5.4 million liters a year, it has just one single malt expression available to American consumers.

Ardmore Traditional Cask

A relatively young whisky, finished in quarter casks to speed up maturation, much like its Beam Suntory stablemate, Laphroaig Quarter Cask. Though no longer in production, it's still relatively easy to find, and it has been repackaged (as Ardmore Tradition) for travel retail.

AGE

No age statement

ALC/VOL

46%

NOSE

Cooked pineapple, honey, papaya, oak, slate, and ever so slightly peated; it grows significantly more herbal with water, along with honey cake, grain, and oatmeal cookies.

PALATE

A thick mouthfeel that opens hot with pumpernickel, oak chips, soap, salt, and earthy peat; water simply underlines all of this. The finish is medium length, with chocolate and mint.

GENERAL

Tastes like a craft bourbon, and not a good one—hot and grainy, unformed, and overly oaked.

PRICE

$

RATING

NR

Ardmore Legacy

Termed "lightly peated," it's made from a mix of 80-percent peated and 20-percent unpeated malted barley.

AGE
No age statement

ALC/VOL
40%

NOSE
Bartlett pear, saccharine, baby vomit, minerality, lemon curd, brownies, and pencil shavings; water adds a bit of creaminess but otherwise ruins the nose.

GENERAL
Boring and thin—sweet and inoffensive.

PALATE
A thin mouthfeel with a lot of grain, lemon cake, vanilla, and a bit of campfire undernote, but not much character; water kills it. The finish dries a bit, with a touch of peat, toasted pumpkin seeds, and minerality.

PRICE
$

RATING

Arran

OWNER: ISLE OF ARRAN DISTILLERS, LTD.

FOUNDED: 1995

REGION: HIGHLANDS

PRONUNCIATION: *AIR-un*

One of the first distilleries founded in the latest wave of Scotch expansion, Arran is the brainchild of Harold Currie, a former Chivas executive. The island of Arran, tucked into the Firth of Clyde on the western coast of Scotland, between the suburbs of Glasgow and the Kintyre Peninsula, was once home to nearly fifty distilleries, but today its namesake is the only one carrying on the tradition. The folks at the distillery no doubt appreciate that heritage, because Arran produces a wide range of expressions for such a new and relatively small company, whose stills churn out just three quarters of a million liters of spirit a year, well below a tenth of what comes out of some of the Speyside stalwarts like Glenfiddich and Macallan. Arran is particularly known for its wine-barrel finishes, and rightly so.

Arran
Aged 10 Years

The distillery's basic, core expression.

AGE
10
years old

ALC/VOL
46%

NOSE

Toasted coconut, vanilla, butterscotch, white wine, raisins, green apple; with water, you get a bit of resin and an almost hoppy, fruity note.

PALATE

Tart dried citrus, coconut, malty creaminess, orange zest, and shortbread; the finish lingers with a slightly drying tart and spice note.

GENERAL

A superb drink for an entry-level expression; bright, bouncy, but not without depths and structure. Strikingly similar to Clynelish, with the citrus and creamy coconut notes.

PRICE

 $

RATING

 ★★★

Arran
Port Finish

Aged for about eight years in ex-bourbon barrels, then finished in ex-port casks.

AGE
No age statement

ALC/VOL
50%

NOSE

Red apples, dried tropical fruit, nutmeg, roasted nuts, leather, vanilla, and a brackish, fungal funk; water adds honey, red currants, and milk chocolate.

GENERAL

Discordant, messy, and intriguingly complex. Not everything works, but it's a beguiling, tasty dram.

PALATE

A medium mouthfeel, tart up front, with cough syrup, bitter citrus, saltwater, grain, and sour cherries; with water, it turns rich and sweet, with red currants, brown sugar, and salt. The finish dries fast; it's slightly medicinal and hot—think spicy cherries, hot peppers, and brine.

PRICE
$$

RATING

Arran
Amarone Finish

Almost rose pink in color; like its brethren, it has spent eight years in ex-bourbon barrels and is then finished in casks that formerly held amarone, a full-bodied Italian red wine.

AGE
No age statement

ALC/VOL
50%

NOSE

Peaches, cherries, vanilla, and a slight oak spiciness, more like a boozy wine than a whisky; water brings out granulated sugar, cake batter, and tropical fruit.

GENERAL

A whisky I can respect, but not like. The finish draws just what the whisky needs from the wine, but nothing more. Still, it's too dry and aggressive for me.

PALATE

A big mouthfeel that opens funky and fishy—think salmon skins—up front, which gives way to baker's chocolate, grape skins, some developing heat, and a slightly metallic tinge. The finish dries quickly, leaving an herbal, slightly vegetal aftertaste.

PRICE
$$

RATING

Arran
Aged 14 Years

Made from a combination of one-third European oak ex-sherry casks and two-thirds American oak ex-bourbon casks.

AGE
14
years old

ALC/VOL
46%

NOSE

Green apples, saline, dough, toast, creosote, tart candy, wet grass; water adds melons, lemon tart, and, after a while, honey and floral sweetness.

GENERAL

Lively, zingy, and sparkly, it's a different whisky than what you're used to, but also what you expect from Arran.

PALATE

Medium-bodied, with melons, sour lemons, cereal; a little water tames it significantly, bringing out bitter cocoa. The finish is long, bitter, and spicy, with the melon and grain notes riding through.

PRICE
$$

RATING

Arran
Cask Strength

An annual, full-throttle expression, with each batch at a slightly different proof. Drawn from a mix of ex-bourbon, first-fill sherry butts, and second-fill sherry hogsheads.

AGE
12
years old

ALC/VOL
52.9%

NOSE

Quite boozy, with clover honey, orange blossom, vanilla crème brûlée, and salt; the sherry notes pour forth with a drop of water

GENERAL

Despite the booze on the nose, it's less aggressive—indeed, much more delicate—than you'd think. Like most Arrans, this one is all about balancing different, competing notes, and it does it so, so well.

PALATE

A thick, meaty flavor, with ripe banana, grapefruit, and tangerine, growing sweeter toward the middle. Water calls forth citrus oil and buttered, peppery toast. The finish is long and slightly dry, with chocolate and hints of sweet and sour sauce.

PRICE
$$

RATING

Arran
Machrie Moor

Machrie Moor the place is a peat bog on the west central coast of Arran, most famous for Bronze Age stone circles. Machrie Moor the whisky is Arran's peated expression, at 14 ppm, released in semiannual batches.

ALC/VOL
46%

NOSE

Woodsy, vanilla, lemongrass, perfume, grapefruit, turned earth, putty, and verbena; water brings out lemon custard, swimming pool, and cigar tobacco.

GENERAL

Tastes like an underaged bourbon. Lacks intensity, despite the angry dog on the label.

PALATE

Medium-thin, with notes of grain, lemon custard, leather, and toast, and a big spice pop at mid-palate; water makes it even grainier. The finish shows ash, tobacco, and wood polish.

PRICE

$$

RATING

Arran
Sauternes Finish

AGE
No age statement

Aged for eight years in ex-bourbon barrels, then finished for an undisclosed span of time in casks that once held Sauternes, a sweet white wine from Bordeaux.

ALC/VOL
50%

NOSE

Honeysuckle, almonds, orange juice, maple syrup, bright floral notes, and an odd, entrancing meatiness in the back; water brings out vanilla, brown sugar, and freshly opened cigarette packs.

GENERAL

Rich and balanced—sweet and dry, fruit and flower, woody and crisp, with an intriguing bit of smoke at the back. Especially for 100 proof, it's light and drinkable.

PALATE

A thick mouthfeel, with fresh tobacco, honey, rum, citrus oils, and pepper at the mid-palate; water calls forth orange extract, Dr. Pepper, and ever-so-slight smoke. The finish pops with chocolate-covered cherries, lemon oil, and a long, peppery note.

PRICE

$$

RATING

Arran
Aged 18 Years

The distillery's oldest release to date and now a part of its core range, the 18 Year Old is aged in ex-sherry hogsheads and ex-bourbon barrels.

AGE
18
years old

ALC/VOL
46%

NOSE

Orange pulp, drawn butter, blueberry syrup, spicy honey, and a late-afternoon sea breeze; with a few drops of water, it transforms into peaches and cream.

PALATE

Dry citrus, cream, spicy vanilla, orange candy, and honey; the long finish shows peaches and black tea.

GENERAL

A perfectly balanced whisky, with clear but not dominant sherry notes. Pair it with a crème brûlée for a double treat at dessert.

PRICE
$$$

RATING

Auchentoshan

OWNER: BEAM SUNTORY

FOUNDED: 1817

REGION: LOWLANDS

PRONUNCIATION: *OAK-en-TOASH-en*

Where once there were dozens of Lowland malt distilleries producing light, aromatic whiskies, today there are just a handful, with Auchentoshan by far the largest and best known—though at just 1.75 million liters per year of output, it's not in the same league as some of the larger Speyside producers. At its founding, the distillery was known as Duntocher, but changed its name to Auchentoshan in 1834. It passed through many hands before, in 1984, landing in the palms of Morrison Bowmore, which was bought by Suntory ten years later. Auchentoshan stays true to the Lowlands style, with short fermentation times and triple-distillation to give its whiskies a light, grainy character.

Auchentoshan
12 Years Old

Auchentoshan's entry-level whisky, aged in ex-bourbon barrels.

12
years old

40%

NOSE

Like a hike in the woods, if those woods also contained toasted coconut, lemon crème brûlée, and ginger; water brings out a buttery fig note.

PALATE

Vanilla, lemon cream, raw honey, toasted nuts, and a fruity mid-palate; water brings forward a juicy roundness. The finish has a big burn for an 80 proofer; it's tannic and slightly peppery.

GENERAL

Like many Auchentoshans, the nose oversells the palate. It's tasty, but the finish comes much too fast.

PRICE
$

RATING
 ★★

Auchentoshan
American Oak

Introduced in 2014 as a replacement to Auchentoshan Classic. Aged in ex-bourbon barrels.

No age statement

40%

NOSE

Apple juice, grain, vanilla, oak, and citrus; water calls forward peach tea, ginger, blanched almonds, and orange zest.

PALATE

A thin mouthfeel, full of grain, almonds, orange zest, and pepper at mid-palate; water adds vanilla and a bit more spice. The finish is peppery and bitter—think wormwood.

GENERAL

A clash between grain and wood notes; it's too young, and the wood seems amped up to cover for it. The result is bitter and spicy, but not particularly tasty.

PRICE
 $

RATING
 ★

Auchentoshan Three Wood

AGE
No age statement

ALC/VOL
43%

Aged ten years in ex-bourbon barrels, then a year each in oloroso and Pedro Ximénez casks.

NOSE
A sherry bomb, with cherry syrup, oranges, balsamic vinegar, fruit punch, and a generally floral aroma; water amps up the juicy notes.

PALATE
Cherry cough syrup, ginger, candied orange peel; water makes it rounder and deeper. It's sweet right to the end, where it's replaced by ginger and bitter herbs.

GENERAL
A new turn from Auchentoshan's usual Lowland lightness; the sherry notes on the nose intrigue with their depth and breadth. But the palate just can't keep up.

PRICE
$$

RATING

Auchentoshan Valinch 2012

AGE
No age statement

ALC/VOL
57.2%

An annual release that varies in proof year to year, Valinch (named for the tool used to pull whisky samples from a barrel) is a cask-strength version of the classic Auchentoshan, aged in ex-bourbon barrels.

NOSE
Roasted vegetables, peach schnapps, aromatic wood, rye bread, Lemon Pledge; water brings out more of the vegetal notes.

PALATE
A thin-medium mouthfeel, with a palate that starts with grain-forward notes, then gets hotter until it reveals strong wood and metallic notes, along with burnt sugar. Water takes down the proof, but doesn't do much for the flavor. The finish is hot and spicy.

GENERAL
Hot and sharp, it lacks any of the rich vanilla notes one would expect from something aged in ex-bourbon barrels.

PRICE
$$

RATING

Auchentoshan
Virgin Oak BATCH II

AGE
12
years old

ALC/VOL
46%

A regular but limited-edition release. Like most American whiskeys, it is aged in new (i.e., unused) American oak barrels.

NOSE
Vanilla, swimming pool, lilies, spicy pear, butterscotch, sawdust, cool ash, and a whiff of dark fruit; water doesn't do much.

GENERAL
Auchentoshan gets credit for this risky innovation. The nose is intriguing, but the oak dominates the palate, and the malt can't quite stand up.

PALATE
Young and grainy, like a small-barrel bourbon—there's a gamey, sweaty quality, like rancio, as well as cloves, honey, butterscotch, and marshmallow sweetness. The finish is long, with preserved fruits, almonds, and bitters.

PRICE
$$$

RATING
★

Auchentoshan
18 Years Old

AGE
18
years old

ALC/VOL
43%

Auchentoshan's oldest expression in its core range, aged in ex-bourbon barrels.

NOSE
Toasted vanilla bean, coconut, peanut brittle, sweet sherry, ginger, and pine resin; water makes it oily and nutty.

GENERAL
Big on the nose, short on the tongue. Solid all around, but a bit too tannic toward the finish.

PALATE
Simple syrup, white pepper, spicy honey, and oak bitterness; with water you get a hint of banana bread. The finish is slightly tannic and minty.

PRICE
$$$

RATING
★★

Auchentoshan 21 Years Old

Aged in second-fill sherry casks.

AGE
21
years old

ALC/VOL
43%

NOSE

Woodsy, juicy, and spicy—think green chilies and green peppers—along with vanilla, pineapple, new leather, and sherry; water brings out a bit of boozy, heathery funk.

PALATE

Sugary up front, then unfolds with pepper, fish skins, orange peel, and baking chocolate; water doesn't do much. The finish is brief, with a white pepper pop.

GENERAL

A perfect example of a Lowland malt, with a surprising spring in its step for a twenty-one year old. The sherry is present but not overwhelming.

PRICE
$$$$

RATING

Aultmore

OWNER: JOHN DEWAR & SONS/BACARDI

FOUNDED: 1896

REGION: SPEYSIDE

PRONUNCIATION: *ALT-moor*

Like its stablemate Aberfeldy, Aultmore was founded near the close of the nineteenth century to provide malt whisky for the blending industry. Aultmore was built by Alexander Edward, the owner of Benrinnes and, later, Oban, who sold a stake to the Pattison brothers shortly before their whisky racket imploded in 1899. The distillery muddled through, and in 1923 John Dewar & Sons bought it, then quickly sold it to United Distillers. Along with Aberfeldy, Craigellachie, and Royal Brackla, Aultmore went back to Dewar and its parent company, Bacardi, in 1998. Though it has recently expanded its single malt offerings, Aultmore remains a benchmark for blenders, who account for almost all its output.

Aultmore
Aged 12 Years

AGE
12
years old

ALC/VOL
46%

Once a rarity, distillery bottlings of Aultmore are now more common, with the entry-level 12 Year Old in particular developing a small but devoted following.

NOSE

Bananas, fresh-baked walnut bread, and toasted coconut; water brings out notes of hay, blanched almonds, and crème brûlée.

PALATE

Pineapple, flower candy, milk chocolate, Juicy Fruit gum, and malted milk balls—and all of these open significantly with water. The medium-length finish is spicy and slightly juicy.

GENERAL

Wonderfully easy to drink—round and fruity. And while it's not cheap for a twelve-year-old whisky, it is, like a child in a Wes Anderson movie, oddly mature for its age.

PRICE
$$

RATING

Aultmore
Aged 18 Years

AGE
18
years old

ALC/VOL
46%

Nothing unique or special about the aging of this whisky—just 18 years of quality sleepy time, which have produced a classic unpeated, un-sherried Speyside.

NOSE

Crème brûlée, cedar, dried ginger, and dessert wine; water makes it smell a bit sweeter.

PALATE

Melon, salted caramels, and pineapple; with water, you find toasted marshmallows, menthol, and vanilla. It builds to a long, spicy, minty finish.

GENERAL

A solid but not great whisky.

PRICE
$$$

RATING

Balblair

OWNER: INVER HOUSE/INTERNATIONAL BEVERAGE COMPANY

FOUNDED: 1790

REGION: HIGHLANDS

Officially founded in 1790 but with roots going back to 1749, Balblair is one of the oldest distilleries in Scotland, well predating the 1823 liberalization of British distilling laws. In 1872 its owners, the Ross family, moved it a few miles away to be closer to a rail line. Like many distilleries, Balblair passed through several hands before ending up with Inver House (which itself has gone through several owners and is now a subsidiary of International Beverage Company, part of Thai Beverage Group). The distillery's new make spirit is meaty and sulfury, but aging transforms that heaviness into fruit, toffee, and spice notes. In 2008 it began to release only vintage-dated expressions. This means it can be hard to keep track of what is available from Balblair year after year; what follows are reviews of some of the most common expressions available as of 2017.

Balblair Vintage 2005

Barreled in ex-bourbon casks in 2005 and bottled ten years later; currently the youngest in the Balblair stable, replacing the 2003 vintage.

AGE
10
years old

ALC/VOL
46%

NOSE
Bright and fresh, with vanilla, milk chocolate, and yeast rolls right out of the oven.

Toasted coconut, yeast rolls, vanilla, floral, and sweet, honeyed malt. The finish is dry, with lingering vanilla notes.

GENERAL
More like a Speyside than its siblings. Water doesn't change much, but it gives the honeyed malt a pretty polish.

PRICE
$$

RATING

Balblair
Vintage 2002 FIRST RELEASE

Matured in ex-bourbon barrels and bottled at ten years old.

AGE
10
years old

ALC/VOL
46%

NOSE

Sponge cake, honey, apple, sawdust, peat, and toffee; water turns it spicy, with apple flesh, white pepper, and perfume.

GENERAL

A big, spicy whisky; slightly bitter, a bit sweet, and grainy. Better without water.

PALATE

Thick with honey cake, cinnamon, and bread, moving to a hot pepper mid-palate; water turns it sweeter, like spicy pears. The finish is on the brief side of medium-length; slightly dry, with lemon zest, vanilla, and bitter almonds.

PRICE
$$

RATING
★★⯪

Balblair
Vintage 2003 FIRST RELEASE

Aged in second-fill ex-bourbon barrels and bottled at twelve years old.

AGE
12
years old

ALC/VOL
46%

NOSE

Oranges, vanilla, coconut, lilies, and apple blossoms; water brings out crisp Granny Smith apples.

GENERAL

Like a spicy Speyside, but a bit grainy for a twelve year old. It's a tad on the narrow side, but still tasty.

PALATE

Sweet and spicy; a medium mouthfeel that builds from a floral perfume entry to a hot, round mid-palate. Adding water brings out vanilla, honey, grain, and apple flesh. The finish is long, hot, and fruity.

PRICE
$$

RATING

Balblair
Vintage 1999 SECOND RELEASE

AGE
15
years old

ALC/VOL
46%

Originally released for the travel retail market, the 1999 vintage is bottled at fifteen years old and aged in a mix of ex-bourbon barrels and Spanish oak ex-sherry butts.

NOSE

Raisins, fruitcake, spiced apples, pancake batter, and toasted coconut; it gets funky and umami-like with water—mushrooms, ginger, and a vague meatiness.

PALATE

Toasted coconut, candied ginger, rich vanilla, spiced pears; water brings out stewed strawberries. The finish is fruity, spicy, and slightly drying.

GENERAL

A delicious drink, with typical north Highland characteristics; fans of Clynelish should seek this one out.

PRICE
$$

RATING

Balblair
Vintage 1990 SECOND RELEASE

AGE
21
years old

ALC/VOL
46%

Aged for twenty-one years in ex-bourbon barrels, then two more in oloroso sherry butts.

NOSE

Rich caramel, chocolate powder, stewed fruit, and vanilla extract; the sherry really comes through with water.

GENERAL

Simply fantastic and an excellent value compared to other malts of similar age. Paradoxically, it's a bit thin without water, but a few drops deepen and round it out substantially.

PALATE

A bit thin and funky, with a rum-like rancio note on top of raisins, rubber, oak, and a spicy mid-palate; it improves with water, showing less rancio and going deeper and sweeter. The finish is long and spicy, a bit tannic, and oaky.

PRICE
$$$

RATING

Balvenie

OWNER: WILLIAM GRANT AND SONS

FOUNDED: 1892

REGION: SPEYSIDE

PRONUNCIATION: *Ball-VEN-ee*

Balvenie shares an expansive campus with Glenfiddich, though the two have their own complete sets of facilities and—it's pretty quickly obvious—very different styles. Glenfiddich is light-bodied and fruity; Balvenie is richer, with honey and dark fruit notes. William Grant founded the distillery six years after Glenfiddich and originally named it Glen Gordon, but soon switched it to Balvenie, after a nearby castle. Though Balvenie produces a hefty 5.6 million liters a year, it has maintained much of its old equipment, including a ninety-year-old malting facility that produces about 15 percent of its malt on-site—one of the few remaining distilleries to do so, to any extent. Under veteran master distiller David Stewart, Balvenie has managed to be both a tradition-minded distillery and an innovative one: Stewart was among the first to "finish" his whisky—first in port casks, and later rum casks—and he was a pioneer in the idea of "marrying" barrels in large oak containers, called tuns, before bottling.

Balvenie DoubleWood

AGE
12
years old

ALC/VOL
43%

Aged first in refill ex-bourbon casks, then transferred to first-fill ex-sherry casks for the last year or so. The Balvenie's basic expression, and it's a high bar for an entry-level whisky.

NOSE

Honey, a touch of sherry, fresh-cut wood, cake batter, and apricots; baking spices emerge with a touch of water.

GENERAL

Not a sherried malt per se; don't expect anything like a Macallan or GlenDronach. The sherry rearranges and accentuates what's there, but plays a supporting role.

PALATE

Smooth mouthfeel, with notes of sherry up front, then shifting to honey, honeydew, cinnamon bread, and a slightly anesthetic quality; the tannic finish lingers with muted spice.

PRICE

$$

RATING

★★★

Balvenie Caribbean Cask

AGE
14
years old

ALC/VOL
43%

A rare rum-finished single malt: After sitting in ex-bourbon barrels for fourteen years, this whisky spends a few months in American oak barrels that have been conditioned with a blend of West Indian rum.

NOSE
Warm, soft, tropical air, with notes of white rum, coconut, guava, and hay; water brightens and sweetens it.

PALATE
Fruitcake-rich, but less fruity than you'd expect; there's dark brown sugar, cane juice, cola, dark malts, and, underneath, a slight bitterness. It finishes with a warm note of cinnamon toast. The aftertaste is remarkably similar to a rich porter.

GENERAL
The rum doesn't dominate, and that's a good thing—the result is an engaging balance, a compelling drink after a light meal.

PRICE
$$

RATING

Balvenie Single Barrel CASK 1422 BOTTLE NO. 80

AGE
12
years old

ALC/VOL
47.8%

A more youthful expression than the 15 Year Old Single Barrel, this one's aged in first-fill ex-bourbon casks.

NOSE
Honey and drawn butter, cedar shavings, and fresh-cut ginger; diluted, it shows bananas and even more honey.

PALATE
Sweet and bitter, with a slightly buttery mouthfeel; it has a strong oak influence, with ginger, cola, and vanilla; those same notes continue through the long finish.

GENERAL
Amazingly complex and rich for a twelve year old; it's well worth the upcharge over the 12 Year Old DoubleWood.

PRICE
$$

RATING

Balvenie
Peat Week 2002

AGE
14
years old

ALC/VOL
48.3%

One week a year, Balvenie loads its on-site kiln with Highland peat. The resulting peated barley goes into a variety of expressions, but recently the distillery began turning out an all-peat expression at 50 ppm.

NOSE

Banana pudding, teriyaki jerky, creosote, soy sauce, cedar, Runts candies; water adds sweet wine and lemon juice.

GENERAL

Despite the high ppm, this is a balanced dram, thanks to its fourteen years in cask and the use of Highland peat, with its smokier, less medicinal character. There's something reminiscent of Japanese cuisine—soy sauce, teriyaki—in here. Details aside, this is simply a gorgeous whisky, from nose to finish, and a great alternative to the typical Islay peated malts.

PALATE

A medium-thick mouthfeel, with a deep and nuanced spice—think barbecue sauce —that turns sweet at the mid-palate. All along, there's an ashy, cigar tobacco, jazzy bass line. Water brings out heather, honeysuckle, and wildflower notes. The finish doubles down on the sweetness without being cloying.

PRICE

$$

RATING

Balvenie
Single Barrel CASK 770 BOTTLE NO. 451

AGE
15
years old

ALC/VOL
46%

Aged exclusively in sherry butts for fifteen years, this whisky is then released barrel by barrel, in batches of about 650 bottles each. No two barrels are the same.

NOSE

Rum raisin, fruitcake, new rubber, and a slightly herbaceous funk; the nose sweetens and the funk relaxes with a bit of water.

GENERAL

Complex, funky, and rich, a bit too much so at times, but adventurous types will love it for an after-dinner treat.

PALATE

Campfire up front, then the fruitcake and dried fruit notes emerge. There's a little perfume in there, alongside a bass line of smoked ham; smoke lingers on the finish.

PRICE

$$$

RATING

Balvenie DoubleWood

Like the 12 Year Old DoubleWood, but aged in first-fill ex-bourbon barrels for another five years before moving to the sherry. A new batch is released annually.

AGE
17
years old

ALC/VOL
43%

NOSE
Port, plums, apple juice, peach tea, oak spice, sweet tobacco, vanilla, and honey; water subtly accentuates it.

PALATE
The oak influence is clear—hot, with ginger, dried tobacco, spiced apple, cola, dried fruit, and citrus; the finish is long and spicy.

GENERAL
A big, solid whisky, with lots of spice. It needs a bit of water to calm it, despite the relatively low proof.

PRICE
$$$

RATING

Balvenie PortWood

Finished in thirty-year-old port pipes, after spending at least twenty-one years in ex-bourbon barrels.

AGE
21
years old

ALC/VOL
43%

NOSE
Rich and creamy, with plum jam, toasted coconut, and orange; water doesn't do much.

PALATE
Nutty, spicy, oaky, with raisins and coconuts up front; the port is present, but not dominant. It's a bit tannic on the long finish, with mint and strawberries.

GENERAL
Just a delicious, well-rounded drink—a stellar example of what expert finishing can do to elevate a malt from above average to outstanding.

PRICE
$$$$

RATING

Balvenie
Aged 30 Years

Aged in a mix of ex-bourbon and European oak ex-sherry casks, then slowly married together. Laid down over thirty years ago, this whisky nevertheless hits the mark in terms of Balvenie's house style—elegant, rich, and captivating in its depths of flavor.

AGE
30
years old

ALC/VOL
47.3%

NOSE

Honey, toasted almonds, linseed oil, dry sherry, chocolate powder, sawn wood, and baked apples; water amplifies the sherry notes and adds a subtle sweetness.

GENERAL

People often ask if very expensive scotch is worth the price. I say it depends—but in this case, the answer is most definitely yes.

PALATE

A medium-weight mouthfeel, with notes of vanilla bean, butter, honey, and cigar; nuts and dark fruits come out with a dash of water. Finishes with a slight burn, followed by a long echo of vanilla ice cream.

PRICE

$$$$

RATING

BenRiach

OWNER: BROWN-FORMAN

FOUNDED: 1897

REGION: SPEYSIDE

PRONUNCIATION: *Ben-REE-ahk*

BenRiach has gone through a star-crossed series of owners and closures since it opened in 1898, at the height of the Victorian-era whisky boom. It closed two years later and didn't come back online until 1965—and even after that, it operated in fits and starts until 2004, when it was bought by entrepreneur Billy Walker and two partners from South Africa. It has been open ever since, even though it's now in the hands of Brown-Forman, the Kentucky-based company best known for Woodford Reserve bourbon and Jack Daniel's Tennessee Whiskey. In recent years, BenRiach has produced a wide variety of expressions—so many that its portfolio has suffered an identity crisis—but under Brown-Forman, its range has begun to consolidate behind a few strong bottles.

BenRiach Heart of Speyside

BenRiach's non-age-statement introductory expression, Heart of Speyside, was recently discontinued.

AGE
No age statement

ALC/VOL
40%

NOSE

Pear, red apple, bright floral notes, Pine-Sol, cinnamon toast, and a Riesling-like minerality; it turns astringent with water, releasing apple candy and graham crackers.

GENERAL

It's a shame BenRiach brought this one to an end—for the price and proof, it's hard to beat. A classic, inexpensive Speyside.

PALATE

Sweet, juicy, and medium-bodied up front, it turns to spiced honey and barley at the mid-palate, accompanied by dried grass notes; water moderates and balances the sweet and spice notes, and adds chocolate, graham crackers, and herbaceous undertones. The finish is short, metallic, and slightly drying.

PRICE

$

RATING

BenRiach
Aged 10 Years

Aged in a combination of ex-bourbon and ex-sherry casks.

AGE
10
years old

ALC/VOL
43%

NOSE
Grilled shrimp, dried fruits, pencil shavings, wet moss, and a hint of smoke; water elicits more fruit notes and a wafting fresh air scent.

PALATE
Honey, baker's chocolate, coffee, roasted almonds, and orange zest; the long, tannic finish has honey and roasted peanut skins.

GENERAL
A straightforward, classic, but not simple, Speyside malt; it's smooth, but not superficial.

PRICE
$$

RATING

BenRiach
Curiositas

BenRiach's other ten-year-old expression is a surprisingly peaty Speyside single malt—and more like an Islay than the typical peated Speyside malt, at that.

AGE
10
years old

ALC/VOL
46%

NOSE
Grilled meat, biscuit box, vanilla, fruit punch candy, iodine, moss, and oak shavings; skip the water—it only weakens it.

GENERAL
The nose is finely balanced between sweet and peat; it's a nice alternative to an Islay, but don't expect anything radically different.

PALATE
Strong but not overwhelming peat notes—campfire, bittersweet chocolate, creamy malt, and a crisp minerality, followed by a long finish with hints of charred meaty bits and a vague minty coolness.

PRICE
$$

RATING

BenRiach
Tawny Port Finish

Sadly, the tawny port finish has been discontinued. Aged primarily in ex-bourbon barrels, it's finished in—you guessed it—tawny port hogsheads.

AGE
15
years old

ALC/VOL
46%

NOSE

Raisins, prune juice, s'mores, thick caramel, campfire, fruitcake, and putty; water brings out Nilla wafers and raspberry tea.

GENERAL

A delectable dram—full of chocolate, fruit, and subtle spice notes. Have it after dinner.

PALATE

Thick and darkly fruity— orange slices, fruitcake, raisins, molasses, dark chocolate; water thins it significantly but balances the dark, rich fruit with a fruit-candy and milk-chocolate note. The finish is quick, dry, and fruity.

PRICE
$$

RATING
★★
★

BenRiach
Madeira Finish

Aged in ex-bourbon barrels and finished in Madeira wine barrels from Henriques & Henriques. Like the port finish, this has been discontinued but still appears on shelves.

AGE
15
years old

ALC/VOL
46%

NOSE

On first nosing it, you'll find an overpowering vegetal, sulfurous note, but it fades quickly, to be replaced by straw, honeysuckle, barley soup, brown sugar, and earthy flowers. Water brings out green peppers, mint leaves, and nacho chips.

GENERAL

The sulfur is off-putting, but let it sit in the glass a few minutes and it's fine. And like a stinky cheese, the delicious, rich palate makes up for the nasal offense.

PALATE

Get ready for a big spice hit, with a touch of hazelnuts and wood smoke; as it sits, a tropical note of dried papaya and caramel emerges. Water lessens the spice and dries out the dram. The finish is short and a bit sweet, with just a wee pop of spicy chocolate.

PRICE
$$

RATING

★★
★

BenRiach Septendecim

Much heavier on the peat than the ten-year-old Curiositas; the balance is less between the malt and the peat than it is the peat and the oak.

AGE
17 years old

ALC/VOL
46%

NOSE
Grilled pineapple, sweet smoke, vanilla, iodine, pipe tobacco, and moss; water sweetens it.

GENERAL
The peat is big on this one, with iodine dominating the nose and palate.

PALATE
Pipe tobacco, iodine, anise, a sour fruitiness at the back, and a warm, spicy, numbing quality; the finish is long and smoky.

PRICE
$$$

RATING

BenRiach Aged 20 Years

Aged exclusively in ex-bourbon barrels, so there isn't much here to hide the basic character of well-aged malt.

AGE
20 years old

ALC/VOL
43%

NOSE
Lavender, crème brûlée, honey, creamy vanilla, bread dough, and cooking oil; with water, you find more oak, a vague savoriness, and a crunchy, fresh vegetable note of celery and carrots.

PALATE
Honey, light cream, ginger candy, vanilla bean, cake batter, and a malty bass line; the long finish is all about chocolate fudge.

GENERAL
For all the themes in the tasting notes, this is not a particularly sweet whisky; it has a rich depth that belies the superficial candy qualities. It's an excellent drink for right after dinner, as a digestif.

PRICE
$$$

RATING

BenRiach Authenticus

A replacement for the popular twenty-one-year-old Authenticus.

AGE

25

years old

ALC/VOL

46%

NOSE

Sweet sherry, vanilla, fruitcake, tropical fruits, oak shavings, and cola.

GENERAL

You'd be forgiven for thinking it's partly aged in sherry barrels. It's less peaty and more sweetly woody than younger expressions—a great pour for a bourbon fan looking to cross over into single malts.

PALATE

Sweet herbal and campfire notes, along with oak and cedar; it's a bit juicy, but also shot through with whiffs of charred meat and wood. The finish is long and a bit tannic, with strong asphalt overtones.

PRICE

$$$$

RATING

Benromach

OWNER: GORDON & MACPHAIL

FOUNDED: 1900

REGION: SPEYSIDE

PRONUNCIATION: *Ben-RO-mahk*

Along with BenRiach and a handful of others, Benromach was part of the late-Victorian-era boom in distillery construction; unlike many, it operated continuously until 1985, when it was mothballed. Over a decade later, Gordon & MacPhail, an independent bottler with a world-famous retail shop in nearby Elgin, bought the distillery and, in 1998, reopened it at a celebration attended by, among others, Prince Charles (a barrel filled for the occasion sits in one of the distillery's dunnage warehouses). Despite global distribution and a respectable range of expressions, Benromach is one of the smallest distilleries in Scotland, producing just over 500,000 liters a year. Though Gordon & MacPhail replaced almost all the equipment, there is virtually no automation at the distillery.

Benromach
10 Years Old

Aged for nine years in a mix of 80-percent first-fill ex-bourbon and 20-percent first-fill ex-sherry casks, after which it goes into first-fill oloroso casks for a year. The malt is lightly peated at 10 ppm.

AGE
10
years old

ALC/VOL
43%

NOSE

Slightly smoky, with teriyaki chicken, roasted peanuts, vanilla extract, chalk, apples, and pears; it loses the peat with a bit of water.

GENERAL

The peat is present, solid, but hardly overwhelming—well integrated and complex. A nice intro class on peaty Speyside malts.

PALATE

Peat, sour cherries, roasted malt, rubber, grilled orange, caramel chews, and a sweetness that grows to an acid sharpness; water adds pencil eraser and strawberries. The rich, lingering finish evokes campfire, caramel chews, and sharper phenols.

PRICE

$$

RATING

Benromach Peat Smoke 2006

Smoked at a sizable 62 ppm and aged in first-fill ex-bourbon barrels. Who said heavy peat was just for Islay?

AGE
10
years old

ALC/VOL
46%

NOSE
Iodine, aloe, light brown sugar, dried apricot, tobacco, and vanilla; water elicits honey and bright fruits.

PALATE
Grilled meat, black pepper, Atomic Fireball, orange juice, and vanilla; the finish is long, with lingering notes of spice, menthol, and smoked salmon.

GENERAL
A perfect pairing with smoked fish. It's a robust peat, but in balance with its sweetness and round spice moments.

PRICE
$$

RATING

Benromach Organic 2010

One of the few single malts made with 100-percent certified organic malt. It's aged for an undisclosed time said to be five to six years in lightly charred, virgin oak barrels sourced from Missouri.

AGE
No age
statement

ALC/VOL
43%

NOSE
Nutty, loamy, with honey, biscuits, ginger, grape soda, and charcoal; water underlines the nuttiness.

PALATE
Grain-forward, with vanilla, black pepper, corn pudding, and a bit of peat; the finish is quick, hitting its note with a pop of spice.

GENERAL
A decent dram, but not an improvement over the less expensive 10 Year Old. Eschew water; it thins out the palate too much.

PRICE
$$

RATING

Benromach Imperial Proof

AGE
10
years old

ALC/VOL
57%

A supercharged version of the standard Benromach 10 Year Old, it's a combination of 80-percent first-fill ex-bourbon and 20-percent first-fill ex-sherry casks. In Britain it's called "100 Proof," British proof measurements being a bit different from American.

NOSE
Cooked bananas, coconut, bacon, and a whiff of smoke, like your sweater after sitting next to a fire; add some water and you get caramel and a mossy, sea-air aroma.

PALATE
Smoky, sherry-juicy, with barbecue chips and a dark floral underside; opens up beautifully with water and finishes with a slightly dry peatiness.

GENERAL
A clear but restrained smokiness that's nicely integrated with a subtle sherry note.

PRICE
$$

RATING

Benromach 15 Years Old

AGE
15
years old

ALC/VOL
43%

A relatively new addition to the core range; it takes the same barrel program used to make the 10 Year Old but tacks on another five years in first-fill ex-oloroso sherry casks.

NOSE
Rich honey, fresh-baked raisin bread, sherry, and vanilla extract; water makes it sweeter, with garlic salt and herbal notes.

PALATE
Honey, sherry, orange zest, iodine, cinnamon, and salt; water tames the peat and makes it a bit sweeter. The finish has lingering peat and cinnamon notes.

GENERAL
A clear upgrade from the 10 Year Old, and worth the higher price.

PRICE
$$$

RATING

Benromach
21 Years Old

A rare bottle worth seeking out for a glimpse of what the old Benromach distillery was into. Aged in first-fill and refill sherry casks.

AGE
21
years old

ALC/VOL
43%

NOSE
Bananas, fresh linen, lavender, honey, toasted nuts, vanilla, and lemon curd; water brings out ginger, malt, and marigolds.

PALATE
A medium mouthfeel, with soap, honey, pepper, cereal grains, candied flowers, and just a touch of creosote; water turns it herbal and grassy, bringing out papaya and spicy pear. The spice lingers on the finish, along with floral candy.

GENERAL
Like crawling under fresh sheets—the floral and linen notes dominate. It's elegant, but rounded, with a depth.

PRICE
$$$

RATING

Benromach
36 Years Old

A fossil from another era: distilled before the Benromach distillery was mothballed in 1983, and aged in first-fill ex-sherry casks.

AGE
36
years old

ALC/VOL
46%

NOSE
Vanilla cake batter, cashews, honeycomb, prunes, and a surprisingly restrained sherry bass line; after sitting a while, milk chocolate emerges.

PALATE
As smooth as a putting green, with a complexly layered sweetness full of honey, sherry, cashews, anise, orange, cream, and tropical fruits; the finish dries under a blanket of graham crackers and oak notes.

GENERAL
The nose unfolds nicely, and the palate is a dream. The finish is a bit abrupt, but it leaves you wanting more. Don't even think of adding water.

PRICE
$$$$

RATING

Blackadder

INDEPENDENT BOTTLER

OWNER: BLACKADDER INTERNATIONAL

Named for a persecuted Scottish minister—and not the Rowan Atkinson sitcom—Blackadder is an independent bottler found mostly in Britain, but with occasional sightings in the United States.

Black Snake VAT NO. 2 / SECOND VENOM

The second release of the second in the Black Snake series, it's a vatting of several barrels from an undisclosed distillery, which are first married in ex-oloroso butts. Non-chill filtered, with no color added.

AGE
No age statement

ALC/VOL
57.7%

NOSE
Artificial fruit candy, moss, sandalwood, creosote, cherry juice, and fig jam; with water, you find grape skins, fresh bread, maple, caramel, roasted meat, and rum raisin.

PALATE
Syrupy with a big sherry hit up front, along with sultanas, dried cherries, leather, and creosote; water adds a rubbery note, yet also sweetens it somewhat. The finish is dry and relatively quick.

GENERAL
A huge whisky, with so much going on—chewy, juicy, and smoky. If you like a like a big, thick single malt, look no further.

PRICE
$$$

RATING

Bladnoch

OWNER: DAVID PRIOR

FOUNDED: 1817

REGION: LOWLANDS

PRONUNCIATION: *BLAD-nock*

Bladnoch is one of the oldest operating distilleries in Scotland; it is also the southernmost, being on the same latitude as the English city of Newcastle. The distillery was founded by the McClellan brothers, John and Thomas, in 1817, and ranked among the larger whisky producers through the nineteenth and early twentieth centuries. It fell silent for eighteen years beginning in 1938, and even after reopening it struggled to return to its former glory. In 1994 Raymond Armstrong, an Irish businessman, bought it from United Distillers, reopening it in 2000. Bladnoch was at risk of closure again in 2014, when Armstrong and his partners decided to liquidate it; fortunately, another entrepreneur, David Prior, who founded and sold a successful yogurt business in Australia, bought it up and restructured its core range. Today it produces the eight-year-old Samsara—reviewed here—as well as the fifteen-year-old Adele and the twenty-five-year-old Talia.

Samsara

Reportedly at least eight years old, and aged in first-fill California red wine casks and ex-bourbon barrels. *Samsara* is a Sanskrit word that means "wandering" or "world," and is used to connote rebirth.

AGE
No age statement

ALC/VOL
46.7%

NOSE
Raw and young, with a big hit of grain, honey, vanilla, and dried fruit notes—think apricots or fruit compote; there's a funky cheese quality, and a looming woodiness in the background.

Full bodied and thick; the opening is winey, spicy, and woody, resolving into creamy caramel, tobacco, and mint; the finish is crisp and malty. Water doesn't alter much.

GENERAL
Overpriced for such a young and under-polished spirit, but an intriguing glimpse at where the distillery is headed.

PRICE
$$

RATING

Bowmore

OWNER: BEAM SUNTORY

FOUNDED: 1779

REGION: ISLAY

PRONUNCIATION: *BO-more*

There is evidence that distilling took place at the Bowmore site well before it officially opened in 1779, making it one of Scotland's oldest. Like Laphroaig down the road, Bowmore has its own malting floor, and malts about a third of its barley needs; the rest comes from Islay's Port Ellen malting facility. (This choice is less for capacity or efficiency, and more because of the different malt characteristics that each facility can produce.) In the 1990s Bowmore was one of the first distilleries to release whiskies at different ages. Bowmore breaks up its malted barley before it's dried, so that it absorbs smoke more easily and peaty phenols less readily, which results in the whisky's signature smooth, smoky character. For a good while in the 1990s and 2000s, many people found a cheap floral quality in Bowmore's whiskies, which some called "French whore perfume."

Bowmore Small Batch

AGE
No age statement

ALC/VOL
40%

Added to the Bowmore core range in 2014 and chopped less than three years later, though you can still find it on shelves, Small Batch was aged in first- and second-fill ex-bourbon barrels.

NOSE

Apples, pears, honey-sweet barley, white pepper, saltwater taffy, and pencil eraser; water adds significant cherry notes.

PALATE

Old rubber, sweet smoke, ashtray, slight minerality; water just ruins it. The finish is all tobacco and ash.

GENERAL

A good mixer, but boring on its own—sweet, oily, without much depth.

PRICE	RATING
$	★

Bowmore
Aged 12 Years

The basic Bowmore, widely considered a baseline introductory Islay expression—peaty, but not too much so. Aged in ex-bourbon and ex-sherry casks.

AGE
12
years old

ALC/VOL
40%

NOSE
Cedar, anise, cake batter, cloves, Bac-Os; water brings out caramel, fresh greens, and a slight char note.

GENERAL
A disappointingly thin palate that could be improved with a slightly higher proof.

PALATE
Watery, with figs, potting soil, sea spray, Bac-Os, tarragon, orange peel, and a sweet mid-palate; water thins it even further but adds a spicy vanilla note. The finish is semi-dry, with lingering hints of campfire.

PRICE
$

RATING

Bowmore
Darkest

Essentially, the Darkest is the 12 Year Old Bowmore that has spent an additional three years in oloroso sherry casks. That certainly contributes to the darker color, but, alas, it also has caramel coloring added.

AGE
15
years old

ALC/VOL
43%

NOSE
Mushrooms, coal tar, red wine, barley soup, pouch tobacco, and black cherry; water amps up the mushroom-y funk.

GENERAL
Despite the misleading name, "Darkest" is an elegant, engaging drink, with a lot of campfire and resiny peat notes, at least for a Bowmore.

Rich and oily, with rhubarb, oregano, sweet tobacco, and grilled meat; water brings chili, menthol, and chocolate. The finish is dry, with mint, tobacco, dried herbs, and barbecue sauce.

PRICE
$$

RATING

Bowmore
Dorus Mor

AGE
10
years old

ALC/VOL
54.9%

Dorus mor means "rough seas" in Gaelic, and it's known as "Tempest" outside the United States. And for good reason—it's a nearly cask-strength ten year old, aged in first-fill ex-bourbon barrels.

NOSE
Raisins, potting soil, cherry cola, vanilla, and cedar; water makes it creamier, with cloves and sweet herbs.

PALATE
Red Hots, blackberry jam, ash, apple pie; water turns it cloyingly sweet. The finish is drying, with lingering cinnamon and campfire notes.

GENERAL
Despite the proof, the peat notes are restrained, offset by sweet and spicy notes.

PRICE
$$$

RATING

Bowmore
The Devil's Cask DOUBLE THE DEVIL

AGE
No age statement

ALC/VOL
56.7%

Aged in first-fill Pedro Ximénez and oloroso sherry casks, and named for a local Islay legend about a merry band of Scotsmen who chased a devil out of a church and through the Bowmore distillery. It's the third and last in the Devil's Cask series.

NOSE
Raisins, ginger, new rubber, blackberry, and cherry wood; with water, it shows stewed fruit and a bit more of that rubber note.

PALATE
Salted chocolate, rubber, cinnamon sticks, and candied orange; water makes it sweeter and smokier. The finish is long and drying, with orange zest and cinnamon sugar.

GENERAL
Water makes a big difference here, and not just because of the high proof. It corrals the sweet and peaty notes, bringing them into a smoky, sugary harmony.

PRICE
$$$

RATING

Bowmore
Aged 18 Years

Aged in a mix of ex-bourbon and ex-sherry casks.

AGE
18
years old

ALC/VOL
43%

NOSE

Sweet peat, rubber, asphalt, iodine, herbs, a bit of sherry, and a lot of barbecue pork; water makes it fruitier.

GENERAL

Just three years older than the Darkest, but significantly richer and deeper.

PALATE

Honey, sweet smoke, citrus zest, orange juice, and ginger, which comes to the front with water; the finish is long and, damn, isn't that honey barbecue chicken?

PRICE
$$$

RATING

Bowmore
Aged 25 Years

Like its younger siblings, the 25 Year Old is aged in a mix of ex-bourbon and ex-sherry casks, though with a higher percentage of the latter.

AGE
25
years old

ALC/VOL
43%

NOSE

Sauna, grassy, eraser heads, milk chocolate, goldenrod, olive juice, plums, and prunes; water brings out a sweet funk of Vidalia onions, brine, and mushrooms.

GENERAL

This is a complex whisky, to be sure, and it has its partisans. But many will find the soapy, floral palate a challenge, which shouldn't be the case for such an expensive pour.

PALATE

Soap, habanero peppers, cinnamon, hazelnuts, geraniums, and violets; water elicits more floral notes, along with cinnamon dust and a nut-skin bitterness. The finish is drying and bitter.

PRICE
$$$$

RATING

Bruichladdich

OWNER: RÉMY COINTREAU

FOUNDED: 1881

REGION: ISLAY

PRONUNCIATION: *Brook-LAD-ee*

Many distilleries have gone through periods of closure and even near-death, but Bruichladdich has been truly born again. Though it operated until 1994, it traded hands many times; when it was closed it was left to rust, and was near destruction when a group of investors led by the entrepreneur Mark Reynier took it over in 2000. The new team preserved as much equipment as possible and began distilling immediately. For the first decade or so of its new existence, Bruichladdich was known for a confounding— though also exciting—array of whiskies, including the legendary Laddie Ten. Today it has largely consolidated its offerings to a few ranges. At its core are the unpeated namesake brand and the peated Port Charlotte, both of which are released as "Scottish barley" bottles, made with mainland grain, and vintage-dated "Islay barley" bottles, made with grain from the island's farms. The distillery also produces a limited-edition, very heavily peated series called Octomore, and an occasional series called Black Art, whose age, peatiness, and finish change from bottling to bottling at the master distiller's whim. Along with Glenmorangie in the Highlands, Bruichladdich has some of the tallest stills in Scotland.

Bruichladdich Scottish Barley The Classic Laddie

AGE
No age statement

ALC/VOL
50%

Bruichladdich gained worldwide attention with its release of the Laddie Ten, a one-time, ten-year-old unpeated whisky. Once those stocks were gone—and it didn't take long—the distillery replaced the Ten with the Classic Laddie. It's unpeated, like the Laddie Ten, but the Classic Laddie is a blend of different ages.

NOSE
Funky barley, saltwater taffy, grainy, butterscotch, honey, and the distinctive Bruichladdich floral notes; water brings out brown sugar and cooked raspberries.

PALATE
A round mouthfeel, with spicy honey, peppermint, and spicy herbs; water ups the spice and adds a bit of chocolate and creamy honey. The finish is long, dominated by spicy caramel and oyster shells.

GENERAL
As an entry-level whisky, it's hard to beat (except on price). That said, fans of the Laddie Ten will tell you it's a big step down from its lauded predecessor.

PRICE
$$

RATING

Bruichladdich Islay Barley 2007

AGE
No age statement

ALC/VOL
50%

As with all Islay Barleys in the Bruichladdich portfolio, this one's made from grain harvested and distilled from a specific farm in a specific year—in this case, Rockside Farms in 2007.

NOSE
Honeyed pear, buttered toast, honeysuckle, and a deep, rich maltiness; water brings out grilled pineapple, cinnamon, and caramel.

PALATE
A rich, creamy mouthfeel, with bubblegum, oak, honey, dark fruits, and toffee; water amps up the sweetness. The finish is long and spicy, with notes of anise and Indian spices, and just a touch of ash.

GENERAL
Straightforward, simple, beautiful—the notes make it sound like a Speyside, but it's more raw, and less precious.

PRICE
$$

RATING

Bruichladdich Port Charlotte Scottish Barley Heavily Peated

AGE
No age statement

ALC/VOL
50%

A non-age-statement whisky using barley from the mainland of Scotland that's been peated to 40 ppm.

NOSE

Salted pork, roasted nuts, iodine, wet hay, white wine, bubblegum, and spring flowers; with water you'll find maple sugar and cocoa powder.

PALATE

A full mouthfeel that's sweet up front, with grass, cherry candy, and maple sugar, followed by a peat effervescence at the mid-palate; water tones down the sweetness and brings out a subtle floral note. The finish is sweet and semi-dry, with a bit of a vegetal note.

GENERAL

A good balance of sweet, salty, and savory notes. A solid whisky, but old timers will not hesitate to tell you how much better the old Port Charlottes were. Since those whiskies are but a memory, you can safely ignore them.

PRICE

$$

RATING

Bruichladdich Port Charlotte Islay Barley Heavily Peated

The town of Port Charlotte, on Islay, was once home to the Lochindaal distillery, and with this expression Bruichladdich is trying to approximate its legendary whisky. As with all expressions in the Port Charlotte series, this one is peated at 40 ppm, similar to other Islay peat bombs. For the 2008 vintage, the barley came from the Coull, Kynagarry, Island, Rockside, Starchmill, and Sunderland farms, right there on Islay.

AGE

No age statement

ALC/VOL

50%

NOSE

Caviar, smoked herbs, baked chicken, tangerines, burnt rubber, charred wood, and a slight nuttiness; water brings out Cinnamon Toast Crunch and fresh rubber gasket.

GENERAL

Delicious—like pulled pork barbecue in a glass.

PALATE

A medium mouthfeel, with the flavor of vinegar barbecue sauce slathered on pulled pork; there's a slightly sweet char note there as well. Water adds grilled fruit and Cinnamon Toast Crunch. The finish is long, woody, and acidic, with a bit of iodine running underneath.

PRICE

$$

RATING

Bruichladdich
The Laddie Ten
Second Limited Edition

AGE
10
years old

ALC/VOL
50%

A "limited" edition of eighteen thousand bottles, this is a reprise of the original Laddie Ten, released in 2011 as the distillery's first regular-production expression, but later discontinued. Unpeated and aged in a combination of first-fill ex-bourbon, ex-sherry, and ex–French wine casks.

NOSE

Mellow to the point of nonexistence, but there are whiffs of honey, grain, lemon zest, and white pepper. A bit more aroma comes out with a few drops of water.

GENERAL

What an odd whisky—a near-absent nose, an oil-thick mouthfeel, and an odd blend of flavors. Still, it's a cult favorite, and a solid choice for an after-dinner dram. If you find it, buy it.

PALATE

An unusually thick mouthfeel, almost like that of a liqueur; it's creamy and peppery, with lemon curd, spicy honey, and sea salt. Water brings out a roasted-nut quality. The finish is semi-dry, with chili peppers and lingering salt.

PRICE
$$

RATING

Bruichladdich
Octomore EDITION 07.4

Named for a nearby farm and former distillery, the Octomore range is a regularly released, limited-edition expression that claims to be the most heavily peated whisky in the world. Each release is a bit different; this one, 7.4, has a peat level of 167 ppm and is aged for seven years in virgin French oak barrels.

AGE
7
years old

ALC/VOL
61.2%

NOSE

Fresh paint, bacon, sawn oak, pine resin, army surplus store, campfire, raisins, toasted marshmallows, cut ivy, and vinegar barbecue sauce; water elicits pumpernickel bread, sherry, and clove-studded orange.

PALATE

Raisin, resin, honeyed caramel, mint, and spiced meats; with water you find campfire, fruit juice, and red wine notes. The sweet-and-spicy finish has a bit of ashtray to it.

GENERAL

A fantastic whisky, and don't let the eye-popping ppm frighten you. The peat is present but integrated; overall, the influence is more in the savory-meat range than campfire and ashtray. Pair it with salmon and blue cheese.

PRICE

$$$$

RATING

Bruichladdich
Black Art 1990 EDITION 04.1

The last in the Black Art series to be concocted by the legendary distiller Jim McEwan, the production of this twenty-three year old is a mystery—hence the name. The only detail the distillery will reveal is that it's unpeated, and drawn from a combination of ex-bourbon and ex-wine casks.

AGE

23
years old

ALC/VOL

49.2%

NOSE

Acetone, honeycomb, lavender, cherry chews, hay, and new car; it grows fruitier with water, and gains a bit of funk and saltwater taffy.

GENERAL

An excellent, evolving whisky, something to savor—contemplate, even—after a big dinner. Water helps enormously.

PALATE

Full-bodied, with grape jam, vanilla pudding, and wood char, moving to cured ham at the mid-palate; water underlines the salty meat character, and smoothes out the transition from sweet to salty/savory. The finish is dry and savory, with a slight note of tobacco ash, chocolate, and cooked stone fruits.

PRICE

$$$$

RATING

Bunnahabhain

OWNER: DISTELL GROUP

FOUNDED: 1887

REGION: ISLAY

PRONUNCIATION: *BOO-na-hav-venn*

Bunnahabhain was founded to provide peaty whiskies to the blending industry, and though it has since dropped almost all its peat to become one of the only more or less unpeated Islay brands, it remains a favorite of blenders: It is a primary component in Cutty Sark, Black Bottle, and Famous Grouse, among others. The distillery ages 90 percent of its whisky in ex-bourbon barrels and 10 percent in sherry casks, all on-site; it also ages casks from the Isle of Mull's Tobermory Distillery (including the Ledaig brand), which is also owned by Distell. Generally, "Boona" is known for its salty ginger note (and for its insanely hard-to-pronounce name).

Bunnahabhain Aged 12 Years

AGE
12
years old

ALC/VOL
46.3%

In 2011, Bunnahabhain jacked up the proof on its 12 Year Old, from 80 to 92.6; not unrelated, it stopped chill filtering its whisky. It's unpeated, but maybe there's something in the air on Islay—whiffs of smoke pervade.

NOSE

Nutty, woody; mushrooms, dried pineapple, orange zest, and a bit of smoke; it pops with water, blooming with fruit punch and wet stones. "Coastal" is a good, if vague, descriptor.

PALATE

Oily, with cherry cough syrup, coffee grounds, cashews, and oak chips; it loosens up with water, getting sweeter, with a pepper spice at the mid-palate. The medium finish is a bit dry and bitter.

GENERAL

Water makes a huge difference here. But it still suffers from too much wood influence.

PRICE

$$

RATING

Bunnahabhain Toiteach

AGE
No age statement

ALC/VOL
46%

Toiteach—pronounced *TOE-chuck*—is Gaelic for "smoky," a good name for Bunnahabhain's first contemporary peated whisky.

NOSE

So there's peat, and a good dose of it—iodine, slate, heather, kielbasa, and campfire encircle sweeter notes of charred pineapple, hay, melon, anise, and fennel. Water tames the peat, bringing out lavender, baked goods, and citrus—think key lime pie.

PALATE

It opens sweet, with a thick brown sugar and cigar note, then builds to hot peppers, salted almonds, campfire, and smoked sweet sausage; add some water to get cherries and Cel-Ray soda. The finish dries toward a hot wisp of campfire and strawberries.

GENERAL

This may be Bunnahabhain's first official peated release of the modern era, but they came to play. It's some serious peat, with some lovely interlacing between sweet, spicy, and smoky notes.

PRICE
$$

RATING

Bunnahabhain Ceòbanach

AGE
No age statement

ALC/VOL
46.3%

Pronounced *KEEOW-bin-ack*, it translates as "smoky mist" in Gaelic. Like its similarly phonetically challenged sibling, Toiteach, it's heavily peated, and in this case a bit more than ten years old, aged in ex-bourbon barrels.

NOSE

Portobello mushrooms, peanut shells, vanilla, dried roses, hints of sherry, and loamy earth; water brings out slate, savory tomato sauce, potting soil, and lavender perfume.

PALATE

Thick and savory: Think mushrooms cooked over a campfire, pine resin, lilacs, maple syrup, and seaweed; water underlines the meaty sweetness. The finish is long and hot, with a bit of mint and potpourri.

GENERAL

Like most Bunnahabhains, peated or not, it unfolds beautifully on the palate, going from sweet to a rolling heat. Some will find it a bit too sweet, though.

PRICE
$$

RATING

Bunnahabhain
Aged 18 Years

Bunnahabhain recently reintroduced this expression, this time au naturale—non–chill filtered, natural color, and at a higher proof.

AGE
18
years old

ALC/VOL
46.3%

NOSE

Caramel, hemp, fresh fig, black-berry jam, cinnamon, nutmeg, Magic Shell, salty (but not briny), and decomposing wood; water brings out caramelized fruit, ginger cola, dried reeds, and geraniums.

PALATE

Viscous mouthfeel that builds to a sweet mid-pal-ate, with cherry tobacco, caramel, and maple sugar; there's also some leather, copper, and black tea. It's more honeyed and floral with water. The finish is hot, with sweet and spicy pepper, and slightly tannic. A bit "coastal" right at the end.

GENERAL

Voluptuous, long, and spicy; it echoes between sweet, spicy, and earthy flavors. A real treat. It marries smoke and sherry expertly.

PRICE
$$$

RATING

Caol Ila

OWNER: DIAGEO

FOUNDED: 1846

REGION: ISLAY

PROCUNCIATION: *Cowl-EE-la*

One of the rare operating distilleries founded between the early- and late-nineteenth century whisky booms, Caol Ila is today by far the largest on Islay, with a capacity of 6.5 million liters per year. It employs a long fermentation process, up to 120 hours, which—along with a high cut—produces a fresh, grassy character. Caol Ila provides a significant amount of whisky for Diageo's flagship blend Johnnie Walker, but curiously, all of that is unpeated. Though the distillery is relatively close to Bunnahabhain, on the northeastern coast of Islay, it is one of the most remote distilleries in Scotland. As Alfred Barnard recalled about his visit to the distillery, "The driver directed our attention to an object about two miles away, which looked like a stump of a tree on a rock but which he assured us was Caol Ila."

Caol Ila
Aged 12 Years

Though it uses a fairly heavily peated malt, the final product is surprisingly sweet and balanced. Aged in ex-bourbon barrels.

AGE
12
years old

ALC/VOL
43%

NOSE

Bright and vibrant, with sweet grassiness, tropical candy (especially banana), nail polish, new car, new tennis-shoe rubber, cured meats, saline solution, and a touch of sulfur. A drop of water darkens the nose, with more iodine and general feintiness.

PALATE

Not as sweet as the nose lets on, but still light—honey-roasted chicken, smoked salt, seaweed, cooked bananas, strawberry chewing gum, and a bit of herbaceousness; the finish is gentle and medium in length, with ash and toasted seeds.

GENERAL

Restrained but direct in its peatiness, this is a solid introduction to the classic Islay style.

PRICE

$$

RATING

Caol Ila
Stitchell Reserve

Named for distillery manager Billy Stitchell, who retired in 2013, it's a non-age-statement expression aged in used and rejuvenated American oak and used European oak casks (unspecified, but probably ex-sherry). Oh, and it's unpeated, too.

AGE
No age statement

ALC/VOL
59.6%

NOSE

Melons, orange blossom, carpet glue, raw shrimp, slightly salty, cherries, and fresh oak shavings; water brings out more melon, green apple candy, white chocolate, and eau de vie.

GENERAL

Big, chewy, hot, rich—there's a lot going on here, and it may overwhelm. But it's a whisky worth getting to know. Despite the unpeated malt, there's an unmistakable Islay-ness to the whisky.

PALATE

A medium mouthfeel, with a load of heat. There's also dark fruits, dried apricot, and lots of oak; water turns it a bit astringent, but also adds dark floral and chocolate malt notes. The finish is long, with rubber, wasabi, fudge, and grilled fruit.

PRICE
$$$

RATING

Caol Ila
Aged 15 Years

Released in 2014, it's made in an "unpeated style" and aged in ex-bourbon casks, then bottled at cask strength.

AGE
15
years old

ALC/VOL
60.39%

NOSE

Caramel, fresh bread, dried hay, Italian herbs, celery, and white chocolate; with water, you'll find apples, melons, dried apricot, leaf piles, and freshly snapped twigs.

GENERAL

A perfect dessert whisky—dark, chewy, woody, and fruity.

PALATE

There's heat up front, of course, but it moderates into raisins, melon candy, orange pekoe tea, and oak dryness; with water, there's a slight seaweed note, dried hay, cherry cough drops, and chocolate. It dries quickly, with residual notes of raisins, dates, and black tea.

PRICE
$$$

RATING

Cardhu

OWNER: DIAGEO

FOUNDED: 1824

REGION: SPEYSIDE

PRONUNCIATION: *Car-DOO*

Practically (but not entirely) alone among Scotch distilleries, Cardhu was run, for many years, by women—first Helen Cumming and then her daughter-in-law, Elizabeth. (Originally it was spelled *Cardhow*; the spelling was changed in 1980.) Before the distillery went legal in 1824, Cumming mère devised ingenious methods for fooling traveling excise men, including disguising the entire distillery as a bakery. The Cummings later grew rich off providing malt whisky to DCL to put in its Johnnie Walker blend. In 1884 Elizabeth Cumming revamped the entire facility and sold its old stills to an enterprising startup distiller who needed secondhand equipment for his new distillery, Glenfiddich. The Cummings sold their distillery to John Walker & Sons in 1893. The distillery is the "brand home" for Johnnie Walker, and the single malt, for various reasons, is by far the most popular brand in Spain.

Cardhu
12 Years Old

A major component in Johnnie Walker, this is a classic, conventional Speyside malt.

AGE
12
years old

ALC/VOL
40%

NOSE
Bright tropical notes, with honey, cooked cream, vanilla, and fresh sea air; water kills it.

GENERAL
Solid but quick; a bit generic.

PALATE
Oysters, spiced honey, smoked chicken, vanilla, bright fruits, and a tiny bit of orange zest; it finishes with a pop of spice.

PRICE
$

RATING

Clynelish

OWNER: DIAGEO

FOUNDED: 1967

REGION: HIGHLANDS

PRONUNCIATION: *KLINE-leash*

Technically, Clynelish was founded in 1819 by the Marquis of Stafford, who chose the site for its proximity to the Brora coal fields. Like so many distilleries, it eventually fell under the ownership of DCL (now Diageo), which built a new facility next door in 1967. It renamed the old facility Brora, and gave the Clynelish name to the new one. (Brora closed for good in 1983.) Clynelish has a distinctive waxy character, which comes from its long fermentations and a policy of allowing gunk to build up in its spirits receiver, thereby reducing the amount of copper that the vapors can interact with. There is only one distillery bottling of Clynelish, but many independent bottlers offer it at different ages. (In 2017 Diageo announced it would reopen Brora.)

Clynelish
Aged 14 Years

Hard to come by until recently, this is the sole proprietary bottling of Clynelish available in the United States.

AGE
14
years old

ALC/VOL
46%

NOSE

Sherry, vanilla ice cream, paraffin, charred wood, spun sugar, hints of bananas, candied pork, cinnamon candy; water brings out sage and grass.

GENERAL

There's so much going on here; it's full-bodied and much richer than you might expect from a fourteen year old.

PALATE

The distillery's famous waxy mouthfeel is unavoidable here; it's round, peppery, and voluptuous, with thyme, banana cream, cinnamon, and a meatiness at mid-palate; the finish is long and semi-sweet.

PRICE
$$

RATING

Cragganmore

OWNER: DIAGEO

FOUNDED: 1869

REGION: SPEYSIDE

PRONUNCIATION: *CRAG-an-more*

Cragganmore was founded early in the Victorian-era whisky boom, and was one of the first distilleries built with the intention of supplying malt whisky for the growing blending industry. Long prized for its slightly peaty, slightly meaty character—the result, in the latter case, of using worm tubs instead of more modern shell-and-tube condensers—the distillery is beloved today by blenders and consumers alike. Cragganmore is located in Ballindalloch, near the southern reaches of Speyside. Despite its connection to blending, Alfred Barnard praised it for being the antithesis of urban distilling and blending: "Presently, and for a moment, the distillery, the object of our visit, appeared to view, in which we were shortly to see the process whereby that admired liquor, 'Mountain Dew,' is compounded, that, in the estimation of many Englishmen, as well as Scotchmen, is superior in sweetness, flavor, salubrity and gusto, to any that science and capital produces in crowded towns and cities."

Cragganmore
12 Years Old

Aged in second-fill ex-bourbon casks, which keeps the oak influence to a minimum.

AGE

12
years old

ALC/VOL

40%

NOSE

Rich bubblegum notes, with cherry, maple, melon, brown sugar, white-flower perfume, and the slightest whiff of peat; leave the water aside.

PALATE

Thin on the entry with Christmas spices, overripe melons, moss, and subtle caramel; lingering spice and tannins on the finish.

GENERAL

Minimalist and inoffensive. And unexciting.

PRICE

$$

RATING

★ ★

Cragganmore Distiller's Edition

DISTILLED 2001 / BOTTLED 2014

After an initial twelve-ish years in ex-bourbon barrels, this expression is one of the few single malts on the market today that's finished in port pipes.

AGE
No age statement

ALC/VOL
40%

NOSE

Lots of high oak notes: butter-scotch, vanilla, strawberries, lychee, and an ever-so-slight hint of smoke; water does nothing.

PALATE

All high notes: honey, vanilla, sweet pipe tobacco, creamy malt, and, out of nowhere, seared scallops; the tannic finish has vanilla, ginger, and menthol.

GENERAL

Quite sweet, without a lot of depth to it, but still an enjoyable dram, and a good example of an elegant, soft Speyside malt.

PRICE
$$

RATING

Cragganmore 21 Years Old

Aged in second- and third-fill ex-bourbon casks.

AGE
21
years old

ALC/VOL
56%

NOSE

Oily, berries, spicy honey, ginger, acetone, moldy paper, baked bananas; water adds a bouquet of violets, roses, and peonies, with a honeydew note.

PALATE

A thick, oily mouthfeel—spicy, herbal, and floral, with toasted coconut, acetone, and grappa; with water you find soap, violets, and strawberries. The finish is semi-dry, with milk chocolate, spearmint, and a slightly herbal edge.

GENERAL

Smoothly floral, and almost no sweetness; a divergence from the usual meatiness one finds in a Cragganmore.

PRICE
$$$

RATING

Craigellachie

OWNER: JOHN DEWAR & SONS/BACARDI

FOUNDED: 1891

REGION: SPEYSIDE

PRONUNCIATION: *Creg-ELLA-kee*

Craigellachie sits at the very heart of Speyside, on the northern edge of Aberlour and just up a hill from the Spey itself. In fact, the site was chosen because it lay at the intersection of several rail lines; in the century and change since, it has also come to sit astride several key regional roads and amid tourist-friendly neighbors like the Speyside Cooperage, the Craigellachie Hotel, and the Highlander Inn, the latter two with world-famous whisky bars. Like its dictionary neighbor Cragganmore, Craigellachie uses worm tubs to condense vapors coming off the still, producing a meaty, sulfurous note. The bulk of the whisky produced at Craigellachie goes into the White Horse blend; its first official single malt only appeared in 2014.

Craigellachie Aged 13 Years

Aged in ex-bourbon barrels.

AGE
13
years old

ALC/VOL
46%

NOSE

Cinnamon applesauce, potting soil, pine, dried oak, moldy leaves, mushrooms, mandarin oranges, and a general but unavoidable meatiness. Water adds tropical fruit notes, and amps up the meat and dankness.

GENERAL

Crisp, dry, and thick. A touch of ash and citrus. Robust and delicious, if not outside the ordinary.

PALATE

A medium mouthfeel, with spicy cigars, crisp Granny Smiths, ash, and mushrooms, turning bitter toward the middle; water tamps down the sweetness, but adds a little lemon zest. The finish is long, with salty, semi-sweet chocolate.

PRICE

$

RATING

Craigellachie
Aged 23 Years

A relatively new release from a very old and coveted distillery that until lately has been shy about bottling its own whisky.

AGE

23
years old

ALC/VOL

46%

NOSE

Cedar, roasted notes, soapy, minerality, maple syrup, and cherries and cream; water underlines the minerality, with slate, chalk, and potting soil.

PALATE

Round and creamy, with orange and lemon, building to a spicy pop at mid-palate; water adds sweet nuts and ginger honey. The finish is long, with grapefruit and white pepper.

GENERAL

The definition of a gracefully aged whisky—rich honey notes, without too much oak influence.

PRICE

$$$$

RATING

★★
★★

Dalmore

OWNER: WHITE & MCKAY/EMPERADOR

FOUNDED: 1839

REGION: HIGHLANDS

Dalmore Distillery was founded in 1839 by Alexander Matheson, whose family had made its fortune through his uncle, Sir James Matheson, a leader of the East India Company and a prime mover behind Britain's campaign to force China to buy opium. But don't worry—in 1891, control over the distillery passed to Andrew Mackenzie, an enterprising tenant farmer on the Mathesons' land. The distillery grew steadily during the twentieth century, with a pause during World War I, when it was used to make mines for the American war effort—in fact, part of the nearby harbor facility is called Yankee Pier. Dalmore began selling single malt (or "self malts") as early as the 1870s, and it soon developed a name for producing richly sherried whiskies, a reputation it continues to embrace today.

Dalmore
Aged 12 Years

This Dalmore expression is aged for nine years in ex-bourbon barrels, then half of it is transferred to thirty-year-old González Byass matusalem sherry casks for another three years while the remainder stays in the bourbon barrels.

AGE

12

years old

ALC/VOL

40%

NOSE

Orange peel, sweet malt, cinnamon, pears, oily ash, and sherry; waters adds a whiff of curry.

GENERAL

The nose is an immediate winner, but the palate takes a bit to open up, like a reluctant flower—give it time, it'll bloom.

PALATE

Intensely smooth, with unsweetened chocolate, coffee, white wine, and a slight bit of pepper; it's not especially sweet, but the finish lingers with a bit of cinnamon.

PRICE

RATING

Dalmore
Aged 15 Years

Like the 12, the 15 Year Old is first aged in ex-bourbon barrels nine years, then dumped into sherry barrels, though in this case all of it goes, split evenly among amoroso, apóstoles, and matusalem oloroso barrels.

AGE
15
years old

ALC/VOL
40%

NOSE
Melons, orange peel, perfume, sherry, and chocolate-covered coffee beans; a few drops and it smells like Ben and Jerry's Cherry Garcia ice cream.

PALATE
Rich, but not sweet; it has a solid, malty backbone, with orange zest, raisins, honey, and a touch of ginger toward the end.

GENERAL
Rich and creamy, but still disciplined and slightly austere, like a portly ex-Marine.

PRICE
$$$

RATING

Dalmore
Cigar Malt Reserve

Designed to complement a cigar—specifically, a Partagás Serie D, Numbers 2 and 4. It's aged in a combination of 70-percent matusalem oloroso sherry butts, 20-percent ex-bourbon barrels, and 10-percent premier cru cabernet sauvignon wine casks.

AGE
No age statement

ALC/VOL
44%

NOSE
Rich, sherried malt, with sweet pipe tobacco, shortbread, and a whiff of cinnamon; vanilla and juniper come forward with water.

PALATE
Toffee, wood notes, glazed bananas, fruitcake, cinnamon dusted on honeycomb, and sherried orange peel, with a dry finish.

GENERAL
One of those "I could nose this all day" whiskies. The palate is woody but not bitter. It's simply a fantastic whisky, with or without a cigar.

PRICE
$$$

RATING

Dalmore
Aged 18 Years

AGE
18
years old

ALC/VOL
43%

Continuing the Dalmore house style, this is aged for fourteen years in ex-bourbon barrels, then transferred for four years to matusalem oloroso sherry butts from González Byass.

NOSE

Sherry, maple, orange zest, leather, chocolate-covered raisins, dry ash, pear; water brings out a nutty, peppery brine note.

PALATE

Stewed cherries, lemon peel, baker's chocolate, almonds, raisins, and dry gin, with a long, medium-dry finish.

GENERAL

A bit sweeter than the younger expressions, and significantly more complex.

PRICE
$$$

RATING
★★★

Dalmore
King Alexander III

AGE
No age statement

ALC/VOL
40%

A complex whisky aged in a sextet of bourbon, port, Marsala, oloroso sherry, Madeira, and cabernet sauvignon casks. It's named in honor of Scotland's King Alexander III, who was saved from a charging stag by Colin of Kintail, of Clan Mackenzie, whose descendants (much) later took ownership of the Dalmore distillery.

NOSE

Genuine Dalmore, but so much more: orange zest, cranberry sauce, raisin bread toast, vanilla bean, sherry, and light toffee. Leave the water aside.

GENERAL

Simply astounding—a perfect balance of robust and nuanced notes, with a finish that echoes for hours.

PALATE

A bit of smoke that opens into spiced fruit, plum jam, raisins, port, almond biscotti, and, toward the middle, black pepper, with a creamy, medium mouthfeel; the finish is long, peppery, and a bit tannic.

PRICE
$$$$

RATING
★★★★

Dalwhinnie

OWNER: DIAGEO

FOUNDED: 1897

REGION: SPEYSIDE

PRONUNCIATION: *Dal-WHINNY*

At one thousand feet above sea level, Dalwhinnie is the second-highest distillery in Scotland, surpassed only by Braeval. The name is derived from the Scots Gaelic word meaning "the meeting place," and indeed it is at the confluence of three old roads, which made it the ideal location for cattle drovers and whisky smugglers long before anyone realized it would be a good place to make whisky, too (well, legal whisky, that is). Like Cragganmore and Craigellachie, Dalwhinnie has worm tubs, but unlike them, its house style is light and grassy—Iain Banks compares it to a fino sherry you might drink before a meal.

Dalwhinnie Aged 15 Years

A simple, classic Speyside whisky, aged in ex-bourbon casks.

AGE
15
years old

ALC/VOL
43%

NOSE
Peaches, almond, strawberries, vanilla, sweet malt, toffee, and apple blossoms; water brings out an oily, nutty rancio note.

GENERAL
This one takes well to water, which tones down the bitterness toward the end and extends the sweet notes. It's a solid, middle-of-the-road Speysider that will surprise with its rich sweetness.

PALATE
Roasted peanuts, cigar smoke, floral tea, apple cider, and grain; water makes the sweetness richer and adds a surprising, pleasing sponge cake note. The finish is drying and slightly bitter, a bit like Earl Grey tea.

PRICE
$$

RATING

Dalwhinnie Distillers Edition

A non-age-statement whisky (rumors say it's about 15 years old) aged in ex-bourbon barrels that has spent an additional year in ex-oloroso sherry casks.

AGE
No age statement

ALC/VOL
43%

NOSE
Very sweet, with honey, peaches and cream, vanilla, and confectioners' sugar; water brings out pear, cider, and floral notes.

PALATE
A medium mouthfeel, with chocolate, sweet cinnamon, and ginger; water adds cedar, orange blossom, and a bit of white wine. The slightly bitter finish is surprisingly meaty and leathery.

GENERAL
Elegant but robust. The finish is a bit of a mess, but not unpleasantly so. Quite easy to drink, this one.

PRICE
$$

RATING
★★

Deanston

OWNER: DISTELL GROUP

FOUNDED: 1964

REGION: HIGHLANDS

Deanston is a rare example of a once-common category, the mill-distillery—that is, a distillery that took the place of a mill, using its water-power capacity to mill grain and perform other whisky-related tasks. In Deanston's case, the mill was already 180 years old when Brodie Hepburn, the distillery's founder, bought it and shut down its weaving operations in 1964. Distilling began five years later. It was closed between 1982 and 1990, when it was acquired by Burn Stewart, a forerunner of its present owner, Distell.

Deanston Virgin Oak

A non-age-statement expression that is matured in refill bourbon barrels, then finished in new American oak casks.

AGE
No age statement

ALC/VOL
46.3%

NOSE
Honeycomb, nougat, malt balls, citrus, and soy sauce; it blossoms with water, revealing bananas, cherries, and a chalky minerality.

GENERAL
A conventional, if slightly spicy, Highland whisky, but a great deal for the money.

PALATE
A thinnish mouthfeel, with mint (think Listerine), Christmas spices, and vanilla; water brings out basil and pepper. The round, dry finish elicits minty chocolate notes.

PRICE
$

RATING

Deanston
Aged 12 Years

AGE
12
years old

ALC/VOL
46.3%

Aged in ex-bourbon barrels, un-chill filtered.

NOSE

Orange zest, rich honey, cinnamon, grain silo, and a whiff of smoke; adding water amplifies the smoke note and adds figs and salty air.

PALATE

Vanilla cream, barley, raisins, and smoke at the mid-palate; there's citrus if you add water. The finish is smoky and quite dry, with just a hint of sweetness.

GENERAL

Complex for a twelve year old, with a solid balance between smoky and sweet.

PRICE
$$

RATING
★★
★

Deanston
Organic

AGE
14
years old

ALC/VOL
46.3%

One of the few single malts available anywhere to go through the rigors of organic certification (by Britain's Organic Food Federation), from the barrels to the barley to the maturation and bottling.

NOSE

Oily and loamy, redolent of French onion soup, mushrooms, miso, and a dollop of honey; water rounds it out and sweetens it, with a nutty, floral, orange-cream quality.

PALATE

Honey, orange marmalade, milk chocolate, fresh grass clippings, and grapefruit; with water you find orange peel and dark chocolate. The finish is clean and spicy, with a continuation of the grassy, chocolatey mid-palate.

GENERAL

The organic designation is laudable, though it doesn't affect what's in the glass. Still, this is a unique, complex, and somewhat messy whisky that's worth seeking out.

PRICE
$$

RATING
★★

Deanston
Aged 18 Years

AGE
18
years old

Like the Virgin Oak expression, the 18 Year Old gets a double shot of Kentucky: It first matures in refill bourbon casks, then it's finished in first-fill bourbon barrels.

ALC/VOL
46.3%

NOSE

Honeycomb, nougat, malt balls, citrus, and soy sauce; it blossoms with water, revealing bananas, cherries, and a chalky minerality.

PALATE

A heady blend of vanilla and wood spices with a mushroomy, rancio through-line; water fleshes it out with mint and chocolate but adds even more wood. The finish is long and full bodied, with leather, white pepper, coconut, and candied ginger.

GENERAL

This is a bourbon lover's scotch. Imagine a marriage of the oily spiciness of Clynelish with the vanilla sweetness of a bourbon.

PRICE
$$$

RATING

Deanston
Aged 20 Years

AGE
20
years old

Aged exclusively in ex-oloroso sherry barrels, then bottled at cask strength.

ALC/VOL
55.5%

NOSE

Cooked mushrooms, prunes, charcoal briquettes, baker's chocolate, fruitcake, miso, and grilled meat; water turns it a bit smoky, with a slight whiff of Necco wafers.

PALATE

Thick on the palate, with fish skins, cookie dough, charcoal, fruitcake, and sultanas; adding water brings out chocolate, green pepper, mushrooms, grilled pork, and peppercorns. The long finish is slightly sweet, but the savory charcoal notes continue through like an electric bass line.

GENERAL

A powerful, dense nose; it's weird but captivating, and delicious. Let it unpack, though; the nose and flavor change with a bit of time and a drop of water.

PRICE
$$$

RATING

Dun Bheagan

INDEPENDENT BOTTLER

OWNER: IAN MACLEOD DISTILLERS

PRONUNCIATION: *Dun BAY-gun*

Along with owning the private-label brand Dun Bheagan, Ian Macleod Distillers owns both Glengoyne and Tamdhu outright. The Dun Bheagan range includes whisky from an undisclosed distillery in each of Scotland's major regions.

Dun Bheagan Highland

AGE
8
years old

ALC/VOL
43%

NOSE

Heather, musty grain, old closet, spice cabinet; water brings out a stale, sweaty funk.

GENERAL

A real miss for the Dun Bheagan line.

PALATE

A medium mouthfeel, with raw nuts, tobacco, black pepper, peas, grain, green bananas, and milk caramels; water underlines the grain notes, but adds a soapy, seaweed quality. The green bananas linger on the finish, which is otherwise dry and quite woody.

PRICE
$

RATING
NR

Dun Bheagan Island

AGE
8
years old

ALC/VOL
43%

NOSE

Crisp—think ocean breezes, beach fire, Bit-O-Honey, and an earthy funk at the back. Water turns it more medicinal, with less honey.

GENERAL

A good, basic introduction to the Island style. It lacks a bit of depth and nuance, but for the price, it's hard to beat.

PALATE

A thin mouthfeel, with smoke up front that builds to a spicy, oak- and chocolate-laden mid-palate; water broadens the taste, adding dried fruit, toffee, coffee, and pepper. The spice notes linger on a dry finish.

PRICE

$

RATING

★

Dun Bheagan Lowland

AGE
8
years old

ALC/VOL
43%

NOSE

Dark fruits, wood polish, heather, raisin box, stale bread, and a bit of butyric funk; water turns it slightly cheesy.

GENERAL

Nothing remarkable here, save for a few off notes. Lots of wood and smoke for a Lowland whisky. The palate is muddled but inoffensive. A solid mixer.

PALATE

A thin sip that's smoky up front, giving way to cinnamon and pronounced wood notes; water adds a bit of sweetness. Ends with a smoky, peppery finish.

PRICE
$

RATING

Dun Bheagan Speyside

AGE
8
years old

ALC/VOL
43%

NOSE

Apple bin, honey, pine, cardboard, and marigolds; with water you'll smell dried wood and apple chips.

GENERAL

Darker and meatier than you'd expect from a Speyside, though it still hits all the right regional notes of floral and honeyed sweetness.

PALATE

Thick and a bit meaty, with baked apples, dried apricots, dried flowers, and solvent; water makes it smoother and a bit sweeter—think apple eau de vie. The finish is dry and lingering, with wood, cinnamon, and a hint of mint.

PRICE
$

RATING

Edradour

OWNER: SIGNATORY

FOUNDED: 1837

REGION: HIGHLANDS

PRONUNCIATION: *Edra-DOO-er*

Like Benromach well to its north, Edradour is an old distillery that fell on hard times, only to be revitalized by an independent bottler looking to branch out. Also like Benromach, Edradour is one of the smallest distilleries in Scotland. It was founded, and run for many years, by a collective of local farmers, and it retains its farm-distillery aesthetic: Though Signatory has significantly upgraded its visitor center and other facilities, it looks much like it did 150 years ago: a collection of white-washed buildings nestled around the Edradour Burn.

Edradour
The Distillery Edition

Aged in ex-oloroso sherry and ex-bourbon casks.

AGE
10
years old

ALC/VOL
43%

NOSE

Maple syrup, cedar, leather, dried hay, pecans, cinnamon, lemon wax, and vanilla; water calls forth a slight vegetal funk, alongside old library mustiness.

GENERAL

Scotch for bourbon lovers—lots of warm spice and vanilla notes. But there's something off about it; the alcohol sits on top of the flavors, while the nose and palate clash.

PALATE

Oily and full, soapy and spicy, with honeycomb, varnish, maple, and sherry; water doesn't do much, except draw the heat back to the mid-palate. The finish is medium in length, oaky and spicy, with figs and smoke.

PRICE
$$

RATING
★★

Edradour
Ballechin

Edradour's heavily peated expression (at least 50 ppm, according to the distillery), Ballechin is aged in a combination of ex-bourbon and ex-oloroso sherry casks.

AGE

10
years old

ALC/VOL

46%

NOSE

Honey-baked ham, cold campfire ash, moldy hay, soap, and leather; with water, you'll find honey, rubber, and herbal tea.

GENERAL

Appropriate coming from a distillery that touts its agricultural leanings, Ballechin is as close to a farmyard as you'll find in a Scotch. That makes for an interesting nose, but a challenging palate.

PALATE

A medium mouthfeel; the entry is rich with honey, leading to a rich, charred sweetness. Water brings out more of the meaty, smoky side of the whisky. The finish is quick and spicy, with soap and ash at the end.

PRICE

$$

RATING

Finlaggan

INDEPENDENT BOTTLER

OWNER: VINTAGE MALT WHISKY COMPANY

Located on an island in Loch Finlaggan, a lake on Islay, Finlaggan is a set of ruins that once served as the seat of the Lords of the Isles, who ruled over most of Scotland's western islands until the fifteenth century. The whisky is a non-age-statement mystery brand, sourced from an unnamed distillery and produced by a company called the Vintage Malt Whisky Company Ltd. Its source is widely debated online, but the company says only that it has always gotten all its whisky from the same single distillery on Islay. Is it Caol Ila? Is it a young Ardbeg? Who knows? In the United States, it can most easily be found at Trader Joe's, alongside TJ's own private-label scotch.

Finlaggan
Old Reserve

AGE
No age statement

ALC/VOL
40%

NOSE

Marine peat, with iodine, old rubber, pine, and campfire hot dogs, along with lemon soap and jerky. Water brings out more iodine, along with vanilla, ash, dirt, and baking spices.

GENERAL

This isn't just good for its price—it has depth, roundness, and complexity, especially surprising given the proof. It's distinctly, but not overly, peaty. Just shows that quality doesn't require a luxury price tag.

PALATE

A thick, buttery mouthfeel, with a sweet and smoky roundness; roasted pork emerges toward the mid-palate. Water kills it. The finish is long and meaty, with iodine and spicy chocolate.

PRICE
$

RATING

Glencadam

OWNER: ANGUS DUNDEE

FOUNDED: 1825

REGION: HIGHLANDS

PRONUNCIATION: *Glen-CAD-am*

A trim, rather nondescript distillery nestled between the North Sea coast and the Cairngorm Mountains, Glencadam is historically a major source for blending whisky. Mothballed by its previous owner, Allied Distillers, in 2003, it was sold to Angus Dundee three years later. Glencadam is known for its grassy, buttery, pear, and flower notes, the result, in part, of its stills' upturned lyne arms, which increase reflux and reduce the sulfur content in the distilled vapor.

Glencadam Aged 10 Years

Aged in ex-bourbon barrels; non-chill filtered and no coloring added.

AGE
10
years old

ALC/VOL
46%

NOSE
Hay, fresh laundry, bubblegum, and grape soda; adding a little water brings out maple syrup–drenched French toast, powdered sugar, and a slight minerality.

PALATE
A medium mouthfeel, with honey up front, followed by tobacco, SweeTarts, and stewed plums; water makes it richer and fuller, with a strand of fresh ginger. The finish is semi-dry, and semi-bitter—pepper and menthol.

GENERAL
Fantastically rich for a ten year old—full, but fresh and youthful.

PRICE
$

RATING

Glencadam
Aged 15 Years

A welcome release, first seen in 2009, from a distillery better known (if at all) for its contributions to some of the leading blends.

AGE
15
years old

ALC/VOL
46%

NOSE

Honey dribbled over papaya, white pepper, toasted coconut, green apples, and caramel chews; with water, you get grilled pineapple.

PALATE

A medium mouthfeel, with stone fruit, toasted coconut, and a peppery Sancerre; water makes it sweeter, like a Pedro Ximénez sherry. The finish is quick, dry, and slightly peppery.

GENERAL

Elegant but booze-forward; it's not especially sweet, but not overly severe either.

PRICE

$$

RATING

GlenDronach

OWNER: BROWN-FORMAN

FOUNDED: 1826

REGION: HIGHLANDS

PRONUNCIATION: *Glen-DROH-nock*

GlenDronach was founded in 1826 by a cooperative of local farmers led by James Allardice, but it was destroyed by fire in 1837 and not rebuilt until 1852. It is among Scotland's lovelier distilleries, with expansive gardens and a mansion on the premises. Like Macallan, GlenDronach specializes in sherry cask aging and finishes; it is also a major part of Teacher's blended whisky.

GlenDronach Original

Aged in Pedro Ximénez and oloroso sherry casks, the 12 Year Old, aka "The Original," is a down-the-line, heavily sherried malt. A more aggressive alternative to the Macallan 12 Year Old.

AGE
12
years old

ALC/VOL
43%

NOSE

Rich, sweet malt, herb-rubbed meat, ash, and a hint of creosote, and tons of sherry—of course. Water brings out a creamy, cherry whiff.

GENERAL

A classic sherried Highland whisky, but quite robust—and yet, somehow, it's not a heavy drink. Pick this for a light after-dinner drink.

PALATE

Creamy sherry, sour cherries, coconut milk, with a pop of ginger at the middle and tannins toward the end; the finish reverts to a creaminess, with spiced chocolate.

PRICE

RATING

GlenDronach Peated

AGE
No age statement

ALC/VOL
46%

This relatively new expression is a throwback to the distillery's olden days, when it used peated malt as a matter of course. Like all modern GlenDronachs, it's then aged in ex-sherry barrels.

NOSE

Like many peated Speyside whiskies, the smoke on this one is muted and less medicinal than its island cousins, blending well with notes of cherry syrup, honeyed pear, and sweet ash; water calls forth more smoke and—there it is—a bit of iodine.

PALATE

Sweetly smoky, with maple syrup, butter, and grilled pineapple; the mid-palate presents a spicy blend of sweet paprika and cinnamon, while the finish has green apple and smoked sausage.

GENERAL

Fun and different than the usual GlenDronach—than most sherried Highland malts, for that matter. Its subtlety will disappoint peatheads, though there's too much peat for the smoke-averse. Best to approach this one with an open mind.

PRICE
$$

RATING

GlenDronach Tawny Port Finish

AGE
15
years old

ALC/VOL
46%

As the name implies, this now-quite-rare version of the discontinued 15 Year Old is finished in tawny port casks.

NOSE

Mushrooms, sulfur, brown sugar, barley soup, Fig Newtons, and raisin bread; with a drop of water, it opens into wood pulp, milk chocolate, cola, and red wine.

GENERAL

Powerful and supple, but elegant. A perfect after-dinner dram.

PALATE

The port really does a number here: It's thick with raisins, cola, nuts, and rancio; water brings out rum raisin, espresso, and prunes. The finish shows chocolate-covered raisins and dried ginger.

PRICE
$$$

RATING

GlenDronach Allardice

AGE
18
years old

ALC/VOL
46%

Named after the distillery's founder, James Allardice, and aged exclusively in oloroso sherry barrels.

NOSE
Raisins, rancio, fruitcake, carnations, and powdered jelly donuts; grows sweeter with water.

GENERAL
Quite a change from the 12 Year Old, though the creamy notes are consistent. The oak influence is clear, but not overwhelming.

PALATE
Dry up front, and not as sweet as you'd expect from the nose—toast, raisins, dried ginger, semi-sweet cream, thick marmalade, menthol, and cola syrup; the ginger persists on the slightly tannic finish.

PRICE
$$$

RATING
★★★

GlenDronach Parliament

AGE
21
years old

ALC/VOL
46%

Named for a parliament of rooks that live in the trees next to the distillery, the 21 Year Old goes back to the oloroso/Pedro Ximénez combo used for the 12 Year Old.

NOSE
Powerful sherry notes, with chocolate fudge, allspice, brown sugar, coffee, citrus zest, and a bit of smoke. Water elicits the smell of orange cream and unleaded gasoline, but in a good way.

GENERAL
Almost like drinking sherry itself—rich, complex, powerful.

PALATE
Raisins up front, then toast, stewed fruit, citric acid, and a touch of tannins and wood smoke; the lengthy finish has lightly roasted almonds and malt.

PRICE
$$$

RATING

GlenDullan

OWNER: DIAGEO

FOUNDED: 1897

REGION: SPEYSIDE

PRONUNCIATION: *Glen-DOO-lan*

Though Glendullan is Diageo's second-largest distillery, at 4 million liters a year, it is relatively unknown as a single malt, with virtually everything it makes going into blends (in particular, Old Parr). The company is trying to change that with the Singleton brand, an umbrella name that covers the single malt output of three distilleries for three global regions: The Singleton of Dufftown goes to Europe, the Singleton of Glen Ord goes to Asia, and the Singleton of Glendullan comes to the United States.

GlenDullan
The Singleton
12 Years Old

Made from a marriage of whiskies aged in ex-bourbon and ex-sherry casks.

AGE
12
years old

ALC/VOL
40%

NOSE
A fruit bomb: raspberry, honey, cherry cough syrup, and fruit cake, with a slight funk at the back; water thins it out and elicits a lavender note.

GENERAL
The oaky bitterness overpowers everything. Like many mediocre whiskies, the nose deceives; the palate reveals.

PALATE
A thick, honeyed mouthfeel, with bitter wood, fruitcake, rum-funk, rubber gasket, and a savory undertone, which comes to the fore and clarifies into grilled mushrooms and wood. The brief finish is bitter and semi-dry.

PRICE
$

RATING
★

GlenDullan
The Singleton
15 Years Old

Made from a marriage of whiskies aged in ex-bourbon and ex-sherry casks.

AGE
15
years old

ALC/VOL
40%

NOSE

Orange blossom, cough syrup, vanilla, acetone, and a general mustiness (think basement carpet); with water you find lavender, cherry cola, and a vague funkiness.

GENERAL

An improvement over the twelve year old, but with the same flaws—unbalanced, overly woody, and bitter.

PALATE

Surprisingly thick at 80 proof, with artificial strawberry, bitter almonds, and so, so much oak. It thins out a bit with water, bringing forth a strawberry and meat combination not unlike baijiu. The slightly sweet finish is brief and dry, with hints of wormwood and dirty metal, like sucking on a penny.

PRICE
$$

RATING

GlenDullan
The Singleton
18 Years Old

The oldest of the Glendullan Singletons, aged, like the others, in a combination of ex-bourbon and ex-sherry casks.

AGE
18
years old

ALC/VOL
46%

NOSE

A subtle, almost nonexistent nose, with sawdust, black tea, rum raisin, and potting soil; water turns it a bit musty, like rotting leaves, though with a hint of juiciness in there.

GENERAL

The best of the three, but still of a type. The metallic notes are hard to move beyond. Even at this price, there are many, many better eighteen year olds.

PALATE

Juicy and metallic, meaty and funky—there's honey, tea leaves, and chocolate; with water you'll get cedar and even more chocolate. The medium finish is dry and bitter, with grape skins, mint, and copper.

PRICE
$$

RATING

Glenfarclas

OWNER: J. & G. GRANT

FOUNDED: 1836

REGION: SPEYSIDE

PRONUNCIATION: *Glen-FARK-las*

One of the only family-owned distilleries in Scotland, and one of the few to still use direct-fired pot stills (perhaps not coincidentally, Springbank also falls into both categories). Glenfarclas was founded in 1836 by Robert Hay; after he passed away, it was purchased by the Grant family, who still own it today. Don't let the heritage fool you: Glenfarclas is a major distillery, popular with blenders and churning out 3 million liters a year. But it's also a cult favorite with single malt fans. Fun fact: During the hard times in the late 1970s, the distillery tried to make extra money by farming crayfish in an unused mash tun.

Glenfarclas
Aged 10 Years

Billed as an aperitif whisky, it's a fine entry-level expression to a much-loved but relatively low-profile single malt brand.

AGE
10
years old

ALC/VOL
40%

NOSE

Butterscotch, dried apricot, and raisins with a subtle graininess; a bit of water brings out brighter fruit notes.

GENERAL

A bit thin and unremarkable, but fine as an everyday drink, especially during the summer. The sherry influence is minimal.

PALATE

Medium-bodied but crisp, with a grainy backbone; citrus, tannins, and lightly toasted bread dominate, leading to a quick, dry finish.

PRICE

$

RATING

Glenfarclas
Aged 12 Years

AGE
12
years old

ALC/VOL
43%

Just two years older than the twelve year old, but the two couldn't be more different. The sherry notes on this whisky are immediate and robust.

NOSE
Loads of sherry notes up front, with burnt butter, cinnamon, and orange pekoe tea.

PALATE
Coffee candy, bright summer fruits, and a bit of mushroom funk underneath; the sherry becomes more pronounced at the finish.

GENERAL
Significantly more complex than the 10 Year Old; compares well with other twelve-year-old sherried whiskies, like the Macallan.

PRICE
$

RATING

Glenfarclas
105 Cask Strength

AGE
No age statement

ALC/VOL
60%

Introduced in 1968, Glenfarclas 105 was the first widely available cask-strength single malt. The "105" refers to the proof (as measured in the slightly different British proofing scale).

NOSE
Honey, acetone, Bit-O-Honey, dried leaves; water brings out caramel cubes and maple notes.

PALATE
Port, maple, dark chocolate, and an umami/soy-sauce undertone; the finish lingers with, deliciously, Tootsie Rolls.

GENERAL
A great pick for bourbon lovers— thick and sweet, with a kick, but surprisingly smooth for such a high proof.

PRICE
$$$

RATING

Glenfarclas
Aged 17 Years

AGE
17
years old

ALC/VOL
43%

The 17 Year Old is sold exclusively in North America, Japan, and at travel retail—a rare instance when giving a bottle to a Scottish friend is not a case of bringing coals to Newcastle.

NOSE

Quite malty, with maple sap, aged rum, and steamed meat; with a drop of water, peppermint and dried apricot emerge.

PALATE

Hoppy, minty, and white-chocolate-y, though not especially sweet; the finish is crisp, with citrus and hop notes.

GENERAL

With the hop notes on the palate, beer lovers will dig this whisky. So will everyone else: It's complex—robust but sophisticated, bright but with significant depth.

PRICE
$$$

RATING

Glenfarclas
Aged 21 Years

AGE
21
years old

ALC/VOL
43%

Aged in a combination of ex-bourbon and ex-sherry (oloroso and fino) casks.

NOSE

Musty at first, then it opens into honeycomb, orange peel, ginger, and cinnamon; water brings out apricot and raspberry.

GENERAL

A finely tuned whisky—sweet, spicy, and minty, it's complex without being precious or fusty.

PALATE

Very sweet and spicy, round and buttery, with an oily mouthfeel and notes of sugar cookies, strawberry candy, honey, and a touch of mint; the candy notes continue through the finish.

PRICE
$$$

RATING

Glenfarclas
Aged 25 Years

One of the oldest whiskies to have been aged exclusively in ex-sherry barrels.

AGE
25
years old

ALC/VOL
43%

NOSE

Fruit cake, brown sugar, and fine leather gloves; water reveals gingerbread and cola.

GENERAL

A good example of age not dictating quality; while this is a fine whisky, the 21 Year Old is simply better. Still, don't turn this down; it's a solid after-dinner drink, and would pair well with aged gouda.

PALATE

Fall spices like cinnamon and nutmeg, along with maple bacon and cola gum—almost like a high-rye bourbon; the mouthfeel is syrupy and the finish is quick.

PRICE

$$$

RATING

Glenfiddich

OWNER: WILLIAM GRANT & SONS

FOUNDED: 1886

REGION: SPEYSIDE

PRONUNCIATION: *Glen-FID-ick*

Glenfiddich is located on a neatly appointed campus that it shares with Balvenie; both distilleries were founded by William Grant and are still owned by his namesake company. Its name means "The Valley of the Deer," hence the brand's iconic stag's head logo. Glenfiddich came first; it was completed in 1886 and began distilling on Christmas Day, 1887. In the 1960s it was the first distillery to market a single malt expression, and today it is the best-selling single malt Scotch in the world and the second-best in the United States, just behind Glenlivet.

Glenfiddich Aged 12 Years

AGE	ALC/VOL
12 years old	**40**%

Aged in a combination of ex-bourbon and ex-sherry casks, the 12 Year Old is one of the best-selling single malts in the world.

NOSE

Rich honey notes, pears, green apple candy, cloves, melon, brown sugar, and an ever-so-slight salinity; water brings out more apple and a hint of nail polish remover.

PALATE

Opens with honey, then moves to fresh ground pepper, cinnamon, berry juice, and vanilla; it finishes with notes of spice and a juicy sweetness.

GENERAL

As you might expect from a worldwide bestseller, this one is solid but unchallenging. Whatever you do, don't add water—it's already perched on the edge of dissolution; a few drops is all it takes to break the flavors apart.

PRICE

RATING

Glenfiddich Bourbon Barrel Reserve

AGE
14 years old

ALC/VOL
43%

First aged in ex-bourbon casks, this whisky is then finished in new, charred American oak barrels for an added kick.

NOSE

Vanilla, cloves, Red Hots cinnamon candy, orange blossoms, and a whiff of iodine; water brings out pancake syrup and honeysuckle.

GENERAL

A step up from the 12 Year Old and certainly a different flavor profile, but it's a bit too oaky, with too much one-note sweetness.

PALATE

Very sweet, with strawberries, cherries, breakfast-cereal sugar, and maple syrup, balanced with oaky tannins, vanilla, and bitterness; the finish has leather, espresso, and a minty, hoppy aftertaste.

PRICE
$$

RATING
★★

Glenfiddich Unique Solera Reserve

AGE
15 years old

ALC/VOL
40%

The solera process, in which new wine, beer, or spirits are vatted with older liquids, is most often associated with sherry production; here, Glenfiddich first ages its whisky in new oak and ex-sherry casks, then lets it spend time in a large vat that the distillers keep half full.

NOSE

Cherry cough syrup, wheat crackers, grain, dark chocolate; water shows nutmeg, cloves, and dried leaves.

GENERAL

Disappointing against its younger siblings, the 15 Year Old is simple and superficial, especially for a whisky with such a complex production process.

PALATE

Figs, bittersweet chocolate, cinnamon candy, and bitter citrus, though water sweetens it significantly; the medium-length finish returns to bittersweet notes of espresso and baker's chocolate.

PRICE
$$

RATING

Glenfiddich EXPERIMENTAL SERIES 01
Finished in India Pale Ale Casks

AGE
No age statement

ALC/VOL
43%

Glenfiddich teamed up with Speyside Craft Brewery to create a customized IPA that, when aged in a barrel, would impart maximum flavor into the wood; later those same barrels were used to finish this non-age-statement single malt.

NOSE
New oak, old bananas, spring breeze, vanilla, cinnamon; water brings out Bananas Foster and woodsy, herbaceous notes.

PALATE
Cedar, cinnamon, cola, and, over time, a pleasant, vague sweetness; finally, at the very end of the finish, hops appear.

GENERAL
An interesting experiment, but ultimately not compelling—Glenfiddich should have let the beer play more of a role here.

PRICE
$$

RATING

Glenfiddich
The Original 1963

AGE
No age statement

ALC/VOL
40%

A limited release, but with a large enough number—some twenty-four thousand bottles—to merit consideration here. Called a "replica" expression, it's a blend of old stocks intended to mimic the profile of the original Glenfiddich Straight Malt, the granddaddy of scotch single malts.

NOSE
Chocolate chip blondies, Bosc pears, ground cinnamon, vanilla, black tea, and a bit of sherry that grows more pronounced with air; water adds a pop of baked pear and chocolate.

PALATE
A thin, watery mouthfeel—tobacco, vanilla cream, grapefruit; water introduces some sherry notes but also dilutes it significantly, even with a few drops. The finish is slightly dry, with lingering tobacco.

GENERAL
The nose engages; the palate underwhelms. It's elegant but lacks depth. The trademark Glenfiddich pear and vanilla are there—a few more ticks up on the proof would transform it.

PRICE
$$

RATING

Glenfiddich Small Batch Reserve

Aged in a mix of ex-oloroso sherry and ex-bourbon casks.

NOSE

Cedar, grappa, honey, vanilla extract, pine needles, and hazelnut; with water, you get molasses cookies and maple syrup.

PALATE

Cherry candy, ginger, mint leaves, flat Coke, juniper, stewed fruit; the finish is long and sweet with a hint of mint and espresso.

GENERAL

A respectably complex, interesting whisky, but it's not quite reaching its potential—as good as it is, you sense that it should be deeper, richer, more complex.

PRICE

$$$

RATING

Glenfiddich Reserva Rum Cask Finish

While this expression has been on the market in Europe for several years, it only recently arrived in the United States. As its name implies, it's a twenty-one year old finished in rum casks.

AGE
21
years old

ALC/VOL
40%

NOSE

Vanilla custard, rum balls, orange candy, and candied ginger—think of a Dark and Stormy. Water adds a buttery undertone.

PALATE

A surprising lack of rum influence on the rather thin palate; there's brown sugar, wood, and citrus, but it's sadly one-note. Water brings out a bit more citrus and tropical fruit. The finish is slightly spicy and bitter.

GENERAL

An enticing nose, but the palate is beyond disappointing—cloying, one note, and even a little water destroys whatever nuance is in the glass.

PRICE

$$$

RATING

Glenfiddich Excellence

Aged for a whole twenty-six years exclusively in ex-bourbon barrels for a clean, direct malt expression—a daring choice for a brand that often relies in part on sherry aging.

AGE
26
years old

ALC/VOL
43%

NOSE

Crisp, clean, and deep, with peach tea, orange blossom, vanilla wafers, pineapple, and a soft meatiness, like lightly roasted chicken.

PALATE

Cinnamon spiciness up front, mellowing to apple, vanilla, honey, and dried tropical fruits; the medium-length finish is clean and crisp, like mint gum, with a bit of creamy oakiness.

GENERAL

A lovely, elegant whisky, like silk lace; the lack of finishing on such an old whisky is a demonstration of just how much good barrel management can do.

PRICE
$$$$

RATING

Glen Garioch

OWNER: BEAM SUNTORY

FOUNDED: 1797

REGION: HIGHLANDS

PRONUNCIATION: *Glen GEAR-ick*

Licensed in 1785, Glen Garioch is one of the oldest distilleries in Scotland, if not the oldest (like a lot of scotch history, it's a matter of debate). It is one of the few malt distilleries—Bruichladdich is another—that only sells a single malt; none of its output goes into blends (though Glen Garioch used to be a main component in Sanderson's Vat 69 blend). During the inflation and fuel-crisis era of the 1970s, the distillery made extra money by using its waste heat to warm several greenhouses, whose produce it then sold.

Glen Garioch 1797 Founder's Reserve

Non-age-statement, aged in ex-bourbon and ex-sherry casks.

AGE
No age statement

ALC/VOL
48%

NOSE
Butterscotch, green apples, white pepper, vanilla cream, cherry juice, and a slight salinity; water turns the green apples red, adding loamy oakiness.

PALATE
Ginger, cherry cola, vanilla, and a mid-palate citrus hit; water doesn't do much. The finish is long and ginger-spicy.

GENERAL
A pleasant but generic drink; no harm in making it an everyday pour, but there are cheaper, more interesting options.

PRICE

RATING

Glen Garioch Aged 12 Years

Aged in ex-bourbon and ex-sherry casks.

AGE
12
years old

ALC/VOL
48%

NOSE
Vanilla, raisin, fresh ginger, freshly sawn cedar, and tropical coconut; water adds rum raisin and more vanilla.

PALATE
Full and round, with coconut, ginger, spicy mango, butterscotch, and orange zest; water brings out biscuit and tobacco. The finish is long, semi-dry, and spicy, with black pepper and ginger.

GENERAL
A huge step up from the Founder's Reserve—spicy and tropical, with intriguing depth, especially after adding a bit of water. A good introduction to the Highland style.

PRICE
$$

RATING

Glen Garioch Virgin Oak

Aged exclusively in new American oak barrels for an undisclosed period of time.

AGE
No age statement

ALC/VOL
48%

NOSE
Not surprisingly, big, hot vanilla hit up front, then sawn cedar, grain mash, lemon water, and cardboard; with water you get even more wood and grain, along with stewed potato and cocoa powder.

PALATE
Medium mouthfeel, with loads and loads of grain notes, along with cedar and chocolate-covered cherries. It turns even grainier with water; there are nuts and fruit juice as well. The finish shows vanilla and pepper.

GENERAL
Pronounced aroma and palate, as you'd expect from new oak, but there's too much grain at the opening. It integrates as it evolves. Tastes very much like a craft bourbon.

PRICE
$$$

RATING

Glenglassaugh

OWNER: BROWN-FORMAN

FOUNDED: 1875

REGION: HIGHLANDS

PRONUNCIATION: *Glen-GLASS-awk*

Glenglassaugh is located on the northeastern coast at the border of the Speyside region. A longtime supplier to blended scotches like Cutty Sark and the Famous Grouse, it shut down production in 1986, one of the many casualties of the drop in global demand during the 1970s and '80s. In 2008 a private investment firm bought and refurbished it; five years later it sold the distillery to BenRiach, which in turn sold it to Brown-Forman in 2016, along with the BenRiach and GlenDronach distilleries. While there are a few pre-1986 expressions on the secondary market, these days Glenglassaugh is known for its three excellent, no-age-statement whiskies.

Glenglassaugh Revival

Aged in a combination of ex–red wine and first-fill ex-bourbon casks, then married and re-barreled in sherry casks.

AGE
No age statement

ALC/VOL
46%

NOSE
Minerality, toast, carpet fibers, charcoal briquettes, and dried moss; water turns it woodsy, with a bit of campfire.

GENERAL
Lots of depth for a young whisky (though the precise age is unstated). The sherry influence is just right.

PALATE
Winey, oily, and nutty, with dry sherry, raisins, and mild pepper; there's very little sweetness, but a certain perplexing minerality at the back. The finish reminds one of a spicy, dry white wine.

PRICE
$$

RATING

Glenglassaugh Evolution

Aged in first-fill ex–Tennessee whisky barrels, reportedly from the George Dickel distillery in Tullahoma. There's no age statement, but it's obviously young, probably three years old.

AGE
No age statement

ALC/VOL
50%

NOSE
Vanilla cream, banana, custard, and drawn butter; water adds notes of charcoal briquettes, fruit, and salt air.

GENERAL
For a whisky with obvious youth, this is complex and bright; imagine drinking it on a cool spring afternoon, with the sun not yet set and the smell of blossoming trees in the wind.

PALATE
A thin-to-medium mouthfeel, with banana custard, vanilla, sweet malt, and a mid-palate burst of spice; water sweetens it, with notes of buttery toffee. The finish is crisp, with tropical fruit notes.

PRICE
$$

RATING

Glenglassaugh Torfa

The distillery's peated, intensely smoky expression, with the initial peat at a respectable phenol level of 20 ppm.

AGE
No age statement

ALC/VOL
50%

NOSE
Sweet, strong peat, centered on a heady blend of sea air, bacon, and a vaguely medicinal note.

GENERAL
Nicely balanced between sweet and smoke; pair it with smoked fish or Chinese food.

PALATE
Chinese-food spiciness, with honey, oak spiciness, toasted nuts, and cantaloupe; the finish blends spice and candied cherries.

PRICE
$$

RATING

Glengoyne

OWNER: IAN MACLEOD DISTILLERS

FOUNDED: 1833

REGION: HIGHLANDS

PRONUNCIATION: *glen-GOIN*

Glengoyne literally straddles the line between the Highlands and Lowlands: The still house sits on the northern side of the Highland Line, but the whisky ages in facilities on the southern side. Though it's not the only single malt made without peat, it's the only one to make it a central part of its sales pitch—it even says so on every label.

Glengoyne
Aged 10 Years

Aged in ex-sherry casks made from European and American oak.

AGE

10

years old

ALC/VOL

43%

NOSE

Pears, light brown sugar, freshly cut grass, candied fruit, slate, new car, Red Hots; water makes the nose oilier and less sweet, with bananas and the aroma of young oak.

PALATE

A medium mouthfeel, full of bright notes of tutti frutti, citrus, vanilla, resin, and cherry cola; water brings out baker's chocolate. It finishes with a long spicy hit, crossed with plums and strawberries.

GENERAL

An excellent drink for such a young age—light in spirit but full of flavor, with a strong American oak influence.

PRICE

RATING

Glengoyne
Aged 12 Years

Aged in ex-sherry casks and first-fill ex-bourbon barrels that have been rebuilt as hogsheads.

AGE
12
years old

ALC/VOL
43%

NOSE

The bourbon influence is unmistakable—oily nuts, vanilla, oak, black cherry juice—as well as a strong whiff of malt; water makes it a bit more herbal, and brings out some of the underlying sherry notes.

GENERAL

Despite the mere two-year gap, it's a clear step up from the 10 Year Old, with a pronounced sherry influence.

PALATE

The sherry comes out on the nose, along with candied orange, rubbing spices, grilled meat, pineapple, and rancio; water makes the sherry more pronounced. The finish is dry, with an echoing hint of spice.

PRICE

$

RATING

Glengoyne
Aged 15 Years

Like the 12 Year Old, it's aged in a mix of ex-sherry and ex-bourbon casks.

AGE
15
years old

ALC/VOL
43%

NOSE

Vanilla bean, rum raisins, banana, grilled pineapple, and a faint umami note, like mushrooms; the sherry pops out with water, along with Nilla wafers and fresh-cut ginger.

GENERAL

Big, juicy, and spicy, it has a serious bourbon profile—this one's a crowd pleaser.

PALATE

A full mouthfeel, with cola gum, burnt marshmallows, drawn butter, and a solid pinch of allspice; water fills it out, adding cocoa powder and a more pronounced sherry note. The medium-length finish is heavy with candied ginger and leaves a bit of sweetness on the lips.

PRICE

$$

RATING

Glengoyne
Cask Strength BATCH 4

Aged in a combination of European and American oak first-fill and refill sherry casks.

AGE
No age statement

ALC/VOL
58.8%

NOSE

Tight, with brown sugar, maple syrup, ashy soil, rich chocolate, figs, and bergamot; it explodes with a few drops of water, revealing oranges, ripe bananas, flowers, butter, ginger, and cigar smoke.

GENERAL

Drinkable at full strength, but it needs some water to open up on the nose and palate. Still, it's a fantastic whisky, with so much to reveal.

PALATE

Full-bodied, with vanilla, fruitcake, dark chocolate, and oranges; with water, you find coffee candy, ginger candy, cigar smoke, and Cel-Ray soda. The finish is slightly anesthetizing, with dark chocolate, almonds, figs, and menthol.

PRICE
$$

RATING

Glengoyne
Aged 18 Years

Aged strictly in refill and first-fill sherry casks.

AGE
18
years old

ALC/VOL
43%

NOSE

The sherry dominates: sweet raisins, baking spices, raisin bread, vanilla, lilies, apple pie, grilled pineapple, linseed oil, and Italian herbs; water brings out perfume and pumpernickel.

GENERAL

An underappreciated all-star; fantastically rich and sugary, yet not cloying or superficial. The sherry notes are dominant, but not overbearing.

PALATE

A thick, generous mouthfeel, with chocolate, vanilla beans, cola, ginger, and dark brown sugar; with water, you find maple syrup, mushrooms, baker's chocolate, and a bit of leather. The finish is long and slightly citrus-inflected, like an Old Fashioned.

PRICE
$$$

RATING

Glengoyne
Aged 21 Years

Aged in first-fill European oak oloroso sherry casks.

AGE
21
years old

ALC/VOL
43%

NOSE

Intensely woody—let it open up a bit. In time you'll find vanilla, caramel, rancio, fresh rubber, cola, ginger, and raisin bread; with water, you'll find rum raisins and barley soup.

GENERAL

A solid drink that needs time and a bit of water to open up. It tastes a bit past its prime, though—the 18 Year Old is where Glengoyne's at.

PALATE

A thick mouthfeel that almost tastes like a rum, for all the wood influence—raisins, rancio, vanilla; with water it shows maple, soy sauce, and a bit of a vague meaty note. The spicy finish has hints of vanilla and sweet and sour sauce.

PRICE
$$$

RATING

Glengoyne
Aged 25 Years

Aged exclusively in European oak ex-sherry casks.

AGE
25
years old

ALC/VOL
48%

NOSE

Dark fruit jam, fig jam, a box of raisins, molasses, a bit of wood polish; with water you find almonds and a loamy, woodsy note.

GENERAL

Fans of Springbank should give this a try (and vice versa). If you like big sherried malts, do not miss this.

PALATE

A huge sherry hit—a mouthy, chewy whisky full of creosote, sated caramel, raisins, rum cake, Christmas spices, and geraniums; water brings out roast meat and jelly. The finish is long and spicy.

PRICE
$$$$

RATING

Glen Grant

OWNER: CAMPARI

FOUNDED: 1839/1840

REGION: SPEYSIDE

It's no coincidence that the Italian drinks giant Campari bought Glen Grant in 2006—Glen Grant has long been among the best-selling single malts in Italy. The distillery, built by the Grant family and originally called Drumbain, has always been enormous; today it produces 5.9 million liters a year, far outpacing all but a few malt producers. Victorian-era demand was such that Glen Grant's owners installed the region's first pneumatic malting drums, a major time- and labor-saving device. It is a remarkably light and grassy whisky, the product in part of a unique set of "tall, slender stills," as the label pointedly reminds you, as well as purifying chambers in the lyne arm, which push back reflux.

Glen Grant Major's Reserve

AGE	No age statement
ALC/VOL	**40**%

Formerly Glen Grant's entry-level expression—it was recently discontinued—it's named for James "the Major" Grant, the son of one of the founders and the man who took the distillery to worldwide fame in the late 1800s and early 1900s.

NOSE

Honey, candied ginger, floral perfume, cream, mango, apples, and lemon; water adds lemon custard, white pepper, and apple skins.

PALATE

A thin-to-medium mouthfeel, with apples, honey, roses, dried papaya, green apple, grain, and light pepper; water intensifies the grain and honey notes. The finish dries a bit, and leaves a lingering bitter note.

GENERAL

Not as sweet as you think, but it's still an archetypal light Speyside whisky. For the price, it's hard to beat, and you could do a lot worse than a glass of this, with a small ice cube, on a hot summer day.

PRICE

$

RATING

Glen Grant
Aged 12 Years

Glen Grant's entry-level age-statement expression.

AGE
12
years old

ALC/VOL
43%

NOSE

Nutty, salty, and buttery, with a tinge of pencil shavings; it's floral, with sweet grass, Lemon Pledge, and vanilla pudding.

GENERAL

A bit too restrained and ethereal to be a real beauty, but still an enjoyable, light dram.

PALATE

Light-bodied, with a slightly bitter entry followed by a buildup of fruit candy, coconut, and waxy texture; water brings out more floral notes but turns it less sweet. The finish is short and dry, with the buttery, nutty spiciness from the nose returning.

PRICE

$

RATING

Glen Grant
Aged 18 Years

An often-overlooked Speyside malt, this eighteen year old was named the second-best whisky in the world in *Jim Murray's Whisky Bible 2017*.

AGE
18
years old

ALC/VOL
43%

NOSE

Apple eau de vie, caramel toffee, powdered sugar, Gummi Bears, fresh tobacco, and an ever-so-slight herbaceousness; it weakens with water.

GENERAL

Disappointing; it's well structured, but it misses many of the complexities of eighteen years in the barrel.

PALATE

Thin-bodied, bright, and floral, with an intense oaky spice-box character; there's jellied fruit and a little soap. Water tones down the soapy floral notes. The finish is long and tastes remarkably like Cel-Ray soda.

PRICE

$$

RATING

Glengyle

OWNER: J. & A. MITCHELL

FOUNDED: 1880

REGION: CAMPBELTOWN

PRONUNCIATION: *Glen-GYLE*

The distillery is called Glengyle, but that name was already owned by another company, so its owners—J. & A. Mitchell, which also owns the neighboring Springbank—decided to avoid a legal battle and instead call their whisky Kilkerran (pronounced *kill-CARE-an*). The original Glengyle opened in 1872, during the boom in Campbeltown distilling, and it was one of the last distilleries to close, in 1925, after the region's whisky industry collapsed. Like Bruichladdich and a few other distilleries, Glengyle is a phoenix: Abandoned for decades—its stocks were sold off, and in the 1940s it was used by a rifle club—it came back to life in 2000 after Mitchell bought and rebuilt it. Like Springbank, Glengyle does all its malting on-site, though unlike Springbank it has a heavier, sootier, oilier character.

Glengyle Kilkerran

AGE
12
years old

Lightly peated and aged in 70-percent ex-bourbon and 30-percent ex-sherry casks.

ALC/VOL
46%

NOSE

Grilled pork, strawberry jam, maple syrup, honey, biscuits, herbal tea, and a whiff of peat; the peat comes out further with water, along with bananas and a general floral note.

PALATE

Medium and oily, it opens hot, then expands with Lexington-style North Carolina barbecue, green apples, green melons, and brine; water elicits black pepper, French herbs, custard, and green grass. The finish is dry, but the spice and fruit linger.

GENERAL

The palate is a bit hot, especially for the proof, but it's still a delicious whisky. It has the honeyed notes of a Speyside and the coastal peat of an Island malt.

PRICE
$$

RATING

Glenkinchie

OWNER: DIAGEO

FOUNDED: 1880

REGION: LOWLANDS

PRONUNCATION: *Glen-KIN-chee*

Known as the "Edinburgh Malt," for its proximity to the
Scottish capital. The area used to be full of distilleries,
thanks to its bounty of barley fields and easy access to the
water to the north and the city just to the west. (The farming
connection remained into the twentieth century, when the
distillery bred prize-winning cattle.) Though Glenkinchie was
founded in 1880, distilling has been going on at the site
since 1825. It's one of a dwindling number of distilleries
to use a worm tub for condensing vapor. Despite being a
Lowland distillery, it merely double-distills its liquid, instead
of the triple-distilling once common in the region.
Today much of its product goes into big blends like Haig
and Dewar's.

Glenkinchie
12 Years Old

A recent replacement to Glenkinchie's
ten-year-old expression.

AGE
12
years old

ALC/VOL
43%

NOSE
Honey cakes, toasted coconuts,
spicy vanilla, papaya, and lemon
zest; with water you'll get more
lemon zest and honey.

PALATE
Thin and creamy—there's
lemon zest, coffee milk,
and toasted coconut; water
doesn't do much. The finish
is quick, bitter, peppery,
and honeyed.

GENERAL
The nose is robust, more like
a Highland malt than a Lowland,
but the palate is too thin
and quick.

PRICE
$$

RATING
★ ★

Glenkinchie
The Distillers Edition

Aged for ten years in a refill cask, it then spends four years in a cask of amontillado—Edgar Allen Poe would approve.

AGE

No age statement

ALC/VOL

46%

NOSE

Smells like breakfast: cinnamon toast, maple syrup, raisins, raspberry jam, and vanilla extract. Water amplifies the sherry notes, as well as adding dried hay and marzipan.

PALATE

Sugary sweet up front, then turns into a woody bitterness at the mid-palate; it's broader and spicier with a dash of water. The finish is nutty and bitter, with a touch of mint.

GENERAL

An excellent nose, but the body is narrower than you expect. Still, the breakfast and sherry notes make it a good choice for a holiday pour.

PRICE

$$

RATING

Glenlivet

OWNER: CHIVAS BROTHERS/PERNOD RICARD

FOUNDED: 1823

REGION: SPEYSIDE

PRONUNCIATION: *Glen-LIV-it*

George Smith, the bootlegger and founder of Glenlivet, was one of the first distillers to apply for a license under the reforms of 1823. His neighbors despised the government and anyone who worked with it, and told him as much; for protection, he carried two loaded pistols wherever he went. Smith had the last laugh: By the mid-1800s, Glenlivet was world famous, and Smith was rich. Sir Walter Scott wrote, in *Saint Ronan's Well*, that Glenlivet was "worth all the wines of France for flavor, and more cordial to the system besides." Distilleries miles away from it were using its name on their labels; wags joked that the valley of Glenlivet was the longest glen in Scotland. In 1881 Smith's grandson George Grant Smith sued to block the use of Glenlivet's name by rivals; the court enforced a compromise that allowed distilleries to use the name as long as they appended it to their own—for example, Aberlour-Glenlivet. The practice only died out a few decades ago. Today Glenlivet is the best-selling single malt in the United States, and it's neck-and-neck with Glenfiddich for the global title.

Glenlivet
12 Years of Age

AGE

12

years old

Arguably the most popular single malt in the world, the 12 Year Old Glenlivet is aged in a mix of European oak casks and ex-bourbon American oak casks.

ALC/VOL

40%

NOSE

Apple candy, honey, flower blossoms, varnish, grass, lemon zest, roasted hazelnuts; water makes it zestier and more floral.

PALATE

A thin mouthfeel that offers all the Speyside favorites—orange zest, honey, vanilla, tropical fruits, and a bit of heat at the mid-palate; it's less sweet with a few drops of water. The finish is long, bitter, and zesty.

GENERAL

It's easy to see why this one's so popular—it has all the crowd-pleasing Speyside notes. It's balanced and delicate but not terribly complex—perfect for an everyday dram, especially for the price.

PRICE

$

RATING

Glenlivet
Founder's Reserve

AGE
No age
statement

Created in honor of Glenlivet's founder, George Smith, it's a non-age-statement expression aged in first-fill and reused bourbon barrels. Not to be confused with a 2010 release, also called Founder's Reserve, and at a much higher price point.

ALC/VOL
40%

NOSE

Green apple candy, cinnamon candy, honey, root beer, cherry soda, vanilla; it falls apart with even a few drops of water.

PALATE

Very sweet up front, a bit cakey even, then it morphs into apples, taffy, Cel-Ray soda, cinnamon, and coffee, which continues through the finish, alongside leather.

GENERAL

A solid but unmemorable whisky. The nose is promising, but it doesn't deliver in taste.

PRICE
$

RATING
★

Glenlivet
15 Years of Age

AGE
15
years old

The 12 Year Old, but then aged for an extra three years in virgin French Limousin oak casks.

ALC/VOL
40%

NOSE

White chocolate, soft oak, grape jam, Play-Doh, green apples, almonds, cooked fruit; do not add water.

PALATE

Coffee, cough drops, cherry candy, cream, chocolate; water elicits sweet malt and a bit more spice, which dribbles, with bitter chocolate, into the brief finish.

GENERAL

A decent dram, though the body is much too thin to enjoy its positive notes.

PRICE
$$

RATING
★

Glenlivet Nàdurra Peated

AGE
No age statement

ALC/VOL
61.5%

Like Glenrothes Peated Cask Reserve (and a similar release from Balvenie, awhile back), this expression wasn't made with peated malt; rather, it was aged for an undisclosed number of years in ex-bourbon barrels and finished, also for an unspecified period of time, in casks that had previously held peated whisky.

NOSE
Ginger, orange, old wood, iodine, bananas, apples, and a clear peat note; water tames down the peat and elicits a creamy vanilla.

PALATE
Bananas, pears, peat smoke, almonds, and vanilla cream; water doesn't do much, despite the high proof. The dry finish has habanero pepper and banana, with an ashy undertone.

GENERAL
A clear but restrained smokiness, and a daring extension for Glenlivet. Fairly smooth for a cask-strength whisky, too.

PRICE
$$

RATING

Glenlivet Nàdurra Oloroso

AGE
No age statement

ALC/VOL
60.3%

Aged, for an unspecified period of time, in first-fill oloroso sherry casks.

NOSE
Raisins, linseed oil, lightly roasted peanuts, rancio, prunes, butter, and chocolate; water underlines the butteriness.

PALATE
A thick mouthfeel, with raisins, orange cream, cinnamon sugar, and a warming sherry bass line; water brings out ginger and coconut. The slightly dry finish continues the ginger spice note.

GENERAL
A deliciously big whisky—a bit too far on the dry side, especially at the end, but still a lot of fun.

PRICE
$$

RATING

Glenlivet
Nàdurra First Fill

As the name implies, it's aged exclusively in first-fill casks, in this case ex-bourbon.

AGE
No age statement

ALC/VOL
59.8%

NOSE

Ripe bananas, vanilla, oak, crème brûlée, apples, soap, marzipan; water mutes the bananas and brings out oak and nuts.

GENERAL

If you like banana candy, you'll love this. It needs water to balance out the nose and palate.

PALATE

Oak, roasted almonds, banana candy, vanilla extract, and a bit of solvent at the mid-palate; water shows rich caramel, coconut, and cooked bananas. The finish is nutty and spicy, with a long finish of banana candy.

PRICE
$$

RATING

Glenlivet
18 Years of Age

Drawn from an array of barrels, including first- and second-fill ex-bourbon casks and ex-sherry casks.

AGE
18
years old

ALC/VOL
43%

NOSE

Orange zest, lilacs, concord grape jelly, maple syrup, tropical fruit, pine, honey tea, vanilla; water amplifies the vanilla and grape juiciness, and adds a toasted note.

GENERAL

What a Speyside should be—rich, elegant, and delicate. It's like a cross between a scotch and a bourbon. Think of it for a lighter after-dinner dram.

PALATE

A thin mouthfeel, with vanilla, plums, honey, and a ginger mid-palate; with water you'll find white raisins and a soft red-wine note. The finish is quick, with fruit, nut, and vanilla notes.

PRICE
$$$

RATING

Glenlivet Archive

Aged in a combination of ex-bourbon casks and ex-sherry butts.

AGE
21
years old

ALC/VOL
43%

NOSE
Orange zest, port, flat cola, dark chocolate, and hazelnuts; with water you get powdered sugar, molasses, and sweet broth.

PALATE
Chocolate, raspberry jam, cedar, hazelnuts, and woody spices; the finish is dark chocolate, espresso, ginger, and leather, which fades into a soft note of bitter herbs.

GENERAL
Nothing surprising, just a lovely whisky, elegant and well-constructed.

PRICE
$$$

RATING

Glenlivet 25 Years of Age

Aged for twenty-three years in ex-bourbon barrels, then finished for another two in first-fill oloroso sherry casks.

AGE
25
years old

ALC/VOL
43%

NOSE
Strawberries, lemon zest, vanilla, old wood, dried figs, almond cookies, and a slight salinity; water calls forth maple syrup, savory herbs, and toasted pecans.

PALATE
Menthol, dark chocolate, coffee, ginger, cough syrup, pipe smoke, raisins, melon; finishes with a minty, slightly tannic freshness.

GENERAL
No bells or whistles, just a spectacular whisky, with high and low notes that tumble over each other across the nose and palate.

PRICE
$$$$

RATING

Glenmorangie

OWNER: LVMH

FOUNDED: 1843

REGION: HIGHLANDS

PRONUNCIATION: *Glen-MORE-an-jee*

Alongside the Macallan and Dalmore, Glenmorangie is among the most self-consciously "luxury" whisky brands (not a surprise, given its ownership). And it's not just posing: Glenmo, as many fans call it, invests heavily in big-ticket items like barrel management—it owns a forest in the Ozarks to ensure its oak supply, and then "rents" barrels to Brown-Forman to be seasoned with Jack Daniel's. And it only uses each barrel twice, a significant expense for a distillery that produces 6 million liters a year. Glenmorangie began life as a brewery, but was converted to a distillery by William Matheson in 1843. Today it is known for having the tallest stills in Scotland, which, along with its very narrow cuts, contribute to its signature honey and floral character. It was also one of the pioneers of cask-strength and wood-finished releases in the 1990s.

Glenmorangie The Original

Aged in first- and second-fill American oak casks.

AGE
10
years old

ALC/VOL
43%

NOSE

Honey, vanilla buttercream, zabaglione, orange flowers, marshmallow, grassy; water adds more butter and salt, and takes the floral notes down a notch.

PALATE

Medium-bodied, with Juicy Fruit, cake batter, mandarin orange, peach, and a touch of oak; water adds body and heat. The finish is gentle and fairly short, with a kiss of ginger.

GENERAL

An average whisky, but a good deal for the price. Mild, crowd-pleasing. Keep water away from it.

PRICE

$

RATING

Glenmorangie Quinta Ruban

AGE
10
years old

ALC/VOL
46%

A sibling to Glenmorangie's Lasanta and Nectar d'Or, after this whisky ages ten years in ex-bourbon barrels, it spends two years in port pipes. The name is a mash-up of Portuguese and Gaelic; "quintas" are the estates where port grapes are grown, while "ruban" is Gaelic for ruby, the color of the port.

NOSE
Raisins, rich honey, figs, fresh flowers, raspberries, rum cake, and pecans; water turns the honey note a bit spicy.

PALATE
Maple syrup, fruit juice, pepper at the mid-palate, though water brings out butter and rum raisin; the finish is long and spicy.

GENERAL
A big, juicy palate, deliciously long and round, with loads of raisins and spice. Water, for once, improves this Glenmorangie.

PRICE
$$

RATING

Glenmorangie Lasanta

AGE
12
years old

ALC/VOL
43%

Like the Original, the twelve-year-old Lasanta is aged for ten years in first- and second-fill American oak casks; it then spends two additional years in Pedro Ximénez and oloroso sherry casks.

NOSE
Big sherry hit up front, giving way to rich bourbon notes of vanilla and caramel, complemented by a rich, sweet bread note, like walking into a bakery; water emphasizes the bread notes, along with sweet cereal and cornbread.

PALATE
A thick mouthfeel, with bourbon-like notes through-out: vanilla, caramel, a bit of cinnamon, confection-ers' sugar, and Cocoa Krispies; the relatively brief finish is burnt sugar and cocoa powder, coming to rest on an echo of sherry.

GENERAL
A wonderful integration of sherry and bourbon influence. They com-plement and energize each other.

PRICE
$$

RATING

Glenmonagie Nectar d'Or

AGE

12

years old

ALC/VOL

46%

Like the Lasanta, it's aged ten years in first- and second-fill American oak casks, but in this case its extra two years of aging are spent in French Sauternes barriques.

NOSE

Kraft caramel chews, butter, vanilla cream, dried flowers, and white wine; water elicits raisins, plums, and fennel.

GENERAL

Deep, rich, more sherry than Sauternes, and well balanced between sweet and dry notes. Like most Glenmorangies, water doesn't help much.

PALATE

The mouthfeel is on the thin side, with a palate of raisins, ginger, toffee, chocolate, and a gentle herbal note; the finish lingers with spicy chocolate.

PRICE

$$

RATING

Glenmorangie Grand Vintage 1990

AGE

No age statement

ALC/VOL

43%

The first in a series of limited releases drawn from the distillery's Bond House No. 1, its largest warehouse and the place where it stores its most promising casks. This expression, bottled in 2016, is aged primarily in ex-bourbon casks, with some ex-sherry tossed in as well.

NOSE

Fruity and floral, almost perfume-like, with green apples, ginger, lemon, and chalk. Water elicits guava, coconut, apple skins, and vanilla bean.

GENERAL

Elegant, intricately constructed, flawless, balanced—but almost to a fault. Perfection can be boring.

PALATE

Creamy and mouth-covering, it has vanilla, apples, orange, biscuits, honeysuckle; water brings out honey, green tea, and a bit of wood. The finish is long and fruity.

PRICE

$$$$

RATING

Glenmorangie Signet

AGE
No age statement

ALC/VOL
46%

An insanely complex whisky, drawn mostly from thirty- to thirty-five-year-old barrels, blended with much younger barrels of whisky made from "chocolate" malt, which is roasted to produce a dark brown color and intense, nutty flavor. The barrels are primarily ex-bourbon, but with a significant minority of them virgin American oak.

NOSE
Like a whisky rackhouse, with intense bourbon, rancio, perfume, floral, cherry cola, and fresh hay notes; adding water brings out an oily honeycomb and espresso tinge.

PALATE
A full-bodied, juicy palate, with dark citrus, cherry syrup, café au lait, and bittersweet chocolate, which is supercharged with a bit of water; the finish brings back the café au lait, as well as a char note, on the back of a numbing dryness.

GENERAL
Bourbon geeks will love this one, though it's unmistakably a Glenmorangie scotch. Like an Everlasting Gobstopper, it changes endlessly on the nose and palate.

PRICE
$$$$

RATING

Glenmorangie Extremely Rare

AGE
18
years old

ALC/VOL
43%

After fifteen years in ex-bourbon casks, thirty percent of this whisky is transferred to oloroso sherry barrels; after three more years, all the barrels are blended together.

NOSE
Surprisingly light for an eighteen year old: fresh pears, honey, pancake syrup, lilacs, chalk, and lemon candy/peel; water brings out butterscotch.

PALATE
Medium mouthfeel with a big, sweet entry; lots of oak influence—caramel, vanilla, and baking spices—as well as a bright, sweet vegetal note, like green peas. The finish is herbal and slightly spicy.

GENERAL
So intensely floral, especially for an eighteen year old. The nose is big and vivacious, like an eau de vie. But the palate is a bit muddled, leaving you to tease out the details. Leave the water aside.

PRICE
$$$

RATING

Glen Moray

OWNER: LA MARTINIQUAISE

FOUNDED: 1897

REGION: SPEYSIDE

PRONUNCIATION: *Glen MURR-ay*

Located on the western outskirts of Elgin, along the River Lossie, Glen Moray is significantly more pleasant an institution than what came before it, long ago: the city gallows. The distillery was long in the control of The Glenmorangie Company, which sold it in 2006 to the French company La Martiniquaise, who wanted its malt to go into its Label 5 and Glen Turner blends. The French haven't let the single malt go to seed, either: Glen Moray has a widening range of expressions, and was an early leader in experimenting with wine-cask finishes. The distillery recently completed a massive expansion, nearly doubling its capacity from 3.3 million liters a year to 6 million.

Glen Moray Elgin Classic

Aged in "mostly" first-fill ex-bourbon casks for about seven years.

AGE
No age statement

ALC/VOL
40%

NOSE
Dripping with honey, pear, vanilla, green apple, banana, and drawn butter. Don't even think of adding water.

PALATE
Sweet up front, with honey, melon, and citrus, then becomes a bit spicy and bitter at the mid-palate; the finish is quick, with lemon-peel bitterness.

GENERAL
You won't find a single malt much cheaper than this—and it says a lot about the category that, for the price, it's pretty good: smooth and easy to drink, with a lovely nose. The palate doesn't deliver much, though.

PRICE
$

RATING

Glen Moray Chardonnay Cask Finish

AGE
10 years old

One of the few single malts in wide circulation to spend time in a white wine barrel.

ALC/VOL
40%

NOSE

A bit like a sherry finish at first, with raisins and caramel, but it moves into honey and rich floral notes, as well as a sharp minerality.

PALATE

All the basics: caramel, honey, dried fruits, vanilla, and a slight nuttiness; the finish is a bit tannic, with a lingering note of caramel chews.

GENERAL

The chardonnay influence is more noticeable on the nose than the palate; like the basic Elgin Classic, the latter is a bit disappointing.

PRICE
$

RATING
★★

Glen Moray Port Cask Finish

AGE
No age statement

The Elgin Classic spends an additional eight months in tawny port barrels.

ALC/VOL
40%

NOSE

Surprisingly crisp and clean, like a grappa; eventually, notes of grape bubblegum, pears, vanilla custard, straw, and minerality emerge.

PALATE

A thin mouthfeel, with honey, pear, grappa, and Juicy Fruit gum; the finish is long and slightly bitter, like black tea.

GENERAL

This one's all about bubblegum, and not in an unpleasant way. But "port" implies a thicker, more robust finishing influence than this whisky delivers.

PRICE
$

RATING
★★

Glen Moray
Elgin Classic Peated

AGE
No age statement

A relatively recent addition to Glen Moray's Classic line, it's evidence that the distillery isn't content simply to produce low-cost whisky—it wants to innovate, even at the lower price points.

ALC/VOL
40%

NOSE
Soft and mossy, with melon, apricot, and a touch of rye bread; adding water brings out chocolate and mint.

PALATE
Apricots and honey, with a spicy mid-palate; water brings out earthy and chocolate notes. The finish is long and full of chocolate.

GENERAL
Lighter and softer than the typical Islay whisky, this is a good introduction to the peated style. There's enough of the Speyside honey to balance out the smoke.

PRICE
$

RATING

Glen Moray
Sherry Cask Finish

AGE
No age statement

Like the other finished versions of the Elgin Classic, this one has spent about seven years aging and then about eight months in Oloroso sherry casks.

ALC/VOL
40%

NOSE
Green apples, toffee, vanilla, unripe pear, cinnamon, and lilacs; there's a bracing minerality running beneath it. Water adds a hit of white pepper.

PALATE
A moderately thick mouthfeel, with notes of prune juice, cocoa powder, port, and mid-palate Asian spices; water calls forth more fruit and winey notes. The finish is spicy—think wasabi—with hints of chocolate powder.

GENERAL
A good value for the price, and a solid introduction to the sherried scotch category.

PRICE

RATING

Glen Moray
Aged 12 Years

Aged in ex-bourbon casks.

AGE
12
years old

ALC/VOL
40%

NOSE

Rich pear, roses, Nilla Wafers, flannel sheets, and a slight tropical fruit note.

PALATE

Vanilla pudding, a bit of cinnamon, and a kiss of citrus, with a quick, dry, slightly spicy finish.

GENERAL

A pleasing, vanilla-inflected nose, but the palate can't match. Still, try it as a mixer, or as a light summer dram.

PRICE
$

RATING

Glen Moray
Aged 16 Years

Aged in a combination of ex-bourbon and ex-sherry barrels.

AGE
16
years old

ALC/VOL
40%

NOSE

Peony, cooking oil, fruit paste, and an ever-so-slight sherry note.

GENERAL

Disappointing for a sixteen year old; it would be better at a higher proof.

PALATE

Thin, with honey, Fig Newton, toffee, and an oaky bitterness at the mid-palate; water brings out roasted malt. The finish is quick and hoppy, like a light pilsner.

PRICE
$$

RATING

Glen Moray
Sherry Cask Finish
Aged 18 Years

An eighteen-year-old, higher-proof version of Glen Moray's standard Elgin Classic, aged in first-fill ex-bourbon barrels.

AGE
18
years old

ALC/VOL
47.2%

NOSE

Honey, halva, fir, roasted peanuts, blackberries, slate, hay, and a whiff of smoke at the back; it grows less sweet and more floral with water.

GENERAL

Glen Moray is best known for its low-priced Elgin Classic series, but its older whiskies are well worth the extra coin. You won't find another eighteen year old for this price, and certainly not one this good.

PALATE

Round and buttery on the tongue, it opens with honey and vanilla, then builds to a spicy berry character. It loses its sweetness with water on the palate, though berries and figs remain. The finish is medium in length, with dried fruit and oak spice notes.

PRICE
$$

RATING

Glen Ranoch

INDEPENDENT BOTTLER

OWNER: ANGUS DUNDEE DISTILLERS

PRONUNCIATION: *Glen RAN-ock*

A smoky, non-age-statement expression bottled under the supervision of the Hillman family, the owners of Angus Dundee Distillers. Speculation on the source abounds; the prime suspects are Glencadam and Tomintoul, which are owned by Angus Dundee.

Glen Ranoch

AGE
No age statement

ALC/VOL
40%

NOSE
Artificial sugar, oak polish, moldering leaves, pine air freshener, ammonia, and caramel; water does nothing for it.

GENERAL
Tastes like the floor of a Home Depot. Stay away.

PALATE
A medium mouthfeel, with fake peach, mushrooms, cigarettes, and mouthwash; water elicits moldy grain. The finish is quick and bitter.

PRICE
$

RATING
NR

Glenrothes

OWNER: EDRINGTON GROUP

FOUNDED: 1878

REGION: SPEYSIDE

PRONUNCIATION: *Glen-ROTH-es*

Glenrothes is the few Scotch distilleries to release whisky according to a vintage-dating scheme: Whisky aged in a particular year is either bottled according to the date of distillation, or blended with other whiskies to make up one or more of the distillery's "reserve" expressions. Glenrothes got a boost in 1923 when Berry Bros. & Rudd, a storied wine and spirits merchant in London, chose it as a key component in Cutty Sark, a new blend, which soon became one of the best-selling whiskies worldwide. In fact, the relationship between Glenrothes and Berry Bros. & Rudd was so tight that for seven years beginning in 2010, the latter owned the brand itself (though Edrington maintained ownership of the actual distillery, and bought back the brand in 2017).

Glenrothes Vintage Reserve

A marriage of malts from ten different vintages, ranging from 1989 to 2007.

AGE
No age statement

ALC/VOL
40%

NOSE
Rich honey, caramel green apples, raisins, figs, candied ginger, cinnamon; with water one finds Lemon Pledge, sherry, and Sprite.

PALATE
A full and surprisingly dry mouthfeel, and a bit of a prickly one, with sherry, vanilla, baking chocolate, rancio, almonds, and lemon cough drops. The finish is prickly and semi-dry.

GENERAL
Decently constructed, but ultimately boring. The palate suffers where the nose shines.

PRICE

RATING

Glenrothes Select Reserve

AGE
No age statement

ALC/VOL
40%

A non-age-statement expression, made from whiskies drawn from a variety of barrels that the distillery says typify the house style—fruity, slightly sherried, and a tad spicy.

NOSE

Lemon zest, honey, blanched almonds, slightly acerbic, and that rubbery taste of an aged rum; water underlines the lemon and rubber, and brings out a certain woodsy note.

PALATE

A thinnish palate, with roasted nuts, lemon, grape skins, and a slight sherry undertone; water makes it creamy and woodsy. The finish is medium-length, with chocolate and—how to put it—Lemon Pledge.

GENERAL

A severe and narrow expression; whatever sweetness exists on the nose is absent on the palate.

PRICE

$

RATING

★★

Glenrothes Bourbon Cask Reserve

AGE
No age statement

ALC/VOL
40%

Unsurprisingly, this expression draws from whisky aged exclusively in ex-bourbon barrels. Formerly known as the Alba Reserve.

NOSE

Vanilla, cherries, caramel, honey, oak, chamomile, and floral notes; water brings out a much sweeter visage, but it soon falls apart.

PALATE

A big honey hit up front, followed by a deep oak note, along with bubblegum, bittersweet chocolate, and hookah tobacco; the finish is long and a bit tannic.

GENERAL

It would improve greatly at a higher proof. As it is, it's uninspired.

PRICE

$$

RATING

★

Glenrothes
Sherry Cask Reserve

Aged in first-fill European oak ex-sherry casks.

AGE
No age statement

ALC/VOL
40%

NOSE

Old peanuts, lemon zest, ginger ale, almonds, slate; don't even think of adding water.

GENERAL

Like the Bourbon Cask Reserve, it suffers from its low proof. It's quite boring.

PALATE

Quite thin mouthfeel, with chocolate, raisins, slate, white wine; the dry finish recalls semi-sweet sherry.

PRICE
$$

RATING

Glenrothes
2001 Vintage

As the name says, this whisky is made from casks put up in 2001; the whisky was bottled in 2012.

AGE
No age statement

ALC/VOL
43%

NOSE

Malt, pepper, sherry, grilled pineapple, and a rich citrus haze; water brings out a buttery sweetness.

GENERAL

A real let-down from the 1998 Vintage expression. It's too thin and one-dimensional.

PALATE

A bit thin, with orange, creamy malt, vanilla, white pepper, dry sherry; water doesn't help much. The finish is dry and cinnamon-spicy.

PRICE
$$

RATING

Glenrothes Peated Cask Reserve

AGE
No age statement

ALC/VOL
40%

Don't be confused by the name. This whisky doesn't use any peated malt—Glenrothes never does. Rather, it's whisky from the 1992 vintage finished in used casks from Islay.

NOSE

Very little overt peat, but there are whiffs of salt air and iodine, some caraway and rye, and an unmistakable aroma of green chilies; it breaks down completely with water.

PALATE

Green chilies, iodine, vegetal, salty chips; the finish is long and, increasingly, sweet.

GENERAL

An odd in-between whisky—peat fans will search in vain for clear peat flavors, while the peat-phobic will react to the iodine and sea notes. Still, as a thing in its own, it's an interesting drink.

PRICE	RATING
$$	

Glenrothes 1998 Vintage

AGE
No age statement

ALC/VOL
43%

The first release of this whisky came in 2009; this, the second, came in 2016. The whisky was aged in first-fill and refill American oak sherry casks.

NOSE

Rich vanilla, honey, black pepper, and gingersnaps; water brings out sweet malt and jam.

PALATE

Peppery, malty, cinnamon sticks; it's sweet up front, followed by a bitter turn, and finally a dry finish. Water lengthens things and slows them down.

GENERAL

Wonderfully rich, but very quick—a complex palate, but a speedy one.

PRICE	RATING
$$	

Glenrothes 1995 Vintage

AGE
No age statement

ALC/VOL
43%

Glenrothes' first vintage expression, bottled every few years beginning in 2010. The barrels are about one-third first-fill ex-sherry casks made from American oak; the rest are ex-bourbon.

NOSE

Honeyed malt, soy, ginger, strawberries, wood polish, vanilla cake batter, and a slight hit of pepper; water brings out an oily, umami quality, and suppresses some of the sweetness.

PALATE

Creamy sherry and orange blossom notes up front, followed by a peppery, juicy mid-palate, an impression that only grows with water. The finish ends quickly, with a slight ginger spice ring.

GENERAL

The nose is captivatingly complex, but the palate doesn't come close to matching.

PRICE

$$$

RATING

★ ★

Glen Scotia

OWNER: LOCH LOMOND GROUP

FOUNDED: 1832

REGION: CAMPBELTOWN

PRONUNCIATION: *Glen SKO-sha*

During the whisky industry's fits-and-starts recovery in the post–World War I era, the Glen Scotia facility was purchased in 1924 by a distiller named Duncan Macallum. When the Great Depression hit, he was forced to close the distillery; he locked the door, stowed the key, and drowned himself in the nearby Crosshill Loch, the distillery's water source. It's said his spirit remains, though no word on whether he helps out with the stills. For most of the twentieth century, Glen Scotia passed among owners who operated it intermittently; for a time it was used sparingly by its neighbor Springbank. In 2014 ownership was secured by Loch Lomond Group, and production picked up again.

Glen Scotia Double Cask

A non-age-statement whisky aged in ex-bourbon casks, then finished in Pedro Ximénez sherry barrels.

AGE
No age statement

ALC/VOL
46%

NOSE
Vanilla cream, peaches, raisin oatmeal cookies, mandarin oranges, and candied ginger; it opens significantly with water, with dried apricots, pears, and cardamom.

PALATE
Figs, dark chocolate fudge, ginger, mandarin orange, ash, and coffee; it dries quickly, but keeps the rich chocolate, figgy note.

GENERAL
The figs are strong with this one—intriguingly rich, dark notes, if a bit dry on the finish.

PRICE
$$

RATING

Glen Scotia
Aged 15 Years

Aged solely in ex-bourbon casks.

AGE
15
years old

ALC/VOL
46%

NOSE

Clover honey, pears, melons, ginger, vanilla, dried apricots; with water it shows ginger snaps, graham crackers, and orange.

GENERAL

Like a classic Speyside, but a bit darker. Opens significantly with water.

PALATE

Not especially sweet, despite notes of vanilla and honey; there's also an oaky note, mixed with grilled meat and a slight smokiness. Water makes it a bit spicy. The finish is a bit tannic, with a whiff of smoke.

PRICE
$$

RATING
★★

Glen Scotia
Victoriana

A non-age-statement whisky, finished in heavily charred barrels (ex-bourbon, presumably) in a nod to what whisky from Campbeltown tasted like in the Victorian era.

AGE
No age statement

ALC/VOL
51.5%

NOSE

A bit musty up front, with tangerines, chocolate-covered raisins, brine, citrus, and just a whiff of peat; water brings out milk chocolate, ginger, pipe tobacco, toffee, and anise.

GENERAL

If dark, rich oak is your thing, grab this whisky. It's delicious, and a good alternative to an Islay peat bomb for your winter after-dinner dram.

PALATE

A thick, round whisky that opens as sweet and spicy, then deepens with oak, dark toffee, and raspberries; water adds more toffee, as well as anise and tropical fruit. The finish is tannic, not surprisingly, with coffee and dark chocolate.

PRICE
$$

RATING
★★
★★

Hazelburn

FOR DISTILLERY INFORMATION REGARDING HAZELBURN,
SEE SPRINGBANK ON PAGE 261.

Hazelburn
Aged 10 Years

AGE
10
years old

Triple-distilled and aged in ex-bourbon casks.
Non–chill filtered and no coloring added.

ALC/VOL
46%

NOSE

Pears, honey, white pepper, and a slight minerality, like slate dust; it gets sweeter with water—think orange pulp.

GENERAL

It's triple-distilled, but nothing like a Lowland whisky—it's full-bodied and complex, especially for a ten year old. Fans of Mortlach or Clynelish will love this.

PALATE

A medium mouthfeel, with notes of peppered steak, vanilla extract, and char; water makes it sweet and darkly fruity—dark berries and cherries dominate. The finish is long, oily, and meaty, with a touch of tobacco. The finish is likewise sweeter with water.

PRICE
$$

RATING

Hazelburn
Aged 12 Years

AGE
12
years old

A lovely unpeated, slightly older, and more refined version of the ten year old.

ALC/VOL
46%

NOSE

Musty books, old wood, rich honey, melon, charcoal bri-quettes, creosote; water sweetens it—sweet barbecue sauce, oranges, talcum powder, and earthy wood ash.

GENERAL

Despite it being unpeated, this dram can't escape its earthy, voluptuous Springbank prove-nance. It's big, deep, and rich, and benefits from a few drops of water.

PALATE

A big, medium-bodied spice bomb, laid over cantaloupe, orange pulp, Gummi Bears, leather, and cigars; water amps up the juiciness, adding vanilla, cake, and spice box. The finish is long and fruity, with a lingering charcoal and ashy note.

PRICE
$$

RATING

Highland Park

OWNER: EDRINGTON GROUP

FOUNDED: 1798

REGION: HIGHLANDS

The northernmost distillery in Scotland—just above its fellow Orcadian, Scapa—Highland Park is also one of the most renowned. In recent years it has emphasized the Orkney Islands' Nordic roots, with limited releases named for Norse gods and various elements of Viking lore. It's not an empty claim: Norway controlled the islands from 875 to 1472 AD, and left its mark—Highland Park's reputed founder was named Magnus Eunson, a preacher who is said to have hidden whisky from the excise authorities under his pulpit. For decades Highland Park was also known for using local peat, which is heavy with heather, and bere, a variant of barley, to create its signature flavor profile; it still uses local peat for 20 percent of its malt, with a phenolic content of 20 ppm.

Highland Park Magnus

AGE
No age statement

Aged in a mix of sherry-seasoned and ex-bourbon barrels, this whisky is named in honor of Magnus Eunson, the distillery's legendary founder.

ALC/VOL
40%

NOSE
Rich honey, berry, honeydew, dried tangerines, and floral notes; water elicits orange, toasted coconut, and fruit juice.

PALATE
A thin mouthfeel, with notes of vanilla, dried wood, toast, coffee, and, at the mid-palate, a drying citrus tang; the finish is darkly tropical, with tangerines and lemon rinds.

GENERAL
Anemic and one-note; a higher proof might help.

PRICE
$

RATING
NR

Highland Park
Aged 12 Years

Aged in a mix of ex-bourbon and ex-oloroso sherry casks made from American oak.

AGE
12
years old

ALC/VOL
40%

NOSE

Sweet biscuits, geraniums, ginger, honey, a slight rubbery note, and a strong boozy hit, which intensifies with water.

GENERAL

The sweet and restrained smoky notes are well assembled, but overall the whisky is a bit basic.

PALATE

Oily, medium-bodied; it opens with peat, then sweetens with marmalade, lemon zest, caramel, and herbal notes. The finish offers cigar, a bit of pepper, and a lingering smokiness..

PRICE

$

RATING

Highland Park
Dark Origins

Fitting its name, this expression uses twice as many ex-oloroso sherry barrels as the core age-statement expressions.

AGE
No age
statement

ALC/VOL
46.8%

NOSE

Lots of bold sherry, along with smoky notes of creosote and old wood, bittersweet chocolate, dates, and grilled citrus; water brightens it significantly.

GENERAL

A lively, almost alive whisky; it evolves noticeably on the palate from sweet to dry.

PALATE

Honey-sweet up front, with smoky and peppery notes building toward the mid-palate; as it moves to the finish, it dries a bit, resolving in a long, smoky, oaky finish. Water brings these various stages together into a unitary experience.

PRICE

$$

RATING

Highland Park Valkyrie

AGE
No age statement

ALC/VOL
45.9%

Valkyrie is part of the distillery's ongoing attempt to highlight the Orkney Islands' Scandinavian ties. Whereas standard Highland Park is made with 20-percent peated malt, Valkyrie is made with 50 percent. It is the first in the three-part Viking Legend series that will also include Valknut and Valhalla.

NOSE
Burnt sugar, fruit syrup, glove leather, heather, dirty grass, sulfur, and a wine-like funk—which emerges even more with water, along with ash, pork, and vegetal notes.

PALATE
A big spice hit up front with a thin-to-medium mouthfeel, expanding into toasted coconut, ash, wood spice, black tea, and mint toothpaste; water makes it sweeter and fruitier, though it also adds a note of charred bits. The spice returns on the finish, though it remains sweet to the very end.

GENERAL
For such a large jump in the peat level, it's hardly noticeable. While not uninteresting, it lacks the heft and richness of the usual Highland Park.

PRICE
$$

RATING

Highland Park Aged 15 Years

AGE
15
years old

ALC/VOL
43%

A relatively rare expression aged in ex-oloroso sherry casks made from toasted American oak. Along with Dark Origins, it has been discontinued.

NOSE
Butterscotch, citrus peel, oak, peat smoke, candied ginger, and dark berries; water sweetens it, with more fruit.

PALATE
The reverse of the 12 Year Old: Opens with sweet raspberry, strawberry, and tropical fruit notes, then moves to a smoky, oily mid-palate; the finish is sweet camphor and a bit tannic.

GENERAL
An impressive, complex whisky, and diverse in its uses—neat, in cocktails, before or after dinner.

PRICE
$$

RATING

Highland Park Full Volume

AGE
No age statement

ALC/VOL
47.2%

Aged exclusively in ex-bourbon barrels, instead of the usual sherry. Bonus: It comes in a box designed to look like a (very small) amplifier, with the volume knob turned to, yes, eleven.

NOSE
Soap, green apples, honey, dried figs, and a hint of peat; water gives it a slight cream note, like cake batter.

GENERAL
In *This Is Spinal Tap*, Nigel Tufnel's amps all go to eleven, for "when you need that extra push over the cliff." Nigel Tufnel would not approve of Full Volume. It only goes to one (star, that is).

PALATE
Astringent, with a bit of spice and honey up front; it evolves into honey, cherry cough syrup, and cinnamon candy. Water adds some estery floral notes, but not much. The finish is dry, short, and a bit soapy.

PRICE
$$$

RATING

Highland Park Aged 18 Years

AGE
18
years old

ALC/VOL
43%

Aged primarily in ex-sherry casks.

NOSE
Big sherry hit up front, with ever-so-slight smoke underneath it; there are dark fruit notes of plums, port, baking spices, and brown sugar, with a slight salinity. Water doesn't do much to it, despite the proof.

GENERAL
A solid, well-built whisky that lacks just enough depth to qualify as great.

PALATE
A medium body delivers vanilla, sherry, and toffee, with a boozy, peppery mid-palate; smoke comes forward at the finish, which is also slightly tannic and spicy.

PRICE
$$$

RATING

Highland Park
Aged 25 Years

Nearly 50 percent of the whisky is aged in first-fill ex-sherry casks, a higher percentage than younger Highland Parks. In 2013 it was the first whisky ever to win a perfect score at the Ultimate Spirits Challenge.

AGE
15
years old

ALC/VOL
45.7%

NOSE

Coastal, briny, dry sherry, with a restrained peat presence, but also old scotch notes of toasted almonds, rancio, linseed oil, and old wood. Water brings out fenugreek and fennel.

GENERAL

A master class in balancing the rough peat and coastal notes of the Highland Park house style with a supple sweetness not always found in its younger (and, in many cases, newer) sibling expressions.

PALATE

The mouthfeel is slightly viscous, with notes of plums and cherries, hints of honey and wood smoke, a tannic backbone, and a spicy undertone that builds to a pop at the mid-palate; water heightens the sweetness and dampens some of the tannins. The finish is slightly spicy, dry, and quick.

PRICE

$$$$

RATING

Inchmoan

FOR DISTILLERY INFORMATION REGARDING INCHMOAN,
SEE LOCH LOMOND ON PAGE 227.

Inchmoan
Aged 12 Years

Named for an island in Loch Lomond, Inchmoan is the distillery's peated line (*inchmoan* means "peat island"). The 12 Year Old is aged in a combination of recharred American oak and ex-bourbon barrels.

AGE
12
years old

ALC/VOL
46%

NOSE
Caramel chews, cold fire pit, roses, black pepper, sulfur, melon candies; with water, you'll find boiled vegetables, orange rind, and more ashiness.

GENERAL
A well-smoked, but not overwhelmingly smoky whisky; it nicely balances sweetly floral, funk, and char influences.

PALATE
A thin-to-medium mouthfeel, with a taste of sweet char up front, followed by a woody, meaty mid-palate. Water turns it sweeter, with a melon tint. The finish is long and smoky.

PRICE
$

RATING

Inchmoan
Vintage 1992

Aged in refill American oak barrels.

AGE
No age statement

ALC/VOL
48.6%

NOSE
Jasmine, minerality, salt, honeysuckle, vegetal peat, slightly juicy; all the notes become more pronounced with water.

GENERAL
A beautiful, well-rounded whisky, with lots of honey and light, but noticeable, smoke.

PALATE
Medium-bodied, with a broadly juicy flavor complemented by ginger, cola, honey, citrus, and sweet smoke; water makes it pop, bringing out bright citrus notes of tangerine and lemon. The finish is slightly bitter, and short.

PRICE
$$$$

RATING

Inchmurrin

FOR DISTILLERY INFORMATION REGARDING INCHMURRIN,
SEE LOCH LOMOND ON PAGE 227.

Inchmurrin
Aged 12 Years

Aged in a combination of ex-bourbon, refill sherry, and recharred casks.

AGE
12
years old

ALC/VOL
46%

NOSE
Honey, straw, heather, fresh ginger, toasted coconut, and oak shavings; water adds more oak and a bit of funk to the proceedings.

PALATE
Waxy, spicy, and oaky, with pears, vanilla, salted caramel, and baking spices; water amps up the spices. The finish has perfume, dried fruits, and sweet and spicy peppers.

GENERAL
Round, light, and grassy, it develops distinct pepper notes as it opens.

PRICE
$

RATING

Inchmurrin
Madeira Wood Finish

Aged first in ex-bourbon casks, then put in ex-Madeira casks for an additional, unspecified time.

AGE
No age statement

ALC/VOL
46%

NOSE
The Madeira hits you right up front: tropical and orchard fruits, white raisins, vanilla, varnish, and a slight savory note. Water brings it down a bit, but adds a slight nutty edge.

PALATE
An oily mouthfeel, with potpourri, cinnamon, juicy bananas, candy shell, apples, and pears, but an oaky astringency takes over quickly; the finish is long, tannic, and peppery.

GENERAL
The cask notes are nice, but they prove superficial on the palate, and in time the oak influence dominates.

PRICE
$$

RATING

Inchmurrin
Aged 18 Years

The Loch Lomond distillery sits on—duh—Loch Lomond, the largest lake in Britain, and Inchmurrin is the lake's largest island.

AGE
18
years old

ALC/VOL
46%

NOSE

Lavender candy, stewed pears, baking spices, vanilla, ginger, caramel, and a very slight peat note; water adds a rich honey, orange, and vanilla sweetness.

PALATE

A medium mouthfeel, with a slight, sweet smokiness, alongside honey, burnt sugar, pipe tobacco, and dried apricots; in time an oak astringency dominates, and continues on through the finish, with an added pop of red pepper flakes.

GENERAL

Given the age, and the stellar nose, you'd expect more from this. The palate is narrow and, in time, overly oaky.

PRICE
$$

RATING

Jura

OWNER: WHYTE & MACKAY/EMPERADOR

FOUNDED: 1810

REGION: HIGHLANDS

PRONUNCIATION: *ZHUR-ra*

The only distillery on its eponymous island, Jura is also one of the oldest licensed distilleries in Scotland. Though relatively remote, it's an easy hop over from Islay next door, and no one should visit one and not the other. Jura is also the site of Barnhill, the house where George Orwell retreated to write *1984*. The Jura portfolio has gone through a complete reshuffling of late; all but the 10 Year Old are out of production, though there are still supplies to be found on liquor store shelves. In 2017 Jura dropped all of its expressions and launched a new ten year old; other expressions will follow.

Jura
Aged 10 Years

Though Jura has offered a ten year old for a while, this is a new expression, the first in the distillery's revamped lineup. Unlike the previous Origin 10 Year Old, it has a complex barrel program, aging in new American oak and ex-bourbon casks, with a finish in ex-oloroso casks.

AGE

10
years old

ALC/VOL

40%

NOSE

Flowers, fabric softener, crushed seashells, and a salty hint of coast; water elicits orange blossom and a slight meatiness.

GENERAL

A nice, inoffensive whisky—good for a warm summer day but unlikely to knock your socks off. It's the pleated khakis of whisky.

PALATE

A thin palate offers blanched almonds, vanilla, peonies, and peach skins; adding water brings out a little spice and citrus. The finish is short, with a slight spiciness combined with the chalky sweetness of Necco wafers.

PRICE

$$

RATING

Jura Superstition

One of the first widely available non-age-statement single malts, it's made from 87-percent unpeated barley and 13-percent peated (to a potent 40 ppm).

AGE
No age statement

ALC/VOL
43%

NOSE
Stone fruits, creamy honey, slight peat, and a slight whiff of brine and malt, which bursts forward with a few drops of water.

PALATE
Opens with cream and honey, malted barley, and campfire; it builds to Pop-Rock spiciness, with a medium finish and lingering smoke.

GENERAL
Lovely—a solid whisky, with something for everyone: cream, peat, honey, and malty sweetness.

PRICE
$$

RATING

Jura Diurachs' Own

"Diurach" is the name for a resident of Jura, and the distillery concocted this whisky in honor of the island's 200 inabitants. It's aged fourteen years in ex-bourbon barrels and two more in ex-amoroso sherry casks.

AGE
16
years old

ALC/VOL
43%

NOSE
Almost like a sherried Speyside—white raisins, honey, salt, cold campfire ash, fish skins, heather. With water, you find more honey, plus a bready, spicy edge.

PALATE
A thick mouthfeel, with orange candy, ginger, nuts, rye bread, marzipan; adding water turns it creamy and zesty, like an orange liqueur. The finish is a bit tannic, but not drying, and with very little spice, just a lingering chocolate and citrus sweetness.

GENERAL
For such a low proof, there's a decent amount going on here, though in the end it's not exciting enough to vault into the superlatives. It's mild and approachable.

PRICE
$$

RATING

Jura
Brooklyn

Jura brought six cask samples to Brooklyn, and asked twelve representatives of the borough's food scene to pick their favorite. The winner has been aged in a mix of bourbon, pinot noir, and amoroso sherry casks.

AGE
No age statement

ALC/VOL
42%

NOSE
Strong sherry and dark wine notes; a touch of peat, short-bread, white pepper, and rain-soaked wood.

PALATE
Smoke up front, expanding into ginger and wheat bread, and resolving into an ash and cinnamon finish.

GENERAL
A nice nose, but a disappointingly one-dimensional palate.

PRICE
$$

RATING
★★

Jura Prophecy

AGE
16
years old

ALC/VOL
46%

Jura claims this expression, its peatiest, is pulled from its "finest and rarest" barrels, but offers very little else by way of information. The name—and the bottle design—come from a legend about an eighteenth-century woman from Jura predicting that one day the last man on the island from the Campbell clan, which ruled Jura at the time, would have one eye and carry his entire worldly possessions in a cart. In 1938 it came true, when Charles Campbell, partially blinded in World War I, went broke and left the island in a cart.

NOSE

Chocolate cake, almonds, banana cream, and a strong peat note that grows stronger with air; with water, you'll find varnish, fish skins, cheese, brine, and old closet.

PALATE

Thick and round, with peat, grain, anise, and salmon skin; water adds peanut brittle and pepper. The finish is smoky and briny, with a lingering salty spiciness.

GENERAL

Jura promises this is a "profoundly peated" expression, which it is compared with the other standard Juras, but nothing when paired with some of the whiskies made across the way in Islay. There's less iodine and rubber, among other things. Still, an enjoyable dram, especially if you're looking for peat, but not too much peat.

PRICE
$$

RATING

Kilchoman

OWNER: KILCHOMAN

FOUNDED: 2005

REGION: ISLAY

PRONUNCIATION: *Kill-HO-man*

Kilchoman is one of the youngest distilleries in Scotland to gain international acclaim, though it's still among the smallest; making just 90,000 liters a year, it is about one one-hundredth of the size of the new, expanded Macallan. It is a self-styled "farm distillery," and, true to form, it grows a sizable amount of its own barley (and buys more of it from Islay farmers) and malts a portion of it on-site. Much of its whisky is still quite young, and it shows, but in a good way—proof that the right ingredients, a solid distiller, and good barrel management are more important than the blunt forces of time in producing a worthy spirit.

Kilchoman Machir Bay

This expression is aged in a mix of three-, four-, and five-year-old ex-bourbon casks, then spends eight short weeks in sherry butts. It gets its name from a spot that, according to the distillery, is the prettiest beach in all of Islay.

AGE
No age statement

ALC/VOL
46%

NOSE
Pine, citrus, iodine, a beach campfire, fresh rubber, seaweed, and powdered sugar; water uncovers the sherry influence, along with raisins and coffee.

GENERAL
Good to begin with, the nose and palate improve significantly with water. Either way, it's a delicious blend of citrus and smoke.

PALATE
Campfire, burnt cookies, grilled oranges, caramel, and raisins; a strong wood note emerges with water, along with smoke reek, cigar ash, and candied orange. The finish is all about campfire and salted caramel.

PRICE
$$

RATING

Kilchoman Sanaig

AGE
No age statement

ALC/VOL
46%

Named for an inlet near the distillery, Sanaig is aged for three to four years in ex-bourbon casks, then another ten months in oloroso sherry casks.

NOSE
Dark citrus, raisin bread, fresh sea air, charcoal, coastal peat, toffee, and pine; with water, you get grass, hay, and a big sherry hit.

PALATE
Chocolate-covered raisins, charcoal, apricots, and grilled fruit; with water, pineapple pops up, followed by smoke and ash. The finish is long and creamy, with citrus, cinnamon stick, and mild smoke.

GENERAL
Creamy, malty, fruity, peaty—a great combo, pulled off perfectly.

PRICE
$$

RATING

Kilchoman 100% Islay 2008 EDITION

AGE
16 years old

ALC/VOL
50%

An annual release, Kilchoman's 100% Islay is literally that: Every ingredient—the barley, the peat, the water—comes from the island, just as every step in the production takes place there.

NOSE
Retrained peat; saltwater and raspberry jam dominate.

PALATE
A robust but balanced flavor, tilting between raspberries and mint on one side and wood smoke and chocolate powder on the other, with a finish that lingers in peat and mint.

GENERAL
Don't let the berry and mint notes fool you—the peat is strong with this one. But the balance between the two makes for an intriguing drink.

PRICE
$$

RATING

Kilchoman Loch Gorm

AGE
No age statement

ALC/VOL
46%

Loch Gorm is a relatively young whisky from Kilchoman, aged exclusively in new and refill ex-oloroso sherry butts. It is a limited annual release, first launched in 2012.

NOSE

Warm campfire ashes, grilled pork, with a slight mossy salinity; a little water brings out beef stew and loam.

PALATE

Extremely peaty, with campfire, cinnamon sticks, baker's chocolate, and dried orange peel, and a quick, dry finish.

GENERAL

A whisky only a peat head could love: not especially sweet or complex, just a roaring, smoky fire of a dram.

PRICE
$$$

RATING

Kilchoman 2008 Vintage

AGE
No age statement

ALC/VOL
46%

Every year Kilchoman releases a vintage-dated single malt, aged exclusively in ex-bourbon barrels. At seven years old, the 2008 is Kilchoman's oldest release to date.

NOSE

The peat is restrained; in its place, raspberries, hay, and soft rubbery notes come forward.

GENERAL

An iron fist wrapped in a velvet glove. The nose is balanced, even subtle, but on the tongue it's a four-alarm peat bomb—but not without some subtlety.

PALATE

Aye, there's the peat! And loads of it: cigar, cherry syrup, chocolate, and campfire. The finish is medium-length, and slightly spicy.

PRICE
$$$

RATING

Kilchoman
Cask Strength

Aged in ex-bourbon barrels, then dumped into bottles without a drop of water added.

AGE
No age statement

ALC/VOL
59.2%

NOSE
Strangely muted, with lemon, charcoal, dried apricots, and oak shavings; water brings out graham crackers.

PALATE
Vanilla, toasted nuts, bananas, and charcoal at the mid-palate; graham crackers, berries, and a bit of mint come out with water. The finish is long and dry, with more of those bananas.

GENERAL
A solid dram, but not much of an improvement from the standard proof.

PRICE
$$$

RATING

Kininvie

OWNER: WILLIAM GRANT AND SONS

FOUNDED: 1990

REGION: SPEYSIDE

PRONUNCIATION: *Kin-IN-vee*

Does Kininvie deserve its own entry in this guide? Technically, it is a still house adjacent to Balvenie, not an independent distillery. It was originally built to provide malt for Grant's Family Reserve, a blend, as its stablemates Glenfiddich and Balvenie were increasingly allocated to their respective single malt expressions. But with the opening of Grant's distilling complex at Ailsa Bay, the demand on Kininvie lessened. It is now a major part of Monkey Shoulder blended malt, and a delicious, if preciously rare, twenty-three-year-old single malt on its own. Like Glenfiddich and Balvenie, it is "teaspooned" (receiving a drop of a different malt whisky) to prevent independent bottlers from reselling it as a single malt; post-teaspoon it is sold as Aldunie.

Kininvie
23 Years Old

Aged in a mix of ex-bourbon and ex-sherry casks. Sold in 375-ml bottles.

AGE
23
years old

ALC/VOL
42.6%

NOSE
Vanilla custard, sherry, lemon cake, and honey galore; water adds cedar shavings and a slightly savory note.

GENERAL
Lovely, just lovely—like liquid dessert. It's a stellar whisky, but for the price. . .

PALATE
A medium, waxy mouthfeel, with rich honey notes, candy-shell sugar, white bread, peaches, and strawberries; water makes it slightly herbal, with a strong caramel note erupting. The finish is long and sweet, with honey and dried fruit.

PRICE
$$$

RATING

Lagavulin

OWNER: DIAGEO

FOUNDED: 1816

REGION: ISLAY

PRONUNCIATION: *LAG-a-VOO-lin*

Many enthusiasts declare Lagavulin the perfect Islay malt—maybe the perfect malt, period. Among others, it is the preferred drink of Ron Swanson from the sitcom *Parks and Recreation* (and of the actor who plays him, Nick Offerman). Though Lagavulin was founded in 1816, its site was previously home to a series of illegal still operations; long before that, it overlooked the harbor for the warships of the Lords of the Isles. Though much of Lagavulin's output is aged on the mainland, it is still very much an Islay expression, full of iodine, rich fruits, and seaweed, thanks in part to its uniquely shaped stills—"so pear shaped they look like they were deliberately modeled on pears," wrote Iain Banks.

Lagavulin
Aged 8 Years

AGE
8
years old

ALC/VOL
48%

Inspired by—but not modeled after—an eight-year-old Lagavulin that Alfred Barnard encountered in the 1880s, it was released in 2016 to commemorate the distillery's 200th anniversary. It was made a permanent part of Lagavulin's range in 2017.

NOSE

Toasted coconut, leather, dying campfire, licorice, and dried hay; water brings out honey, old woodshed, grain silo, and, after opening a bit, fresh-baked raisin challah.

GENERAL

Young and vibrant—proof that well-made single malts don't have to be aged into the double digits. Loads of fruit and candy, but balanced against smoke and grain notes.

PALATE

On the thin side, it opens sweet, but darkens and dries, with a bit of smoke; there's vanilla and cinnamon stick throughout. Water adds a bit more sweetness in the form of candy shell and bubblegum. The finish is long and sweetly vegetal, like grilled zucchini and barbecue chips.

PRICE

$$

RATING

Lagavulin
Aged 16 Years

AGE
16
years old

ALC/VOL
43%

A classic—perhaps the classic—Islay single malt, with a robust amount of peat, but enough nuance to let a wide range of flavors shine through. Think of Guns N' Roses' "November Rain," with Slash paired with a piano and full orchestra. Aged in a mix of American and European oak casks.

NOSE

So much going on—smoked cherries, if that's a thing, grassy and mossy, bergamot tea, chlorinated swimming pool, roses, and of course the unmistakable iodine and rubber. It gets a bit sweeter with water, showing caramel and maple syrup.

PALATE

Very sweet up front, with toffee and spicy chocolate, then moving quickly to charcoal and heavily grilled meats, smoked fish, cinnamon, and campfire; through it all, iodine and honey dance in a frenzied tango. The finish is long and floral.

GENERAL

Like drinking a symphony—it's impossibly complex, yet each piece is clear.

PRICE
$$

RATING

Lagavulin
Aged 12 Years

Finished in exclusively American oak barrels.

AGE
12
years old

ALC/VOL
57.7%

NOSE

Meyer lemon, cherry candy, salted caramel, soot, and wood smoke; with water, it's waxy, with pepper, Play-Doh, and grilled pork. Very little brine.

GENERAL

Smoky as hell—big, powerful, but not overwhelming. It's a stripped-down version of the standard 16 Year Old—clear and direct. Not for everyone, but a winner for peat fans.

PALATE

Thick, big, peppery, and meaty, with smoked fish and campfire smoke; water adds a certain juiciness, and it's sharper and somehow drier. The finish shows oatmeal, salt, and a slight sweetness.

PRICE

$$

RATING

Lagavulin
Distillers Edition, 2016

This an annual, limited variant on the sixteen-year-old expression, typically finished in Pedro Ximénez casks.

AGE
No age statement

ALC/VOL
43%

NOSE

Spicy orange marmalade, old rubber, pumpernickel bread, pickled ginger, and sweet peat; water turns it sweeter and savory, with hot dogs, sweet barbecue sauce, licorice, and bubblegum.

GENERAL

Deliciously complex, rolling in waves from its initial burst of honey on the palate to a dry, savory finish.

PALATE

Full and waxy, with honey, sultanas, barbecue, and grilled pineapple, growing drier toward the finish; water adds even more honey and sherry notes. The finish is dry, with a lingering savory, peppery note.

PRICE

$$$

RATING

Laphroaig

OWNER: BEAM SUNTORY

FOUNDED: 1815

REGION: ISLAY

PRONUNCIATION: *La-FROYG*

Like its fellow Ileachs Kilchoman and Bowmore, Laphroaig malts a portion of its own grain, about 20 percent, because its distillers believe that the on-site kiln produces a unique, creosote character, full of tar and iodine. Whatever the details, the peat used for its in-house malting has a higher-than-normal moss content. (Of course, man cannot live by creosote alone, so the balance of the malt comes from the Port Ellen maltings, also on Islay.) For a good chunk of the twentieth century, Laphroaig was under the control of Bessie Williamson, a secretary-turned-distillery manager who inherited it when her boss and the previous owner, Ian Hunter, passed away. She owned and ran it from 1954 to 1967, when she sold it to Schenley Industries, an American company. Laphroaig is also known for one of the most infamous distillery accidents in Scotch history: In 1847 one of its owners, Donald Johnston, fell into a boiling vat and died.

Laphroaig
QA Cask

AGE
No age statement

ALC/VOL
40%

"QA" stands for *Quercus alba*, the Latin name for plain old American white oak. Actually, this whisky gets the QA treatment twice—first in a standard maturation in ex-bourbon barrels, then again in new charred barrels. Available in travel retail only.

NOSE
Tar, charcoal, vanilla, ashtray, burnt toast, and brine, growing sweeter with air; adding water brings out bananas, freshly sawn wood, and strawberries.

PALATE
A thin, light mouthfeel, with vanilla, nuts, marshmallow fluff, and cigar ash; water blows it out completely. The finish is quick and unremarkable, with hints of char and cinnamon.

GENERAL
There aren't many travel retail bottles reviewed in this book, for two reasons. It's a good bet you'll only see them in European airports, and their quality swings widely—as this bottle demonstrates, many of them aren't worth the carry-on space.

PRICE
$

RATING

Laphroaig
Select

AGE
No age statement

ALC/VOL
40%

To make this expression, Laphroaig aged its whisky in oloroso sherry butts, virgin American oak, "PX-seasoned" hogsheads, quarter casks, and first-fill ex-bourbon casks, then married them to create six different profiles. Fans then picked their favorite—hence "Select."

NOSE
Campfire, rubber tire, chlorinated water, new car, cumin, lemon candy, old wood, and tobacco ash; with water you get dark fruit and graham cracker notes.

PALATE
A thin body with raspberry up front, roasted, herbed meats, and blandly bitter; the crisp finish leaves a hint of mint and campfire.

GENERAL
Select is not much of a selection, unless you're making cocktails.

PRICE
$

RATING

Laphroaig
Aged 10 Years

AGE
10
years old

The classic Laphroaig and largely unchanged for seventy-five years.

ALC/VOL
43%

NOSE

Iodine, old cigar smoke, hay, campfire, cedar shavings, buttered toast, salty sea air; over time cherry and sweet berries emerge. Water amps up the cherry note.

GENERAL

Hard to fault, though it is to peat what the meat-lovers' option is to pizza. If you love peat, you'll love this; if you're looking for more, you might not find it.

PALATE

A light mouthfeel with a palate that opens sweet, then darkens with roasted meat, burnt toast, oak, and Cynar amaro; the sweetness never leaves, though, and resolves into butter, saltwater taffy, and apricot. With water it gets sweeter, with a touch of sherry. The finish is long, with oak and campfire notes.

PRICE

$

RATING

Laphroaig
Cask Strength BATCH 6

AGE
10
years old

Non-chill filtered and bottled at its natural strength out of the cask.

ALC/VOL
58%

NOSE

Vanilla, pancake syrup, rum, patchouli, papaya, camphor, linseed oil, and forest; water makes it more volatile, with sweet brandy, ginger, and chlorinated water.

GENERAL

For such a high proof, this one works even without water—the alcohol integrates nicely with the big flavors and round mouthfeel.

PALATE

Thick mouthfeel, with cola, ginger, menthol, grilled fish skins, chicken soup, grilled orange, hot dogs, and mulled wine; the finish lingers with sweet ginger, burnt rubber, a bit of stone fruit, and a slightly anesthetic tingle.

PRICE

$$

RATING

Laphroaig Quarter Cask

AGE
No age statement

ALC/VOL
48%

Officially a non-age-statement expression, this one's aged for about five years in traditionally sized casks, then placed in "quarter casks"—about twenty-one gallons—for another seven months. (Smaller casks have a higher surface-to-volume ratio, thus speeding up the aging process.)

NOSE
Dried wood, rubbing spices, sea air, cherry syrup, grilled lamb, rosemary, and smoked salmon; with water it gets sweeter and a bit smokier, with brine and saltwater taffy.

PALATE
A medium mouthfeel that opens with smoky caramel and chocolate, then morphs into spice, brine, seaweed, and campfire ash; as on the nose, water makes it sweeter, with chocolate dominating. The finish is long and bittersweet, a bit tannic, with notes of grilled orange slices.

GENERAL
It starts off solid, but the more time you spend with it, the less impressive it becomes. There's not as much complexity in the body as the older Laphroaigs—though also less peat.

PRICE
$$

RATING

Laphroaig Triple Wood

AGE
No age statement

ALC/VOL
48%

Non–chill filtered and with no age statement, it's aged sequentially in ex-bourbon barrels, quarter casks, and oloroso sherry butts.

NOSE
Cherry juice, vanilla, stubbed-out cigar, wet leaves, smoked fish, a whiff of sherry, and buckets of smoky lapsang souchong tea; water makes it brighter and fruitier, but it also brings out charred wood.

PALATE
Pipe smoke, smoked fish, apple pie, and burnt marshmallow; the peat heat hits in the mid-palate, along with blackberry, then trails into a gently smoky, bitter, and salty finish, with some hints of graham cracker.

GENERAL
A decently complex palate; the peat and sweet notes are a bit unbalanced, but it's an enjoyable, intriguing drink.

PRICE
$$

RATING

Laphroaig
Aged 15 Years

AGE
15
years old

ALC/VOL
43%

A limited-edition release to mark the distillery's 200th anniversary. Sadly no longer in production, but still found in out-of-the-way liquor stores. If you find it, buy it.

NOSE

Wild berries, forest air, papaya, dark flowers, jackfruit, Band-Aids, spearmint, and fruit gum; tropical notes pop with water, along with oak smoke, maple, and cherry gum.

GENERAL

Big, spicy, juicy, and redolent of tropical fruits—more powerful than one would expect from a moderate proof. One of the best Laphroaigs, and it's a shame it's no longer in production.

PALATE

Medium and slightly oily, with maple and berry sweetness up front, riding an undertone of smoky barbecue. Water underlines and clarifies the sweet meatiness. Finishes with grilled melon and sweet ash.

PRICE
$$

RATING

Laphroaig
Cairdeas 2016

AGE
15
years old

ALC/VOL
51.6%

Every year Laphroaig releases a limited-edition bottling, each time with a twist, under the label "Cairdeas"—Scots Gaelic for "friendship." In 2016, the distillery finished fully matured whisky in Madeira casks (similar to what Glenmorangie did with its 2016 Private Edition release).

NOSE

Dark flowers, herbed butter, sweet wine, old wood, and the slightest whiff of asphalt; with water, you get vanilla cake and baking spices.

GENERAL

As it usually does with Cairdeas releases, Laphroaig knocks this one out of the park: The peat and Madeira are perfectly balanced, and the smoke jumps out immediately on the palate, but never overwhelms the sweet creaminess underneath.

PALATE

Butterscotch, citrus peel, creosote, smoked spice, cocoa, cream; water makes it significantly sweeter, like sweet and spicy barbecue sauce. The finish is oaky, tannic, and drawn out along citrus zest and dried apricots.

PRICE
$$

RATING

Laphroaig Lore

AGE
No age statement

ALC/VOL
48%

Laphroaig's latest addition to its core range, Lore is said to mark the passage of knowledge from one generation of distillers to another—embodied here in a marriage of whisky of different ages (seven to twenty-one years old) from different casks, including sherry butts and quarter casks.

NOSE
Creosote, dark fruits, Red Delicious and green apples, raisin bread, campfire, and sawdust; with water you get bread dough, green raisins, salty air, burnt sugar, and melting ice.

PALATE
Clean and crisp notes, like smoky winter air, though there's also bacon, anise, and a powerful combination of oak and cedar smoke; with water it gets sweeter, including roasted marshmallows and smoked fish. The finish is long, tannic, and a bit smoky, with more of that bacon.

GENERAL
Pleasant, but a bit one-note in its smokiness. There's very little sweetness, even with water. But the smoke isn't nuanced or robust enough to please a peat head, especially for the price.

PRICE
$$$

RATING
★★

Laphroaig Aged 18 Years

AGE
18
years old

ALC/VOL
48%

Laphroaig's most expensive, hardest-to-find whisky in its core range, and even more rare since the distillery discontinued production in 2015. Snap one up if you can.

NOSE
Green apples, salty biscuits, cherries, charred wood, iodine, and blood oranges; water elicits vanilla and lemon custard.

PALATE
Vanilla and caramel open up the full-bodied palate, with plums, slight wood smoke, and a decent pinch of pepper at the mid-palate; water brings out citrus and spice. The finish is long and peppery, and slightly anesthetic.

GENERAL
All those years in the barrel certainly tame the peat notes; the entry is smooth as silk, building to a pleasant spice pop in the middle.

PRICE
$$$

RATING
★★
★★

Laphroaig
Aged 25 Years

A mix of whiskies aged in second-fill ex–oloroso sherry and ex-bourbon casks. It's bottled at cask strength, so the proof will vary.

AGE
25
years old

ALC/VOL
45.1%

NOSE

Quite mild for a Laphroaig—the sherry greets you up front, followed by roast pork, rubber, and a bit of tar; water brightens it a bit.

GENERAL

A stunning marriage of peat, sherry, and American oak notes; it's restrained but in no way boring. Sublime.

PALATE

Silky smooth and mature; there's a peaty bite, but it's restrained, allowing notes of stone fruits, apples, and roasted meat to come forward. Water amplifies the peat. The finish is long, sweet, and sour.

PRICE

$$$$

RATING

★ ★
★ ★

Ledaig

FOR DISTILLERY INFORMATION ABOUT LEDAIG (PRONOUNCED *LETCH-egg*), SEE TOBERMORY ON PAGE 274.

Ledaig
Aged 10 Years

Peated at a light 37 ppm, with malt from Port Ellen maltings on Islay.

AGE
10
years old

ALC/VOL
46.3%

NOSE

Graham cracker, barbecue, creamy bananas, inner-tube rubber, sea air, grilled oranges, dark honey, campfire, and herbs; water elicits perfume, dill, hay, and cocoa powder.

GENERAL

The peat seems big up front, but it fades quickly, to reveal sweetness and fruit. Zesty and pleasant.

PALATE

Sweet peat, with a medium mouthfeel, grilled orange, and a woody astringency; with water it grows more bitter—oak and ash—plus saltwater taffy. The finish is long, with salt, lemon, more grilled orange, meat, and wood.

PRICE
$$

RATING
★★

Ledaig
Aged 18 Years

A smoky, maritime peated malt finished in ex-sherry casks.

AGE
18
years old

ALC/VOL
46.3%

NOSE

Funky—like a washed-rind cheese, tobacco, tangerines, leather, and peat reek; water turns it even funkier.

GENERAL

The funky nose is not entirely pleasant, but the palate is a dream—a complex, peaty, sweet dream.

PALATE

A medium, slightly oily mouthfeel, with much less funk—instead, there's sweet peat, brine, cloves, orange zest, and raisins; it's even rounder and brawnier with water. The finish is dry and a bit tannic, with ash and sweet brine.

PRICE
$$$

RATING

Ledaig
Marsala Finish

The 18 Year Old, finished for an extra year in Marsala wine casks.

AGE
19
years old

ALC/VOL
46.3%

NOSE
Rubber, dark fruits, wood polish, dried figs, and sultanas; the dried fruits come out even more aggressively with water.

GENERAL
What a difference a year and a barrel finish can make—the 18 Year Old is nice enough, but this is a whole new level. Oaky and smoky and sweet as hell.

PALATE
A round, oily mouthfeel, with roasted jalapeño and green peppers, honey, grilled pork, cherry juice, and orange zest; water makes it even sweeter and smokier. The finish is a bit ashy and slightly tannic, but a sweet edge burrows its way through.

PRICE
$$$

RATING

Lismore

INDEPENDENT BOTTLER

OWNER: WILLIAM LUNDIE &. CO

Owned by William Lundie &. Co., Lismore is a true "silent" malt: no one knows where it comes from, and Lundie isn't talking. Oddly, though it is named after an island off Scotland's western coast, its style is pure Speyside.

Lismore

AGE
No age statement

ALC/VOL
40%

NOSE
Orange drink, cherries, floor polish, herbal tea, and intense floral notes of lavender and honeysuckle; water opens and deepens it, even at such a low proof.

PALATE
White wine, wet grain, metallic; water doesn't do much. The finish is astringent and cloying, though a bit spicy with water.

GENERAL
Like many low-end single malts, the nose is fine, even above average, but the palate is a wreck—diluted, unclear, uninteresting.

PRICE
$

RATING
NR

Lismore
Aged 15 Years

AGE
15
years old

ALC/VOL
40%

NOSE
Vanilla, black tea, honey, sweetly floral, caramel, and a whiff of oak; it gets loamy and nutty with a bit of water.

PALATE
A thin, wan mouthfeel, with pumpkin, vanilla, and cocoa powder; water adds a bit of citrus, vanilla, and diluted orange drink. The finish is quick and smooth, with a sheen of mint.

GENERAL
Like the non-age-statement expression, the nose entrances, but the palate disappoints. One can only imagine what it would be at 86 or 92 proof.

PRICE
$

RATING

Lismore
Aged 18 Years

AGE
18
years old

ALC/VOL
43%

NOSE

Anise, port, soy, horehound candy, and rum raisin; water brings out brown sugar and a distinct minerality.

PALATE

Medium mouthfeel, spicy up front, salty, tamarind; with water it's richer and darker. The short finish is slightly jammy and peppery.

GENERAL

A great whisky for the price—a bit thin on the palate, and not quite round enough, but with enough complexity to pull it through.

PRICE
$$

RATING

Lismore
Aged 21 Years

AGE
21
years old

Maybe the best part about this whisky is the packaging: It comes in a faux-leather-wrapped tube.

ALC/VOL
43%

NOSE

Rubber gasket, linseed oil, stale chips, overripe bananas, and mushrooms; a little water brings out caramel and vanilla.

PALATE

A thin-to-medium mouthfeel that opens with vanilla, then grows astringent and spicy; the finish is short and astringent. Water underlines the spiciness with ginger and white pepper.

GENERAL

A bit like a bourbon with its spice and vanilla notes, but if anything it's over-oaked, with too much wood influence. Water is important here—despite the low proof, it's a must.

PRICE
$$$

RATING

Loch Lomond

OWNER: LOCH LOMOND GROUP

FOUNDED: 1966

REGION: HIGHLANDS

Loch Lomond is said to better resemble a Japanese distillery than a Scotch one, in that this one facility can produce an array of whisky styles (its namesake expressions are reviewed here; for Inchmoan and Inchmurrin, see their separate entries). Its wide range of stills can produce both single malt and grain whisky; it is also the birthplace of the "Lomond still," an innovative pot still with rectifying plates arranged above it, so it can act like a column still if need be. Its current owners, the Loch Lomond Group, say it can produce eleven different single malts, with a capacity of 15 million liters of malt whisky and an astounding 18 million gallons of grain whisky a year. It is designed to operate independently; it even has its own cooperage. It is also one of the few still-operating distilleries to be opened by American investors in the post-war whisky boom—in this case, Duncan Thomas and Barton Brands. The latter took over and closed the site in 1984; fortunately, it was soon bought and revived.

Loch Lomond Aged 12 Years

Aged in three types of barrels—first-fill, second-fill and re-charred ex-bourbon.

AGE
12
years old

ALC/VOL
46%

NOSE

Vanilla ice cream, earthy, heather, honey cake; water brings out coastal earthiness, and a bit of smoke.

GENERAL

Lush and oily, juicy and sweet, with very little burn—a real sipper, as they call them in Kentucky.

PALATE

Medium-bodied, floral, and intensely sweet—milk chocolate, candy shell, vanilla bean, and peach candy; water smoothes it further. The finish is all about orange blossom and grapefruit.

PRICE
$$

RATING

Loch Lomond
Aged 18 Years

Made from lightly peated malt and aged in ex-bourbon casks, this is the distillery's flagship expression in the United States.

AGE
18
years old

ALC/VOL
46%

NOSE

A light, soft nose, with freshly sawn wood, sea salt, sweet grains, dried almonds, hay, and nutmeg; water brings out sun-baked upholstery, more almond, vanilla, and citrus zest.

PALATE

Sweet malt up front, balanced by a slight smokiness, along with plump raisins, gingerbread, and burnt orange; the drying finish finds pepper and gingerbread.

GENERAL

The long finish evolves and echoes back to the palate; given the lack of smoke on the nose, its presence on the palate is surprising. All in all, a well-priced, underappreciated eighteen year old.

PRICE
$$

RATING

Longmorn

OWNER: CHIVAS BROTHERS/PERNOD RICARD

FOUNDED: 1893

REGION: SPEYSIDE

John Duff founded Longmorn in 1893, and BenRiach next door two years later, to take advantage of the late-Victorian whisky boom; a few years later, it all collapsed, and Longmorn closed. Duff sold it to James Grant in 1899; eventually it merged with Glenlivet and Glen Grant, which in 1977 flowed into Seagram, and later into the hands of Chivas Brothers and its parent, Pernod Ricard. Longmorn provides a sizable amount of the malt that goes into Chivas's blended expressions, and only recently has become regularly available in official bottlings. Masataka Taketsuru, the father of Japanese whisky, worked briefly at Longmorn, and it is said he modeled Nikka Distillery after it.

Longmorn
Aged 16 Years

An upgrade from the previous fifteen-year-old release, aged in ex-bourbon casks.

AGE
16
years old

ALC/VOL
48%

NOSE
Caramel, fresh leather, vanilla toffee, fabric softener, white port, and melon; water adds a luscious floral intensity.

PALATE
Thick, with cake batter, dates, leather, ash, and spice at mid-palate; with water, you'll get mangos and dried tropical fruit. The finish is semi-dry, with raw almonds, chocolate, oranges, and salt.

GENERAL
Tons of tropical fruits, flowers, raisins, and thick sweetness. Delicate but robust. Gorgeous.

PRICE
$$$

RATING

Longrow

FOR DISTILLERY INFORMATION SEE SPRINGBANK ON PAGE 261.

Longrow
Peated

Previously known as Longrow C.V., it's a non-age-statement expression aged in ex-bourbon casks. All Springbank whiskies (except for Hazelburn) are a bit peaty, but this is significantly more peated than the rest.

AGE
No age statement

ALC/VOL
46%

NOSE
Creamy, waxy whiffs of saltwater taffy, sweet smoke, leather, marzipan, and vanilla; water makes it slightly sweeter.

PALATE
A medium mouthfeel with a palate that opens sweetly, then moves through savory to smoky; water enhances but doesn't fundamentally alter the palate. The long finish shows smoke, seaweed, and spicy pepper.

GENERAL
Islay fans looking to branch out should give this one a shot—it's solid on the peat, but different: more smoky than phenolic, sweeter and less heavy on the iodine. Peat-curious folks should also give it a try before stepping up to an Ardbeg.

PRICE
$$

RATING

Longrow
Aged 18 Years

The oldest and most refined of the Longrow line.

AGE
18
years old

ALC/VOL
46%

NOSE

Grilled lemon, charcoal, creosote, honey, strawberry, cigarettes; water brings out berry juice, barbecue sauce, and grilled pork.

GENERAL

Searing spice and peat, but with enough juicy sweetness to balance it. Combined, it's a remarkable, bold whisky.

PALATE

Chewy, with blackberries, sweet barbecue sauce, charcoal, burnt caramel, cigarette tobacco, and a bubbling spice at the middle; adding water brings out buttered toast and tropical fruit. The lengthy finish is all about chocolate, citrus oil, and raspberry jam.

PRICE

$$$

RATING

Macallan

OWNER: EDRINGTON GROUP

FOUNDED: 1824

REGION: SPEYSIDE

PRONUNCIATION: *Mick-ALLEN*

Though today it is one of the world's leading luxury spirit brands, Macallan began as an illicit distilling operation on a hillside estate in Speyside (though there is some debate over whether it's actually in Speyside, and the bottles specify only "Highlands"). The Macallan is the BMW of single malts: expensive, but worth the money, and with a relatively moderate starting price that escalates rapidly, with some bottles reaching six figures at auction. Among other things, it is famous for its "curiously small stills," which it claims provide body and texture to stand up to the distillery's signature sherry-cask regimen. Despite its luxury trappings, Macallan is an enormous distillery, which after a recent $150 million expansion will churn out about 14 million liters a year. Macallan has also invested heavily in its wood program: It buys the wood directly, has it fashioned into casks, and then loans the casks to sherry bodegas for seasoning for up to three years.

The Macallan Fine Oak 10

AGE
10
years old

ALC/VOL
46%

Unlike the traditional Macallan expressions, the Fine Oak range is aged in a combination of bourbon and sherry-seasoned casks—a concession to the scarcity of true ex-sherry barrels and a nod to drinkers who want a lighter drink.

NOSE

More sherry than you'd expect: blackberry jam, marzipan, mint, green apple, and a slight feintiness. The nose disappears with water, then purrs back with cocoa and vanilla.

PALATE

There's very little sherry here; instead, there's sweet cinnamon up front, morphing into cherry cough syrup, biscuits, and a touch of cigarette ash. The finish is dry, short, and lightly herbal.

GENERAL

Innocuous, perfectly serviceable aperitif whisky—as one panel member put it, it's "the Jack Daniel's of scotch."

PRICE
$$

RATING

The Macallan 12 Years Old

AGE
12
years old

ALC/VOL
43%

Aged exclusively in ex-sherry barrels, this is the classic entry-level Macallan malt.

NOSE

Deep, rich sherry notes of cherry, roses, roasted nuts, fruitcake, oak furniture, and malt; water calls forth a bit more fruit.

PALATE

Quite sweet, with candied pecans, maple syrup, and cherry gum, it then darkens into a leathery, gingery mid-palate and a quick finish.

GENERAL

A multipurpose crowd-pleaser—the single malt to buy for people who say they don't like scotch.

PRICE
$$

RATING

The Macallan Double Cask

A curious take on the traditional Macallan—new American oak is fashioned into barrels in Spain, where it is "seasoned" with sherry before shipping to Scotland. The whisky is also aged in sherry-seasoned European oak—hence the "double cask."

AGE
12
years old

ALC/VOL
43%

NOSE
Muted, with whiffs of oak, varnish, ash, and fruits; there isn't a whole lot of sherry. Water brings out some cocoa.

PALATE
Quite sweet, with bubblegum, then quickly transitioning to a musky, ashy flavor with dates and leather; the finish is mild, with red fruits and bitters.

GENERAL
Not a noticeable improvement over the Fine Oak 10, except for the higher price tag.

PRICE
$$

RATING

The Macallan Classic Cut

A one-time release from the Macallan, Classic Cut is aged in a combination of sherry-seasoned American oak and sherry-seasoned European oak, and bottled at cask strength.

AGE
No age statement

ALC/VOL
58.4%

NOSE
Vanilla, plums, dried figs, raisins, and a hint of matchstick; water turns it sweeter, with strawberry milk and brown sugar.

GENERAL
A powerful, hirsute whisky, and quite enjoyable for that—but it lacks evolution and benefits from a good dose of water.

PALATE
Thick—think cherry syrup—with notes of dried fruits, potpourri, unsweetened chocolate, baking spices, and cotton candy; adding water dries it out significantly. The finish is long, bitter, and woody.

PRICE
$$

RATING

The Macallan Fine Oak 15

AGE
15
years old

Same as the 10 Year Old, with five more years of age and a slightly higher proof.

ALC/VOL
43%

NOSE
Soft and fruity, with creamy vanilla, dried fruits, fresh paint, cherry Coke, and linseed oil; an ashy, chocolate note comes out with water.

PALATE
Sweet up front, followed by raisins, honey, pineapple, vanilla, and almond skins; the medium finish is muted and undistinguished.

GENERAL
Nice up front, then thins out quickly. It's more nuanced than the Fine Oak 10, but don't expect the complexity of traditional Macallans.

PRICE
$$$

RATING

The Macallan Fine Oak 17

AGE
17
years old

Aged in a combination of ex-sherry and ex-bourbon barrels.

ALC/VOL
43%

NOSE
Rich tropical notes—baked banana and melon, honey, balsam, and a hint of sweet smoke; water calls forth baking spices.

PALATE
Creamy vanilla, golden raisins, light toffee, and the softest hint of smoke; the raisins and toffee dribble down the finish.

GENERAL
Muted, elegant, and almost refreshing, but ultimately uninteresting.

PRICE
$$$$

RATING

The Macallan 18 Years Old

AGE
18
years old

The iconic baller single-malt, it's aged exclusively in ex-sherry casks.

ALC/VOL
43%

NOSE

A sherry bomb—raspberry jam on biscuits, fresh-picked strawberries, toast, and a slight hint of citrus; water only weakens it.

PALATE

Hella smooth, with a toasty, malty backbone, alongside figs, baker's chocolate, and muted ginger, and a lingering sherry finish.

GENERAL

The nose beats the palate, which is flavorful but—like so much of what constitutes luxury products these days—a bit characterless.

PRICE
$$$$

RATING

The Macallan Rare Cask

AGE
No age statement

Made from a combination of sixteen different sherry-seasoned casks, at different ages, drawn from the top one percent of the distillery's barrels—a testament to Macallan's sophisticated wood-management program.

ALC/VOL
43%

NOSE

Fresh-hewn oak, vanilla, raisins, grapefruit, dried apricots, creamed butter, sea air, and a hint of mint and smoke.

PALATE

Sweet up front, then deepening into rye crisps, chocolate mint, strawberry candy, and a muted maltiness; the finish continues the mint, like a slowing bass line.

GENERAL

Critics like to hit on the Macallan's use of sherry-seasoned casks, as opposed to true ex-sherry casks, but at least in this case, it doesn't matter. Rare Cask is what a sherried malt should be—light, almost playful, without losing complexity. And it's only available in the United States.

PRICE
$$$$

RATING

MacDuff

OWNER: JOHN DEWAR & SONS/BACARDI

FOUNDED: 1960

REGION: HIGHLANDS

Like Glengyle in Campbeltown, MacDuff does not have clear title to its own name, and so it produces whisky under a different one—in this case, The Deveron. MacDuff, despite its Shakespearean name, is a relatively young distillery, having been built in the late 1950s with then-ultra-modern conveniences like indirect steam heating. Though relatively unknown in the United States, The Deveron is a top seller in European markets, especially France and Spain.

The Deveron
Aged 12 Years

Aged in ex-bourbon casks.

AGE

12
years old

ALC/VOL

40%

NOSE

Honey-covered bananas, vanilla cream, baking spices, and plum jam; water adds a hint of grilled meat and cooking oil.

GENERAL

Generic and unremarkable.

PALATE

A thin and slightly oily mouthfeel, with grape soda, milk chocolate, and honey; water destroys it. The medium-length finish shows a slightly menthol aftertaste.

PRICE

$

RATING

The Deveron
18 Years Old

Aged in ex-bourbon casks.

AGE
18
years old

ALC/VOL
40%

NOSE
Green apples, toffee, fresh sliced ginger (like what you find on a sushi plate), and honey; it comes together with water, revealing honeyed malt and orange candy.

PALATE
A thin mouthfeel, with malt, honey, orange zest, and pepper at the mid-palate; the finish is smooth, with just a tickle on the tongue.

GENERAL
Full flavored and surprisingly supple.

PRICE
$$$

RATING
★ ★
★

McClelland's

INDEPENDENT BOTTLER

OWNER: BEAM SUNTORY

McClelland's is the archetypal bottom-shelf single malt: of unknown origin, bottled at the lowest possible proof. McClelland's has four expressions, each oriented around one of Scotch whisky's main regions.

McClelland's Lowland

AGE
No age statement

ALC/VOL
40%

NOSE
Wet moss, butyric acid, ash, cabbage, and radishes; water adds a varnish note.

GENERAL
Avoid this whisky. There's a wide range of alternatives available for a few dollars more.

PALATE
Bland and thin, with ash, bitters, and a vague cinnamon note. Water underlines the ash and cinnamon. The finish is nonexistent, save for a lingering pepper note.

PRICE
$

RATING
NR

McClelland's Highland

AGE
No age statement

ALC/VOL
40%

NOSE
Varnish, oak, stale raisins, wet hay, stale gym bag, and butyric acid; water does nothing.

PALATE
Thin, with stale grain, bitters, ash, and an abundance of wood; water adds a cinnamon dash. The finish is quick.

GENERAL
Like the Lowlands, this is one to avoid.

PRICE
$

RATING
NR

McClelland's Islay

AGE
No age statement

ALC/VOL
40%

NOSE
Sweet barbecue sauce, charred meat, cigar ash, cleaning solution, and engine oil; water underlines the ashiness and calls forth rubber tires.

PALATE
Thin and feinty, with match heads and cigarette ash, but also a surprising, hoppy, citrus sweetness. Water tamps it all down. The finish lingers with anise and ash.

GENERAL
It tastes worse than it sounds— the cigar and cigarette ash dominates the nose and palate. But if you're looking for a smoky whisky as a mixer, this will do.

PRICE
 $

RATING

McClelland's Speyside

AGE	No age statement
ALC/VOL	**40**%

NOSE
Green apples, pencil graphite, wet cardboard, sulfur; water underlines the funky wetness.

GENERAL
Even for a budget whisky, this is bad—likely the result of subpar barrels and poor barrel management. Aside from everything else, it's not representative of "Speyside" at all.

PALATE
Thin, with cocoa powder, cornmeal, ash, and wet barley; water adds a bit of citrus and white pepper. The finish is long, ashy, bitter, and vegetal.

PRICE
$

RATING
NR

Mortlach

OWNER: DIAGEO

FOUNDED: 1823

REGION: SPEYSIDE

PRONUNCIATION: *MORT-lock*

Known affectionately as "the Beast of Dufftown," Mortlach is a famously meaty, rich whisky, and until recently almost all of it went into blends, in particular its Diageo stablemate Johnnie Walker. It still does, but in the past few years Diageo has released more of it as a single malt. Mortlach means "bowl-shaped valley," and that bowl shape is important: In 1010 King Malcolm II defeated an invading army of Danes by waiting for them to reach said valley and then breaking open a dam upriver, flooding the valley—and the Danes. Mortlach is famous for having six stills of different sizes, which it uses for a unique distillation regimen: After the first wash still, 80 percent of the distillate goes directly to the spirit still, while the other 20 percent goes through an intermediate still called the "Wee Witchie," where it is distilled three more times, after which just the hearts of that last run go into the spirit still with the rest of the batch. As a result, Mortlach says its spirit is distilled 2.81 times. Confused? Sure. But if that's what it takes to produce Mortlach's distinctive spirit, so be it.

Mortlach
Rare Old

Aged in a combination of ex-bourbon and ex-sherry barrels, creating a Mortlach with a subtler-than-usual sherry influence.

AGE
No age statement

ALC/VOL
43.4%

NOSE
Deep-roasted coconut, nutty, cooked banana, dark cherry, and port in the back; adding water brings out Fig Newtons, a clean floral air, and spicy cherry candy.

GENERAL
The finish is too quick for such a strong start, but the palate is lovely while it lasts.

PALATE
A thick mouthfeel, with roasted nuts, dark chocolate, cherry, a bit meaty, cola, violet candy; with water you get cassis, cloves, more sherry, and a stronger savory note, like ham. The finish is quick, and slightly numbing, with chocolate and nutmeg.

PRICE
$$$

RATING

Mortlach
18 Years Old

More like the "Beast of Dufftown" sherry bomb that Mortlach is known for.

AGE
18
years old

ALC/VOL
43.4%

NOSE

Rich, dark sherry notes—dark fruits, cherry, tobacco, dried figs, old oak furniture, saddle leather, spiced sausage, caraway seeds, campfire, and sawdust; water adds cola, mint, and spiced meats.

PALATE

There's a mess of sherry here, too, with raisins, apple bark, dried mint, toasted coconuts, marzipan, port, and dark tropical fruits; the finish is herbaceous and tannic, with a long, sweet, and slightly spicy echo.

GENERAL

Lovely from beginning to end; balanced and elegant with plenty of oomph. But you'll pay dearly for it.

PRICE
$$$$

RATING
★ ★
★

Mortlach
25 Years Old

The oldest in the Mortlach range, aged in refill ex-bourbon casks.

AGE
25
years old

ALC/VOL
43.4%

NOSE

Perfume, minerality, cherry syrup, orange zest, and honeycomb; water brings out Pez candy, chalk, herbs, and a touch of sherry.

GENERAL

A lovely, smooth, meaty dram, much bigger than the proof would have you believe. Superb.

PALATE

Much less sweet than the nose, with a thin-to-medium mouthfeel that shows Mortlach's trademark meatiness. A juiciness pops up at the mid-palate among mineral and herbal notes; there's grapefruit oil and chocolate-covered espresso beans as well. It opens significantly with water. The medium-length finish is sharp and bitter; the wood influence shines through at the end.

PRICE
$$$$

RATING

Muirhead's

INDEPENDENT BOTTLER

OWNER: PICARD VINS & SPIRITUEUX

PRONUNCIATION: *MURE-heds*

Muirhead's dates to 1824, when it opened as a wine merchant in Edinburgh. A few decades later it branched into blended whisky, for which it is still best known. Since 2008, when it was acquired by Picard Vins & Spiritueux, it has released sourced Speyside single malts under its Silver Seal line.

Muirhead's Silver Seal

Somewhat hard to find in the United States, the 12 Year Old is still by far the most common of Muirhead's Silver Seal line.

AGE
12 years old

ALC/VOL
40%

NOSE

Flowers and melon candy, honeycomb, raspberries, orange cream, and mushrooms. Adding water amps up the berry notes.

GENERAL

One of the few whiskies for which a low proof actually works—the elegant floral notes dominate on the nose, and the palate is flavorful and interesting despite the relative lack of alcohol. Especially for the price, you can't go wrong with this one.

PALATE

Light-bodied and a bit oily, it's floral, almost soapy up front, then sweetens toward the mid-palate with notes of orange cream and dried tropical fruits; water brings out wood and pencil shavings. The finish dries to a zesty nib. There's a bit too much bitter woodiness on the end.

PRICE
$

RATING

Oban

OWNER: DIAGEO

FOUNDED: 1794

REGION: HIGHLANDS

PRONUNCIATION: *OH-bin*

Oban the distillery practically predates Oban the town. While the former has grown to global prominence, the latter is still home to only about 8,500 people, tucked into a seaside corner of the Scottish Highlands. The distillery is one of the oldest in Scotland, and still one of the most isolated on the mainland. But it has survived, and flourished, thanks to a rail line that early on connected Oban to Glasgow. On a personal note, my maternal grandmother's family comes from Oban, though both at the time and up to the present none of my ancestors or (now distant) relatives had much to do with the whisky industry.

Oban
Aged 14 Years

The backbone of the Oban range, the 14 Year Old reflects the distillery's geography, poised between the maritime smokiness of islands and the robust maltiness of the Highlands.

AGE
14
years old

ALC/VOL
43%

NOSE

Rich and fruity, with sherry, cherries, and honeyed pears, along with vanilla and notes of iodine, rubber, and sweat; it really opens with water, showing cola, cedar, rye, and salty air.

PALATE

Sweet up front, with muted baking spices, orange peel, dark chocolate, and espresso; the finish is medium in length, minty, and fresh.

GENERAL

Deliciously crisp and bright, with a delightful, gentle smokiness.

PRICE
$$

RATING
★★
★

Oban
Little Bay

Following on the success of Talisker Storm, another non-age-statement single malt from Diageo, the drinks giant introduced Oban Little Bay in 2015 to similar acclaim, putting this small distillery on the global map. (For those wondering about the name, it's a bit redundant: *oban* means "little bay" in Scots Gaelic.)

AGE
No age statement

ALC/VOL
43%

NOSE
Apple eau de vie, cinnamon, milk chocolate, bread dough, cloves, brine, seaweed, dried fruit; a bit floral. Water just ruins the fun.

PALATE
Fried bread, fresh malt, cold ash, plums, mangos, hints of leather, and black pepper; the finish is short, refreshing, and slightly minty.

GENERAL
Light but flavorful, Little Bay is an elegant but slightly severe whisky, like a Thomas Mann novel in liquid form.

PRICE
$$

RATING
★ ★

Oban
Distillers Edition

Though technically a non-age-statement expression, the Distillers Edition is an annual release of Oban's standard 14 Year Old that has spent an extra six to eighteen months in a Montilla fino sherry cask. It draws on just 300 barrels a year.

AGE
No age statement

ALC/VOL
43%

NOSE
Strong sherry influence, with red apples, drawn butter, orange peel, chocolate powder, and a slight whiff of smoke. Don't waste it on water.

PALATE
Big sweet sherry hit up front, then it steps aside to reveal cherry, honey, herbs, almond, and a whiff of smoke; the finish is medium in length, and a bit tannic and gingery.

GENERAL
A good example of how a well-applied dose of sherry aging can transform and improve a standard whisky.

PRICE
$$

RATING
★ ★
★

Oban
Aged 18 Years

Like the Distillers Edition, the 18 Year Old is drawn from just 300 barrels a year. Formerly a limited-edition product, it's now part of the Oban core lineup.

AGE

18
years old

ALC/VOL

43%

NOSE

Brine, chalk, honey, cola, ginger, dried grass, and chocolate-covered fruit; water brings out a citric note, like grapefruit, and an earthy spice note, like turmeric.

GENERAL

Tastes more Speyside than Highlands, despite the brine on the nose. The layers of herbs, spices, and chocolate entrance. A smooth, surprisingly elegant drink.

PALATE

A medium mouthfeel, with tropical fruit, toasted coconut, dried ginger, candied apple, and a big spice pop in the middle; with water, you'll find vanilla extract, nuts, chocolate, and melons. The spice carries through to the finish, with just a bit of lingering fruit.

PRICE

$$$

RATING

★ ★
★ ★

Port Askaig

INDPENDENT BOTTLER

OWNER: ELIXIR DISTILLERS

PRONUNCIATION: *port ESS-keeg*

Port Askaig is a range of anonymous whiskies from Islay, released at different ages and proofs—though only the 110 Proof is available in the United States. The brand's namesake is a village on the northeast coast of the island and one of the main entry points for tourists.

Port Askaig 110 Proof

The only Port Askaig release available in the United States, the 110 Proof is non-chill filtered, with no coloring added—but the distillery it came from remains a secret.

AGE
No age statement

ALC/VOL
55%

NOSE
Butterscotch, black tea, charred wood, and oily smoked fish; it sweetens with water, with candy citrus and grilled fruit.

GENERAL
A delicious whisky, even if its source is unknown (many speculate Caol Ila). It's bold and engaging from start to end.

PALATE
A thick, big mouthfeel—nutty, creamy, and spicy at mid-palate, there's vanilla, tobacco, citrus candy, and burnt sugar. With water, you'll find wood and cake batter. It dries on the finish, with black tea and anise.

PRICE
$$

RATING

Pulteney

OWNER: INVER HOUSE/INTERNATIONAL BEVERAGE
COMPANY

FOUNDED: 1826

REGION: HIGHLANDS

PRONUNCIATION: *PULT-nee*

Until the opening of Wolfburn in 2013, Pulteney was the northernmost distillery on mainland Scotland. It was founded by James Hendersen in 1826; it eventually passed into the hands of Buchanan-Dewar, after which it came under control of DCL, which closed it from 1930 to 1951. It was later owned by Allied Distillers before passing into the hands of Inver House. Pulteney's hometown of Wick was once the herring capital of Europe, and it still maintains a strong connection to the sea and fishing. Not coincidentally, Old Pulteney, as the whisky is known, has one of the most overtly briny, seashore-evocative noses and palates around.

Old Pulteney Aged 12 Years

Aged exclusively in ex-bourbon barrels, this is Old Pulteney's flagship (har har) expression.

AGE
12
years old

ALC/VOL
43%

NOSE

Subtle, with vanilla, white chocolate, honey, cola candy, and butterscotch; tangerines emerge with a little water.

PALATE

Vanilla wafers, high floral notes, cocoa powder, and a touch of woodiness, with a quick, dry finish.

GENERAL

This is a well-regarded, award-winning whisky, but it's hard to get excited about it. A solid, slightly boring dram.

PRICE

RATING

Old Pulteney Navigator

A non-age-statement marriage of malts aged in bourbon and sherry barrels, this bottle is named in honor of the distillery's maritime heritage.

AGE
No age statement

ALC/VOL
46%

NOSE
Opens with a hit of green apples, then slides into cinnamon, black pepper, and crisp new-make spirit; water brings out popcorn and perfume.

PALATE
Tastes very young, with lots of cereal, table salt, matzoh, and a bit of apple at the back; the finish has a lingering spice.

GENERAL
The apple notes are nice, but the saltiness on the palate over-whelms the experience.

PRICE
$

RATING
★★

Old Pulteney Aged 17 Years

Aged in 90-percent ex-bourbon and 10-percent ex-sherry casks, insiders consider it a better whisky than the 21 Year Old.

AGE
17
years old

ALC/VOL
46%

NOSE
Vanilla, apricots, leather, geraniums, seaweed, and a bit of wood, peat, and green apples; water brings out a huge feinty hit.

PALATE
Orange peel, oak, grilled pear, brine, and tobacco, with a medium, apple-centric finish.

GENERAL
My tasting panel loved its com-plexity, but I found it too briny.

PRICE
$$$

RATING
★★

Old Pulteney
Aged 21 Years

Like the 17 Year Old, the 21 Year Old is a marriage of ex-bourbon and ex-sherry casks. Jim Murray named it the World Whisky of the Year in 2012.

AGE
21
years old

ALC/VOL
46%

NOSE

Cream liqueur, white pepper, a whiff of smoke, saltwater taffy; water makes it smell like the seashore.

PALATE

Cel-Ray soda, ginger, cola, chocolate graham crackers, and a bit of wood smoke; the finish is silky smooth and quick.

GENERAL

Many insiders prefer the 17 Year Old over this older version, but I found the 21 Year Old more complex and balanced. Still quite briny, but with a lot else going on.

PRICE
$$$

RATING

Old Pulteney
Aged 35 Years

Aged in a combination of ex-sherry and ex-bourbon casks. The price is partly justified by the handsome wood box it comes in, closed by a solid brass dead bolt.

AGE
35
years old

ALC/VOL
42.5%

NOSE

Quite feinty and umami, with fresh paint, drawn butter, lemon, fresh-sawn oak, roasted nuts, and fresh sea air; water calls forth maple and a whiff of pine.

PALATE

Creamy vanilla, raisins, biscuits, licorice, shortbread, and sea salt; needs a lot of time to open up. The finish is mild and dry.

GENERAL

Lots going on in this whisky, but it takes patience to let the liquid open up. A solid drink, but perhaps a bit pricey.

PRICE
$$$$

RATING

Royal Brackla

OWNER: JOHN DEWAR & SONS/BACARDI

FOUNDED: 1817

REGION: HIGHLANDS

Royal Brackla is the first of only two distilleries to receive a royal warrant, having been granted the status in 1835 after a visit from King William IV. For a relatively obscure whisky, at least in the United States, it has a massive output at 15 million liters a year—much of that, obviously, going into blends. Surprisingly, perhaps, the distillery has yet to capitalize on the fact that it is located roughly on the same site as the main actions in *Macbeth*—the distillery sits on the Cawdor Estate, which is still owned by the earl of Cawdor, whose title Macbeth won in battle.

Royal Brackla
Aged 12 Years

Aged in ex-bourbon barrels and then finished, for an unstated length of time, in first-fill oloroso sherry casks.

AGE
12
years old

ALC/VOL
40%

NOSE
Honey, floral, grassy, buttered toast, ginger, rum raisin, baking spices, tangerines, and tobacco ash; water dries it a bit, but also brings out some sweet cocoa powder, red apples, and a whiff of smoke.

GENERAL
A complex and generally well-balanced whisky, though much drier than one would expect with so many fruit notes. At a slightly higher proof—and if it weren't chill filtered—it would be a knockout.

PALATE
A thin-to-medium mouthfeel, with a juicy palate of coconut, toffee, and stewed apples and plums; water turns it a bit salty, with cracked pepper and graham crackers. It dries out on the finish, though a bit of pepper and stewed fruit lingers.

PRICE
$$

RATING

Royal Brackla Aged 16 Years

Like the 12 Year Old, it's aged in ex-bourbon barrels and finished in first-fill ex–oloroso sherry casks.

AGE
16
years old

ALC/VOL
40%

NOSE

Salty and waxy, with miso, celery, cedar, flint, and grape juice; there's also peppercorns, green apples, bananas, and dill pickles. Water elicits root vegetables, endives, ginger, and an ashy metallic note.

PALATE

A medium, waxy body, with leather, tobacco, sultana grapes, dill pickle, and a slight wood smoke note. Water brings out cooked figs and chocolate. The short finish has bits of smoke and honey.

GENERAL

A solid, if not stellar, whisky, and a no-brainer if price weren't an option. But it carries a steep price tag for an expression bottled at 40% alc/vol. Compare it with a similarly aged Dalmore, though less sweet.

PRICE

$$$

RATING

Scapa

OWNER: CHIVAS BROTHERS/PERNOD RICARD

FOUNDED: 1885

REGION: HIGHLANDS

Located on Orkney and the second most northern distillery after Highland Park, Scapa is in many ways an atypical maritime whisky. Its malt is unpeated, and its finished whisky has a fresh, orchard-fruit nose and a round, sweet palate. It was almost destroyed by fire during World War I, but sailors stationed nearby rushed to put it out. Scapa is one of the few distilleries to use a Lomond still—outside of Loch Lomond, of course—but it stopped using the still's adjustable plates in 1979. Still, it benefits from the large amount of copper that the Lomond still provides to produce that fruity, fresh characteristic.

Scapa Skiren

Skiren means "glittering bright skies" in Old Norse, a reminder that Scotland, especially the north, has long attachments to the Scandinavian lands. Matured in first-fill ex-bourbon casks.

AGE
No age statement

ALC/VOL
40%

NOSE
Honey on toast, green apples, pear juice, buttery, vegetal, anise, and waxy, tropical fruit; water dampens the honey and brings out lemon juice, along with sweet cream, toffee, and graham crackers.

GENERAL
Surprisingly light and fresh for a whisky from Orkney, but the oak notes remind you of its hard, forbidding birthplace. A solid, multipurpose whisky, and one that will be wonderful to watch develop.

PALATE
Round notes of honey, sweet cream, toffee, a tang at mid-palate, and a slight bitterness toward the end. Water makes it more herbal, with melons; it still has some spices, but water generally kills it. The finish is medium in length; it dries a bit, with wood, raw almonds, and a bit of grain.

PRICE
$$

RATING

Scapa
Glansa

In Old Norse, *glansa* means "shining storm-laden skies," which is a lot to pack into six letters in English, but then the Old Norse were used to shining storm-laden skies. Like Glenrothes Peated Reserve, Glansa is aged in ex-bourbon barrels and then finished in barrels that previously held peated whisky.

AGE
No age statement

ALC/VOL
40%

NOSE
A restrained nose featuring red apples, cardboard, lavender, pencil shavings, and tropical fruits; water opens it up, with beeswax, maple, cardboard, and lemon curd.

PALATE
Thin on the tongue, and a bit smoky up front; eventually, candy shell, smoked chocolate, and putty emerge. Water brings out ash, turpentine, and beeswax. The finish is long and ashy, with a touch of sea air and a saccharine sweetness underneath.

GENERAL
A paradox: Water helps the nose, but ruins the palate. Generally, Glansa is thin and uninteresting; the hint of peat is all it has going for it.

PRICE
$$

RATING

Smokehead

INDEPENDENT BOTTLER

OWNER: IAN MACLEOD DISTILLERS

Smokehead is an unspecified single malt produced by Ian Macleod Distillers, the same company that owns Glengoyne, Tamdhu, and the soon-to-reopen Rosebank distilleries. While the company will confirm that Smokehead's source is on Islay, there's much debate about which distillery in particular. Some say it's a young Ardbeg; others Lagavulin; others go off the island and guess Talisker. But assuming that Ian Macleod is true to its word, the best bet is Caol Ila—it fits the profile, and that's by far the largest distillery on the island, with stocks to sell.

Smokehead

Produced by Ian Macleod from an undisclosed distillery. There's no age, either. The point here is the peat.

AGE

No age statement

ALC/VOL

43%

NOSE

The peat is smooth and light, with orange, match heads, leather, honey, dried wood, chocolate, and rubber; water shows ash, bacon bits, and toast.

PALATE

Thin and tannic, with generic wood and smoke notes, along with dried apples, paprika, and pipe tobacco; it gets sweeter with water, and shows more dried fruit. The finish is quick, with pepper and tobacco.

GENERAL

For a mystery product without even an age stated, the bar is going to be high. Smokehead doesn't cut it. If you like peat, it's worth trying, but don't expect much. Otherwise, there are better peated whiskies at a lower price.

PRICE

$$

RATING

Speyburn

OWNER: INVER HOUSE/INTERNATIONAL BEVERAGE COMPANY

FOUNDED: 1897

REGION: SPEYSIDE

Speyburn may not sit at the top of anyone's desert-island whisky list, but it's a solid, affordable everyday dram (according to the whisky writer Charles MacLean, it is the best-selling single malt in Finland). And even if you pass by it on the shelf, should you find yourself in Speyside, don't do the same with the distillery: Designed by the renowned distillery architect Charles Doig, it is one of the prettiest in Scotland, set amid a small glen with a towering kiln chimney and rough-stone walls on most of its buildings. (If you decide to go, call ahead, as it is open by appointment only.)

Speyburn Bradan Orach

Scots Gaelic for "golden salmon," Bradan Orach is aged in ex-bourbon barrels.

AGE
No age statement

ALC/VOL
40%

NOSE
Honey, pear, vanilla custard, Pop Rocks, pancake batter, dead flowers; water brings out perfume, acetone, and bananas.

PALATE
Pears, honey, grassy; the finish is short and slightly bitter.

GENERAL
You won't find many single malts at a cheaper price. But for a little bit more, you can find several better ones.

PRICE
$

RATING
NR

Speyburn
Aged 10 Years

Aged in a combination of ex-bourbon and ex-sherry casks.

AGE
10
years old

ALC/VOL
43%

NOSE

Red apples, dried herbs, light honey, Turkish delight, fresh-cut strawberries; water intensifies the honey and brings out more fruit.

PALATE

Honey, fino sherry, and vanilla pudding, building to an astringent, cinnamon spiciness; the finish is short, spicy, and dry.

GENERAL

There's a lot going on in the nose, but the palate doesn't quite deliver. Still, for its price, this is a solid spirit.

PRICE
$

RATING
★★

Speyburn
Arranta

Aged exclusively in first-fill ex-bourbon casks for an unstated period of time. The name is inspired by the Scots Gaelic word for "intrepid."

AGE
No age statement

ALC/VOL
46%

NOSE

Cinnamon, pepper, sawn wood, drawn butter, honey, a bit of citrus, candy shell, and kissed mint; water calls forth pear, soap, ginger, and a slight nuttiness.

PALATE

Floral, a bit smoky, with tropical fruit, pear, and spicy strawberries; with water, it gets soapy, woody, and a bit astringent. The finish is spicy, woody, and bitter.

GENERAL

Like the 10 Year Old, the nose is more impressive than the palate, which is both bourbon-like and quite soapy, especially with water.

PRICE
$

RATING
★★

Speyburn
Aged 15 Years

Aged in American and Spanish oak casks.

AGE

15
years old

ALC/VOL

46%

NOSE

Rich with dried fruits, mushrooms, cake batter, overripe apples, orange rind, and butter; water brightens it with citrus and candy.

GENERAL

A a unique, affordable fifteen year old, with a lush texture and layers of flavor. Well worth the clams.

PALATE

An oily, medium-to-thick mouthfeel, with notes of lemon, orange, coffee, umami, and spicy dark cocoa; water elicits spiced cake and floral notes. The finish is slightly spicy, with pops of fruit and chocolate.

PRICE

$$

RATING

Speyside

OWNER: HARVEY'S OF EDINBURGH

FOUNDED: 1962

REGION: SPEYSIDE

Speyside was built by an ex–Royal Navy officer named George Christie in 1962, but production didn't commence until 1990. After Christie died in 2011, it was sold to Harvey's of Edinburgh. The bulk of the distillery's output—which, at about half a million liters a year, is not all that much—goes to Taiwan.

Speyside
Aged 12 Years

Known simply as "Spey" in Asia, Speyside 12 Year Old is a conventional, even anodyne, whisky.

AGE
12
years old

ALC/VOL
43%

NOSE

Barley, burnt sugar, popcorn, red apple, acetone, wood, orange peel; water brings out bready, citrus notes.

GENERAL

There's some round, lush Highland aromas on the nose, but the palate is disappointingly one-note.

PALATE

Some oil and funk up front, followed by bubblegum, dried fruit, and spices; it sweetens with water. The finish is quick and dry.

PRICE

$

RATING

Springbank

OWNER: J. & A. MITCHELL & COMPANY

FOUNDED: 1828

REGION: CAMPBELTOWN

Springbank was founded in 1828 by a smuggler and moonshiner named William Reid. His tenuous relationship with the law made it difficult to run a legal distillery, and so in 1837 he sold it to his in-laws, the Mitchell family, who have owned it ever since, making Springbank one of just a handful of family-owned distilleries in Scotland. Though it has a capacity of 750,000 liters a year, Springbank produces a wide variety of expressions under three brand names: the unpeated Hazelburn, the lightly peated Springbank, and the heavily peated Longrow (see Hazelburn and Longrow reviews under their own entries). Springbank is the only original Campbeltown distillery still in operation; Hazelburn and Longrow are named for defunct distilleries, but are no longer made at their respective namesakes—the original Hazelburn is now used as warehousing; Longrow was demolished, and its site is now the Springbank parking lot. Like Mortlach, Springbank is semi-triple-distilled, with a portion of the distillate making a pit stop at an intermediate still before proceeding to the spirit still (Hazelburn, however, goes through a true triple-distillation).

Springbank
Aged 10 Years

Aged in a combination of ex-bourbon and ex-sherry casks. The classic Springbank, a combination of fire and earthiness, what Iain Banks called "a real surf and turf whisky."

AGE
10
years old

ALC/VOL
46%

NOSE

Fruity and waxy, redolent of spicy pears, sweet smoke, sweet mustard, and salt air; water calls forth orange marmalade, wood smoke, moss, and vanilla.

PALATE

A thick mouthfeel with peat reek, grilled pork, orange extract, and salt water; a few drops of water dries it out a bit and adds citrus zest to the mix. The finish is briny and peppery—think smoked fish–flavored Pop Rocks.

GENERAL

Astoundingly supple and complex for a ten year old, but it would be a winner against many single malts twice its age. Recommended as a peated whisky for people who don't like peat.

PRICE
$$

RATING

Springbank
Cask Strength

Springbank's 12 Year Old is always bottled at cask strength, but the proof levels vary from batch to batch.

AGE
12
years old

ALC/VOL
56.3%

NOSE

Honey, ashtray, burnt rubber, wax, grilled chicken, and raisins; with water you'll find match heads and a richer meat note, like grilled pork.

PALATE

A thick and oily mouthfeel, with an ashy, meaty minerality that blends well with high notes of orange candy, caramel, and sweet char; hot pepper develops at the mid-palate. Water amps up the pepper. The finish is long, sweet, and smoky—think grilled orange slices.

GENERAL

An Olympian whisky at a mortal's price. Deep, dark, robust, but without the burn you'd expect from such a high proof. It develops in the glass, especially with water.

PRICE
$$

RATING

Springbank Green

AGE
13
years old

ALC/VOL
46%

Made with organic barley—hence the "Green" in the name—and aged in sherry butts.

NOSE
Sweet peat, grilled seafood, seaweed, honey-glazed meat, salt, and a slight minerality; water tones down the peat and brings out salty crackers.

PALATE
Medium, with notes of green vegetables, sweet smoke, and grilled fruit; water calls forth ginger, chocolate, and tobacco. The finish is slightly dry, crispy, and minty.

GENERAL
Pricy, but worth it. It's a peated whisky for non-peat lovers. At ten years old, it's a surprisingly mature and complex spirit.

PRICE
$$$

RATING

Springbank Aged 15 Years

AGE
15
years old

ALC/VOL
46%

Like the 10 Year Old, this is aged in a combination of ex-bourbon and ex-sherry barrels.

NOSE
Vanilla, green apple candy, scrambled eggs, seaweed, and a beach fire; it opens significantly with water, exhibiting lemon zest and a slight but clear funk.

PALATE
Oily and creamy, with almond paste, ash, spicy peppers, and grilled shrimp; the sherry peeks out a bit with water. The finish lingers with smoke, heather, shellfish, and vanilla.

GENERAL
Unlike the 10 Year Old, the 15 shows very little sherry influence. It's drier and earthier than its younger sibling, too.

PRICE
$$$

RATING

Springbank
Aged 18 Years

Aged primarily in ex-sherry hogsheads.

AGE
18
years old

ALC/VOL
46%

NOSE

Briny and kelpy, like a fish tank, with caramel, wood ash, barbecue sauce, and French herbs; maple syrup, raspberry jam, and a meaty umami note emerge with water.

PALATE

Medium mouthfeel, with sweet chocolate and cherries up front, followed by spice and smoked oysters at the mid-palate; water underlines the spice. The finish is dry, spicy, and just a bit sweet.

GENERAL

What the ironborn of the *Game of Thrones* series would drink—herbal, sweet, balanced, and, above all, brawny.

PRICE

$$$

RATING

Stronachie

INDEPENDENT BOTTLER

OWNER: A.D. RATTRAY

PRONUNCIATION: *STRUN-ah-key*

Stronachie is a single malt produced at the Benrinnes distillery but owned and marketed by A.D. Rattray, a prominent independent bottler. The whisky takes its name from the Stronachie distillery, which was shuttered in 1928.

Stronachie
10 Years Old

Despite the *Man for All Seasons*, retro English label, this is a relatively new expression, introduced by A.D. Rattray in 2014. Aged in ex-bourbon and ex-sherry casks.

AGE
10 years old

ALC/VOL
43%

NOSE

Linseed oil, pencil shavings, pancake syrup, cocoa powder, and shaved wood; water brings out candy sugar and cedar.

PALATE

A thin mouthfeel; sweet, minty, creamy, cinnamon. The finish is brief and spicy, redolent of hot pepper, leather, and toasted nuts.

GENERAL

A terrible nose; the palate is more inviting, but still unimpressive.

PRICE
$

RATING

Stronachie
Aged 12 Years

Not significantly different from the 10 Year Old, except for the obvious two years.

AGE
12
years old

ALC/VOL
43%

NOSE

Honey, linseed oil, beeswax, dried fruit, malt, biscuits, and heather; water makes it sweeter and a bit woodsy.

GENERAL

A standard Speyside, but over-priced.

PALATE

Thin-bodied, with orange peel, honey, oak, and an onslaught of pepper at the mid-palate; water brings out soy sauce, spice cake, and an earthy must. The finish is short, save for a tingle of lingering heat.

PRICE

$$

RATING

Stronachie
18 Years Old

Big brother to the 12 Year Old.

AGE
18
years old

ALC/VOL
46%

NOSE

Fresh coconut, banana bread, slightly herbal; it really opens up with water, to show sweet crackers, black tea, and smoked fish.

GENERAL

A big step up from the 12 Year Old. A bit too sweet, but not unmanageable.

PALATE

A medium, slightly oily mouthfeel, with overripe pear, dried fruit, and savory notes of meat and mushrooms; water brings out candied ginger and soap. It dries quickly, with a bit of strawberry sweetness.

PRICE

$$$

RATING

Talisker

OWNER: DIAGEO
FOUNDED: 1830
REGION: HIGHLANDS

Though Talisker is a lovely whisky, it has a not-so-lovely origin story. Its founders, Hugh and Kenneth McAskill, were clearance landlords, meaning they used recently passed laws to evict small tenant farmers from their land. In search of new sources of revenue, they founded the Talisker distillery in 1830 (naturally, they also raised sheep). Though it is only moderately peated (25 ppm), Talisker is known for its campfire-and-seaweed character, thanks to its complex distillation process—it features very tall wash stills and a purifier pipe, but also worm tubs that reduce the spirit's contact with copper. Until 1928 it was triple-distilled, and until 1972 the distillery malted its own barley. It was a favorite of Robert Louis Stevenson, among many, many others over the years.

Talisker
Distillers Edition

Akin to the Distillers Edition from Oban—another Diageo distillery—this Talisker is the standard ten year old, aged in ex-bourbon casks, then finished for a few more months in amoroso sherry casks.

AGE
10
years old

ALC/VOL
45.8%

NOSE

Toast, salt air, dried pipe tobacco, roast chicken, citrus, vanilla, honey, and a bit of sherry; water just dilutes it.

GENERAL

A brilliant marriage of restrained peat and sherry notes. The nose is deep and luscious; it's almost a shame to have to drink it.

PALATE

A peaty backbone, with vanilla, honeycomb, fruit juice, and a bubblegum-sweet mid-palate; the finish dries on the tongue, with chili flakes and campfire.

PRICE
$$

RATING

Talisker
Storm

Diageo unveiled this whisky in 2013 to rave reviews, winning *Whisky Advocate*'s Highland/Islands single malt of the year. To achieve its "darker" profile, the whisky is aged in a combination of ex-bourbon and "rejuvenated" casks, in which the insides have been scraped and recharred.

AGE
No age statement

ALC/VOL
45.8%

NOSE
Sweet smoke, sausage, stewed cherries, a slight salinity, the eggy creaminess of vanilla crème brûlée; water brings out a bit of bright berries.

PALATE
Light smoke, bacon, lemon, lentil stew; it's sweeter with a bit of water. Smoke lingers on the finish.

GENERAL
While the whisky has its fans, it's hard to see why one would pick the Storm over the 10 Year Old, given their similar price points.

PRICE
$$

RATING

Talisker
Aged 10 Years

AGE
10
years old

ALC/VOL
45.8%

One of the truly classic single malts, yet very much cut from its own cloth. The 10 Year Old is an introduction to the Talisker range, but make sure to stop and enjoy it before pressing on to older expressions.

NOSE
Campfire, roasted meat, barbecue chips, paprika, sweat, citrus, potting soil, mushrooms, rye bread, and chlorine; water elicits sherry and cherry notes.

PALATE
Taco meat, popcorn, sweet cinnamon, smoky but not overly so; water makes it sweeter. The finish is minty and musty, like menthol cigarettes.

GENERAL
A unique but all-purpose whisky; have it on a cold evening before dinner, or pair it with smoked seafood during a meal. Or just kick back beside the fire afterward.

PRICE
$$

RATING

Talisker
Aged 18 Years

AGE
18
years old

ALC/VOL
45.8%

The same as the 10 Year Old—aged in ex-bourbon barrels—just with an additional eight years on it.

NOSE
Dashi broth, green bananas, grape skins, broken granite, sea air, wet rope, bonfire smoke, strawberries, and caramel; with water, you'll find barley soup, seaweed, peat, and Irish Spring soap.

PALATE
A thick mouthfeel with a big hit of strawberries and sweet bread up front, then a dash of peat, smoked meat, dill, and seaweed; water makes the smoke more assertive but the fruit notes remain. The long finish shows saltwater taffy, beef broth, chocolate, and minerality.

GENERAL
Balanced but robust, literally smack between Islay and the Highlands. There are worlds to discover in this whisky.

PRICE
$$$

RATING

Talisker
Aged 25 Years

The 25 Year Old was once only available as part of Diageo's Special Releases series, at cask strength. It's now part of the core range, and at a more manageable proof.

AGE
25
years old

ALC/VOL
45.8%

NOSE

Moss, white pepper, salty meat, cracked rocks, deli ham, cloves, toasted almonds, sweet grass, and honey; water elicits campfire smoke, cherries, dried ginger, flowers, and the incense-soaked air of an old church.

PALATE

Full-bodied and smoky, with a savory, cherry-smoke, peppery palate; water turns it drier and spicier. The long, complex finish has pencil shavings, Ritz crackers, and salt.

GENERAL

For the typical American palate, this whisky has it all—salty, savory, smoky, sweet, spicy. It is hard to imagine a better single malt than this.

PRICE
$$$$

RATING

Talisker
Aged 30 Years

AGE
30
years old

ALC/VOL
45.8%

Like the 25 Year Old, the 30 used to be part of Diageo's Special Releases series, released at cask strength, but is now in the core range (albeit in limited quantities).

NOSE

Sharp and musty, with root beer, honeysuckle, pears, incense, cigar ash, and turmeric; water adds maple syrup, leather, ginger, and jerky.

GENERAL

Less sweet and less smoky than the 25 Year Old, and slightly less interesting—though still an amazing expression. Between the two I'll take the 25, but I won't argue against the 30 either.

PALATE

Smoked meat, menthol, and a deep fruitiness at the mid-palate; water adds orange peel, tea, and a bit of ash and dried ginger. The medium-length finish has cocoa and more smoked meat, along with ash and black pepper.

PRICE

$$$$

RATING

Tamdhu

OWNER: IAN MACLEOD DISTILLERS

FOUNDED: 1897

REGION: SPEYSIDE

PRONUNCIATION: *TAM-doo*

Tamdhu was founded at the height of the Victorian whisky boom, with all the care and precision that came with a mature industry gaining mastery of its means of production—Barnard called it "perhaps the best designed and most efficient of its era." Not surprisingly, Tamdhu suffered the swings of twentieth-century whisky production, mostly recently sitting unused from 2010 to 2012. Though Edrington Group sold it to Ian Macleod in 2011, Tamdhu continues to supply whisky for Edrington's Famous Grouse blend.

Tamdhu
Aged 10 Years

AGE
10
years old

Aged in American and European ex-sherry casks, a "high proportion" of them first fill. Most of this expression goes into Famous Grouse, J&B, and Cutty Sark.

ALC/VOL
43%

NOSE
Rich sherry notes up front, with vanilla cream, raisin bread, toffee, nutmeg, and chocolate-covered cherries; water brings out roses.

PALATE
Orange peel, vanilla, chocolate fudge, and dried apricots; it develops a slight smokiness at the mid-palate and dries out toward the finish, which bounces between tannic and minty notes.

GENERAL
A solid, everyday sherried malt, and a surprisingly complex ten year old—proof that age isn't everything. Compare it with the GlenDronach 12 Year Old.

PRICE
$$

RATING

Tamdhu
Batch Strength BATCH NO. 001

Aged exclusively in ex-sherry casks and bottled without an age statement. The distillery releases the expression in numbered batches. The Batch No. 1 was *Whisky Advocate*'s "Speyside of the Year" in 2015.

AGE
No age statement

ALC/VOL
58.5%

NOSE
Slightly burnt toast, roasted peanuts, vegetable oil, raisin cookies, and a box of chocolates.

PALATE
Seesaws between sweet and spicy—baked banana, honey, malt, and orange juice play against ginger powder, orange zest, and black tea, which lingers on the finish.

GENERAL
Redolent and thick with sherry, but it's smooth enough to drink neat, even at this high a proof.

PRICE
$$

RATING
★ ★
★

Tobermory

OWNER: DISTELL

FOUNDED: 1798

REGION: ISLANDS

PRONUNCIATION: *TOE-burr-murray*

Tobermory, located on the island of Mull, was founded as Ledaig in 1798 by John Sinclair, a kelp merchant—a fact that the distillery honors today by making an aggressively peated range of expressions called Ledaig (see Ledaig reviews under its own entry on page 223). The stills at Tobermory have boil bulbs and S-shaped lyne arms, and the fermentations are on the short, reasonable side. In 2017, the distillery announced a two-year closure for renovations. Its visitor center remains open and sells Tobermory 10 Year Old and various Ledaig expressions; Tobermory 15 Year Old, however, has been unavailable since 2016.

Tobermory
Aged 10 Years

Sadly discontinued in 2017, at least temporarily, but still widely available, and for sale at Tobermory's visitor center. Aged in ex-bourbon casks, with a slight peat influence from the water, not the malting.

AGE

10
years old

ALC/VOL

46.3%

NOSE

Nutty, putty, waxy, mineral, graham cracker, oatmeal, cardboard, rubber sheet; mushrooms, tapioca, strawberries, and mint come out with water.

GENERAL

Lovely—complex and layered, balanced, and structured.

PALATE

A medium mouthfeel with sweet grain up front, unfolding with cherries and hot chocolate, then moving into saltwater taffy and ginger notes; there's a berry and musty sweetness that emerges with water. The finish is spicy, with peppercorns and more ginger.

PRICE

$$

RATING

Tobermory
Batch Strength NO. 1

Like the 10 Year Old, but aged fourteen years
in ex-bourbon casks and then another year in
ex–González Byass oloroso sherry casks.
Discontinued in 2016.

AGE
15
years old

ALC/VOL
46.3%

NOSE

Wood smoke, caramel, raisin
bread, blanched almonds, black
cherry gum, and a slight maritime
note; water elicits menthol, cedar
shavings, and red-wine barrels.

GENERAL

Very woody, slightly peaty, with a
good dollop of sherry notes—a
splendidly balanced combination.
Have it in place of dessert.

PALATE

Thick and sweet—almonds,
raisins, dried fruit, ginger,
and an oak astringency; it
rounds out with a drop of
water, showing dark
chocolate and figs. The finish
is long and spicy, with a
slight fruity minerality.

PRICE
$$$

RATING
★ ★
★ ⭒

Tomatin

OWNER: TAKARA SHUZO

FOUNDED: 1897

REGION: HIGHLANDS

PRONUNCIATION: *Toe-MAH-tin*

At one time Tomatin was the largest distillery in Scotland, with an impressive twenty-three stills up until the early 1970s. Now it is down to twelve, but it still produces a respectable 5 million liters a year. It was the first distillery to be bought by a Japanese firm, in 1986. The whisky has always been popular with blenders, and it is only in recent years that a wide range of official single malts have hit the market. Following the trend of peated Speysiders, Tomatin released Cù Bòcan in 2013.

Tomatin Dualchas

Aged in a combination of ex-bourbon and virgin oak casks. Pronounced *DOOL-kass*.

AGE
No age statement

ALC/VOL
43%

NOSE
Lemon tea, pineapple, vanilla, red apples, and Italian herbs; water merely mutes it.

PALATE
Vanilla, a bit of woodiness, nutmeg, pineapple, lemon, pine; water thins it out significantly, but adds a floral note. The finish is dry, sharp, and slightly smoky.

GENERAL
A solid dram for the price, and more interesting than you'd expect. It wears the American oak influence on its sleeve, and is more complex and interesting for it.

PRICE

RATING

Tomatin
Aged 12 Years

AGE
12
years old

ALC/VOL
43%

Previously bottled at a disappointing 80 proof, this whisky, partially aged in sherry casks, got a big bump up in proof and quality with its 2010 relaunch.

NOSE

Buttered popcorn, white raisins, pineapple, and candied apple, but not much sherry to speak of, even after adding water.

PALATE

Here's the sherry: coconut, toffee, figs, cherries, malt, and dried apricots; water amplifies the sherry and fruit notes. The finish is quick and dry.

GENERAL

Superficial, but well priced, and with some decent fruit action. Just don't expect a lot of sherry.

PRICE
$

RATING
★ ★

Tomatin
Aged 14 Years

AGE
14
years old

ALC/VOL
46%

This whisky spends 13 years in ex-bourbon barrels, and then about a year in tawny port pipes.

NOSE

Butyric funk, mushrooms, black-berry jam, vanilla, caramel chews, maple syrup, and chewing gum; it calms down with water, bringing out red wine and baking spices.

PALATE

Chewy, woody, and foresty; there's sweet heat up front, then the heat dies down and milk chocolate and cherry bubblegum take over. Water makes it sweeter—chewing gum, caramel, and white wine. The finish is long and hot.

GENERAL

The initial funk on the nose clears up after a few minutes, letting the chocolate and berry notes shine through.

PRICE
$$

RATING
★ ✦

Tomatin
Aged 15 Years

Exclusively matured in ex-bourbon casks, a rarity for Tomatin.

AGE
15
years old

ALC/VOL
43%

NOSE

Green apple candy, Anjou pear, vanilla bean, Nerds, and toasted wood; it pops with water, evoking herbs, pencil shavings, figs, and grain.

GENERAL

Delicious. So much going on, and worth exploring at length. Just a year older than the 14 Year Old, but a mile above in quality.

PALATE

Thick and juicy, with dark fruit candy, oak, and a bit of clover honey; it mellows with water, which brings out bubblegum and sweet malt. The finish leaves a lingering sweetness and a touch of spicy pepper.

PRICE
$$

RATING

Tomatin
Aged 18 Years

Aged in ex-bourbon barrels, then finished in oloroso sherry casks.

AGE
18
years old

ALC/VOL
46%

NOSE

Ginger, cola, candied lemon, raisins, cloves, sweet smoke, and hay; water adds orange zest.

GENERAL

A bit heavy on the sherry, but still a right tasty dram. Don't add water.

PALATE

Sweet sherry up front, then cinnamon sugar, rum raisins, prunes, and dried apricots; the finish is dry, with lingering pepper and sherry notes.

PRICE
$$

RATING

Tomatin
Cù Bòcan

AGE
No age statement

ALC/VOL
46%

According to local lore, a spectral hound called Cù Bòcan has wandered the woods surrounding the village of Tomatin for centuries. It's only fitting that the name of a hellhound should grace the distillery's peated release, which is made for one week a year and aged in a mix of first-fill ex-bourbon, ex-sherry, and virgin oak casks.

NOSE

Estery and floral, with toasted seeds, apple brandy, banana pudding, Juicy Fruit, and a meaty smokiness; water opens it up with baking spices, watermelon candy, leather, and bacon, and, over time, chocolate, butter, and vanilla.

GENERAL

A nice, moderately smoky alternative to Speyside, without getting all Islay.

PALATE

Spicy, sweet, and a bit chewy up front, with slight smoke, giving way to spearmint, wood chips, vanilla, and tangerine; it thins out with water, revealing ginger, berries, juniper, and smoldering fire. The finish is long and quite tannic.

PRICE

$$

RATING

★★
★

Tomintoul

OWNER: ANGUS DUNDEE DISTILLERS

FOUNDED: 1965

REGION: SPEYSIDE

PRONUNCIATION: *TOM-in-tool*

Tomintoul was part of the wave of high-volume, no-fuss distilleries built during the postwar decades; today it cranks out 3.4 million liters a year. It was founded by a joint venture between two whisky brokers, who were later bought out by the Scottish and Universal Investment Trust in 1973; five years later that trust was bought by, of all things, the London and Rhodesia Mining and Land Company. Eventually it landed in the hands of the blender Angus Dundee, which also owns Glencadam.

Tomintoul Aged 10 Years

Aged in ex-bourbon barrels.

AGE
10
years old

ALC/VOL
40%

NOSE

Fragrant orange, dry sherry, lemon polish, amaretto, vanilla, unbaked yeast rolls, and grass; water brings out dried leaves, mildewed hay, and almonds.

GENERAL

Inoffensive and gentle, per its nickname. Surprisingly robust for an 80-proof ten year old, and better than most of its older siblings.

PALATE

Cherry pie up front, with a medium mouthfeel, building to a black-pepper heat and oak bitterness; water brings out red apple, biscuit dough, and mint. The finish dries quickly, but the heat lingers.

PRICE
$

RATING

Tomintoul
Aged 12 Years

The same as the 10 Year Old, with two extra years spent in ex-oloroso sherry barrels.

AGE
12
years old

ALC/VOL
40%

NOSE

Fruit basket—oranges, cherries, and tangerines; there's a lipstick waxiness, a sherry sweetness, and a celery zestiness. Water adds a bit of funk, with grappa and orange drink.

GENERAL

A step up from the 10 Year Old—deeper, more flavorful—but still uninspiring.

PALATE

A syrupy mouthfeel, with celery, cherries, grilled pineapple, vanilla, and oak. It's sweet up front, growing astringent toward the middle; water brings out semisweet chocolate, gentle flower notes, bitter herbs, and Robitussin. The finish is quick, with hot pepper, mint, and a tinge of fruit.

PRICE

$$

RATING

Tomintoul
Aged 14 Years

Same as the 10 Year Old, with four more years in ex-bourbon barrels, and without coloring added or chill filtering.

AGE
14
years old

ALC/VOL
46%

NOSE

Pastry crust, amaretto, marzipan, leather, and pear juice; water turns it less sweet, with oak bitterness, celery, white wine, and a slight savory note.

GENERAL

Despite the added age and higher proof, the 14 Year Old pales against the 10 and 12 Year Olds.

PALATE

A big sweet note up front—pineapple juice and vanilla—then astringency, heat, and Pop-Rock spiciness; water kills it, reducing it to a general sweetness. The finish is short, dry, thin, and brittle.

PRICE

$$

RATING

Tomintoul
Aged 16 Years

Aged in ex-bourbon barrels.

AGE
16
years old

ALC/VOL
40%

NOSE

Apples, cherries, roasted nuts, dried bananas, and malt; water reveals potato chips, mangos, and custard.

GENERAL

Light, fresh, and bland.

PALATE

On the thin side of medium-bodied, with coffee candy, dried coconut, orange peel, crème brûlée, and black pepper; it turns creamy with a few drops of water, showing honey, vanilla, pear skins, and a soft hint of tobacco. The finish is drying, with honeycomb and apple skins.

PRICE

$$

RATING

Tomintoul
With a Peaty Tang

A lower-proof replacement for Tomintoul's Old Ballantruan peated single malt brand. It's a marriage between four- to five-year-old peated whisky with eight-year-old unpeated whisky, to produce a "peaty tang."

AGE
No age
statement

ALC/VOL
43%

NOSE

Burnt herbs, bacon, old rubber shoe soles, ash, heather, vinegar, and anchovies; water ruins it, reducing its nuances to a vague heather and herbal note.

GENERAL

The nose promises a standard but substantial peated whisky, but the palate is beyond disappointing—generically smoky, with no character or depth.

PALATE

Thin and generically peaty; it has an herbal sweetness on the front, then rubber, unsweetened chocolate, and charred oak chips; as with other Tomintouls, water ruins it. The finish is short, ashy, and slightly bitter.

PRICE

$

RATING

Tomintoul
Old Ballantruan

AGE
10
years old

ALC/VOL
50%

Though it's hard to know from the label, Old Ballantruan is produced by Tomintoul as the distillery's foray into peat. It was recently replaced by the more obviously branded "Tomintoul With a Peaty Tang" expression, though the latter comes in at a lower proof. If you can find Old Ballantruan, grab it.

NOSE

Barbecue sauce, apple cider vinegar, cinnamon, dried apricots, old attic, and Cherry Swisher sweets; with water you'll find citrus zest, burnt sugar, and graham crackers—think s'mores.

PALATE

Thick lapsang souchong tea, barbecue sauce, and sweet tobacco, all of which are amplified with a few drops of water; the long finish is ashy, minty, and slightly dry.

GENERAL

Surprisingly smoky for a peated Speyside; it's a bit sweet, but it would make an excellent, if pricey, mixer.

PRICE
$$

RATING

Tormore

OWNER: CHIVAS BROTHERS/PERNOD RICARD

FOUNDED: 1958

REGION: SPEYSIDE

Tormore is widely considered to be the most beautiful distillery in Scotland, complete with fountains, lawns, and topiaries. It was designed by Sir Albert Richardson, who also built the Manchester Opera House. And yet inside it is very much a practical postwar facility, efficiently producing up to 3.7 million liters of whisky a year.

Tormore
Aged 12 Years

A down-the-line Speyside usually found in blends, but available occasionally in this official bottling, aged in ex-bourbon barrels.

AGE
12
years old

ALC/VOL
40%

NOSE
Freshly cut melon, pressed apples, licorice, grass, and buttered toast; water makes it darker and richer, less sweet, and a bit meaty. There's cookie dough and dried fruit.

GENERAL
A gentle, boring palate, but not unpleasant; it would benefit significantly from a bump in proof.

PALATE
A thin-to-medium mouthfeel, with fruit up front and an umami meatiness at the back, with a whiff of peat smoke wafting through. Not surprisingly, water kills it. The finish is medium in length, with a grapefruit citrus note.

PRICE
$

RATING

Trader Joe's

PRIVATE LABEL

OWNER: ALEXANDER MURRAY & CO

For the rock-bottom price, Trader Joe's single malt is quite good. Alexander Murray & Company has supplied it since 2004, though neither the supermarket chain nor the intermediary will reveal the source of the whisky itself.

Trader Joe's Highland

AGE
10
years old

ALC/VOL
40%

NOSE

Clover honey, hay, almonds, cherry juice, and Werther's Originals; water amps up the hay notes and adds touches of black pepper and powdered sugar.

GENERAL

Decent for the price—and the secret provenance. Like many budget whiskies, though, the nose overpromises, and it's downhill from there. Cocktail-friendly.

PALATE

Dry and thin, with solvent, salt, a bit of heat, white raisins, honey, and floral notes; water turns it a bit rubbery, but sweeter. The long finish has white pepper, herbs, and cardboard.

PRICE

$

RATING

Tullibardine

OWNER: PICARD VINS & SPIRITUEUX

FOUNDED: 1949

REGION: HIGHLANDS

PRONUNCIATION: *Tull-ih-BAR-deen*

Though beer and spirits have been produced on the site since at least 1488, when James IV stopped there to buy ale, the modern Tullibardine distillery was only opened in 1949—the first to be built in Scotland since the Victorian-era whisky bubble popped in 1899. It stood silent from 1994 to 2003, and in 2011 it was bought by the French company Picard Vins & Spiritueux. Like Glen Moray, also owned by a French firm, Tullibardine's Gallic connections have led to an emphasis on wine-barrel finishes (Picard also owns the Burgundian winery Chassagne-Montrachet). Practically adjacent to Tullibardine is Gleneagles, one of Scotland's most famous hotels and a renowned set of world-class golf courses.

Tullibardine Sovereign

A non-age-statement single malt aged in first-fill ex-bourbon barrels.

AGE
No age statement

ALC/VOL
43%

NOSE
Intensely floral—lilacs, mostly—with banana Runts, grape must, and rubber cement; water makes it sweeter and richer, with a hint of strawberries.

PALATE
A thin mouthfeel, and quite grain-forward, with vanilla, taffy, and corn pudding; adding water just kills it. The finish is medium in length, dry, and somewhat salty.

GENERAL
Astringent, woody, and in the end, rather bland.

PRICE
$

RATING

Tullibardine 228 Burgundy Finish

AGE
No age statement

ALC/VOL
43%

Aged in first-fill ex-bourbon barrels, and then for an extra twelve months in 228-liter ex-Burgundy casks from Château de Chassagne-Montrachet, which is owned by the same company that owns Tullibardine.

NOSE
A bit weak on the nose, but there's maple toast, lemon peel, butter, peppery honey, nuts, and strawberry syrup; it turns a bit musty with water (there's salted caramel in there as well).

PALATE
A thin mouthfeel that starts off sweet and grows spicier; overall, it's bit jammy, with toasted vanilla, chocolate, and orange. With water you'll find maple butter and black pepper. The toasted vanilla lingers on the finish.

GENERAL
As with many of Tullibardine's wine-finished expressions, the nose and palate are promising at the very beginning, but fall apart quickly. Still, this is the best of the bunch.

PRICE
$$

RATING

Tullibardine 225 Sauternes Finish

AGE
No age statement

ALC/VOL
43%

Named for the number of liters in a traditional Sauternes cask, this expression starts in first-fill ex-bourbon barrels and is then finished in Sauternes casks from Château Suduiraut.

NOSE
Indistinct, but there's diluted grape Kool-Aid, pine resin, and honeysuckle; water elicits honey barbecue sauce.

PALATE
Candy-sweet up front, giving way to creamy, grainy notes; water doesn't alter much. The medium-length finish is sweet and peppery, then a bit drying.

GENERAL
An unimpressive attempt to give a Continental gloss to an average whisky. Nothing about it expresses "Sauternes."

PRICE
$$

RATING

Tullibardine 500 Sherry Finish

After spending time in first-fill ex-bourbon casks, it's finished for 12 months in 500-liter Pedro Ximénez sherry butts.

AGE
No age statement

ALC/VOL
43%

NOSE
Waxy, toasted coconut, acetone, white pepper, raisins, and honeycomb; water evokes vanilla and cedar.

GENERAL
Promising up front, but it falls apart completely. Superficially interesting, but there's nothing there.

PALATE
A thin mouthfeel with nuts and stewed fruits up front, followed by vanilla cream, mouthwash, and an oak astringency. The astringency follows to the finish, where there's a bit of sweet and spicy nuts.

PRICE
$$

RATING

Tullibardine The Murray

A twelve-year-old, cask-strength expression, aged exclusively in first-fill ex-bourbon barrels, this whisky is named after the second Marquess of Tullibardine, William Murray, who joined the Jacobite Rising and fought in the Battle of Sheriffmuir, not far from the present-day distillery, in 1715.

AGE
No age statement

ALC/VOL
56.1%

NOSE
Cedar chest, fresh hay, lemon cookies, vanilla frosting; a drop of water really brings out the oak and vanilla.

GENERAL
There's a lot going on here, and without water it tastes a bit unbalanced. A few drops brings it into line, though.

PALATE
Opens with sweet notes of vanilla, lemon icing, artificial citrus, Flintstones vitamins, and new-make spirit; water makes it more floral and richer, with notes of sweet cherries. The finish is surprisingly smooth, with just a slight bite at the end.

PRICE
$$

RATING

Tullibardine
Aged 20 Years

Aged in first-fill ex-bourbon barrels.

AGE
20
years old

ALC/VOL
43%

NOSE

Chocolate powder, roasted meat, sweet smoke, dark fruits, oatmeal cookies, and a clear, but not over-powering, oak presence. Water really opens it up, with intense floral, grape, honey, and extra-aged bourbon notes.

PALATE

Floral, maple syrup, and apricots, with a spicy mid-palate that water tones down significantly; the finish is long, reverberating with sweet and sour notes.

GENERAL

A superb whisky that tastes more expensive than it is. There's nothing surprising about it; it's simply a beautifully rendered, honey-sweet Highland single malt.

PRICE
$$$

RATING

Tullibardine
Aged 25 Years

Aged in ex-sherry hogsheads.

AGE
25
years old

ALC/VOL
43%

NOSE

A puff of rye-like herbaceousness, followed by dark honey glaze, grilled meat, toasted coconut, and orange zest; water and time bring out a whiff of sherry and smoke.

PALATE

A thick mouthfeel, redolent with honey, malt, meat rub, dried apricots, and dried coconuts; water brings out a bit of smoke and bananas. The long, malty finish is a bit tannic.

GENERAL

A big improvement on the already-solid 20 Year Old, this whisky demonstrates what a few years and a different barrel program will do to the same distillate. The palate is big and bold, with strong similarities to Clynelish and Arran.

PRICE
$$$$

RATING

Wolfburn

OWNER: AURORA BREWING

FOUNDED: 2013

REGION: HIGHLANDS

One of the youngest distilleries in Scotland, but one that already has a sizable international following. It is also one of the smallest in terms of production, at just 115,000 liters per year, and it is the most northern distillery on the Scottish mainland. The current distillery stands on the site of an older distillery, which operated from 1821 to 1837 but was more or less obliterated in the intervening years.

Wolfburn Northland

AGE
No age statement

Aged for three years in ex-Islay quarter casks, made from American and Spanish oak.

ALC/VOL
46%

NOSE
Pears, lemon zest, limestone, rubber, cookie dough, chamomile tea, nuts, and new-make spirit; water elicits strong notes of burnt sugar and fruit.

PALATE
A medium mouthfeel, with vanilla cream, lightly smoky, light brown sugar, peach syrup, and flowers; water makes it slightly smokier and spicier, like smoked paprika. The finish is minty and refreshing.

GENERAL
A rich, complex whisky for such a young expression. Fresh and clean—this would make a wonderful summer drink. Definitely a distillery to watch.

PRICE
$$

RATING

Wolfburn Aurora

Like the Northland, but with a twist: Here just 40 percent of the barrels are ex-Islay quarter casks; the rest are 40-percent first-fill ex-bourbon barrels and 20-percent first-fill ex–oloroso sherry hogsheads.

AGE
No age statement

ALC/VOL
46%

NOSE
Intense honey, sweet potato, sherry, uncooked dough, and floral notes; water elicits spiced apples, roses, and ripe bananas.

PALATE
A big, round mouthfeel, with buttercream, honey, baking spices, and a bit of grain; water adds a ginger note. The finish tastes like cinnamon candy, with an echo of grain.

GENERAL
Very much like a sherried Speyside—elegantly, richly sweet, but not cloying. Perfect for after a light summer meal.

PRICE
$$

RATING
★★★

Acknowledgments

Clay Risen

It's convention to thank one's family last. I'll thank them first: Joanna, Talia, and Elliot, you were a font of humor, wisdom, and above all patience through the course of writing this book, whenever I needed it, and even when I didn't.

George Scott of Scott & Nix, Inc. was, as always, my drinking buddy and brain trust.

The many publicists, distillers, merchants, marketers, retailers, bartenders, and bar owners who helped out along the way are too numerous to thank individually, but you know who you are. I hope you know that without your help, this book would not exist.

No one did more to make this book a reality, though, than the people who made up the tasting panel. The book may have my name on it, but it is built on your ideas, arguments, and friendship.

Scott & Nix, Inc.

Many thanks go to the publishing group at Quercus, including Nathaniel Marunas, Amelia Iuvino, Amanda Harkness, Elyse Gregov, and Michelle Morgan.

We thank Susannah Skiver Barton for a careful read of the manuscript.

We thank Nathan Sayers for his beautiful photographs.

We thank the local and far-flung merchants who helped us acquire bottles, including Lakshmi Massand of Manor House Cellar and Michael Dolega of BQE Wine & Liquors in Brooklyn.

Many thanks to the distilleries and their representatives who sent sample bottles to our offices for review.

We thank the many people from novice to expert who shared good cheer with us and whose impressions contributed to the whisky accounts of the book. The following pages profile the core group of our tasting panel that met in our offices every week to sample and combine our collective brains to try and tease out the nuance that makes malt whisky from Scotland such a beautiful thing.

Most of all we thank Clay Risen for his wit, words, and extraordinary work ethic.

We welcome comments, questions, and suggestions for other whiskies to include in future editions of this guide. Feel free to email us at whisky@scottandnix.com.

Susannah Skiver Barton began her whisky journey at the University of Edinburgh, where she was a member of the Water of Life Society. She's currently senior whisky specialist and digital editor at *Whisky Advocate* magazine, where she writes frequently about the subject and regularly tastes whiskies from around the world.

Elizabeth Emmons fell in love with whisky upon her first sip of Laphroaig fourteen years ago and has since had an avid interest in the history and craft of the spirit. Elizabeth is a contributing writer to the online whisky magazine "The Whiskey Reviewer," and is an active member of various whisky and spirit tasting groups and judging panels in New York City.

Josh Feldman is a well-regarded whisky blogger known for detailed historical essays at "The Coopered Tot" (www. cooperedtot.com). A fixture in the New York whisky scene, Josh leads tasting events and presents about whisky history. He works and has also led events at The Morgan Library, where he is network administrator.

Kurt Maitland started his whisky journey with drams of Jameson in college and has been exploring the wider world of whisky/whiskey ever since. He currently is the deputy editor of the popular "Whiskey Reviewer" website and the curator of the Manhattan Whiskey Club.

Pradeep Massand is the owner of Valley Stream Wine & Liquor. After a full career in information technology, Pradeep shifted gears to devote all his efforts to become an expert in wine and fine distilled spirits.

Reid Mitenbuler is the author of *Bourbon Empire: The Past and Future of America's Whiskey*. He has written about spirits for *The Atlantic, Whisky Advocate, The Daily Beast,* and *Slate,* among other publications.

Pitchaya Sudbanthad lives and writes in Brooklyn and Bangkok. His debut novel is forthcoming from Riverhead Books.

Liza Weisstuch is the senior editor at Lonely Planet's "Budget Travel" and an American contributing editor to *Whisky Magazine.* Her work has appeared in the *New York Times,* the *Washington Post,* the *Boston Globe,* and msn.com. She has developed her well-rounded spirits education by visiting more than seventy-five distilleries in thirteen countries.

Recommended References and Resources

Herewith a partial selection of books and other resources I consulted in the writing of this book. I can recommend them all for more information regarding the fascinating history and culture of single malt. Naturally, there are scores of excellent websites devoted to the interest and enjoyment of whisky and other drinks. Listed below are the ones I follow closely, along with several magazines covering the world of whisky.

Banks, Iain. *Raw Spirit: In Search of the Perfect Dram.* London: Century, 2003.

Barnard, Alfred. *A Visit to Watson's Dundee Whisky Stores.* London: Sir J. Causton & Sons, 1891. (facsimile Aaron Barker, 2016)

Barnard, Alfred. *The Whisky Distilleries of the United Kingdom.* New York: A. M. Kelley, 1969. Reprint of 1887 edition.

Daiches, David. *Scotch Whisky: Its Past and Present.* London: Andre Deutsch, 1969.

Glenlivet Distillery. *The Glenlivet: The Father of All Scotch.* Aberdeen: Aberdeen University Press, 1989.

Gunn, Neil M. *Whisky and Scotland.* London: George Routledge and Sons. 1935.

Jackson, Michael. *Michael Jackson's Complete Guide to Single Malt Scotch, 7th ed.* New York: DK, 2015. Updated by Dominic Roskrow and Gavin D. Smith.

Jefford, Andrew. *Peat Smoke and Spirit: A Portrait of Islay and Its Whiskies.* London: Headline Publishing, 2004.

MacDonald, Aeneas. *Whisky.* Edinburgh: The Porpoise Press, 1930. Reprinted 2006.

McDowall, R.J.S. *The Whiskies of Scotland.* London: John Murray, 1967.

Offringa, Hans. *The Road to Craigellachie Revisited: A Journey of Discovery Through the World of Scotch Whisky With an Occasional Detour to Some Other Interesting Places.* PLACATK: Conceptual Continuity, 2012.

Paterson, Richard and Gavin D. Smith. *Goodness Nose: The Passionate Revelations of a Scotch Whisky Master Blender.* Glasgow: Neil Wilson, 2010.

Ronde, Ingvar. *Malt Whisky Yearbook, 2016 and 2017.* Shrewsbury: MagDig Media Ltd.

Saintsbury, George. *Notes on a Cellar-Book.* London: Macmillan & Co Ltd, 1920. Reprinted 2008 by University of California Press, ed. by Thomas Pinney.

Stirk, David. *The Distilleries of Campbeltown: The Rise and Fall of the Whisky Capital of the World.* Castle Douglas: Neil Wilson, 2005.

Townsend, Brian. *Scotch Missed: Scotland's Lost Distilleries.* Castle Douglas: Neil Wilson, 2004.

Weir, R.B. *The History of the Distillers Company: 1877-1939.* Oxford: Oxford University Press, 1995.

Wilson, Ross. *Scotch: The Formative Years.* London: Constable, 1970.

Websites

The Coopered Tot | cooperedtot.com
Josh Feldman covers all things whisky, with a keen eye for history.

Drink Hacker | drinkhacker.com
Not exclusively whisky, but the authors know their single malts.

Drink Spirits | drinkspirits.com
Like drinkhacker.com, not exclusive to whisky, but there are lots of news and reviews of brown spirits to be found here.

K&L Spirits Journal | spiritsjournal.klwines.com
> The official blog of California retailer K&L Wine Merchants.

L.A. Whisk(e)y Society | lawhiskeysociety.com
> A curated collection of reviews and news about the world of whisk(e)y.

Malt Madness | maltmadness.com
> Johannes van den Heuvel's vast and impressive online repository of singe malt history, maps, reviews, and more. Although currently dormant, many years of excellent info is still available.

Malt Maniacs | maltmaniacs.net
> An international consortium of whisky lovers posting all things whisky. Mostly active now at its Facebook group page, "Malt Maniacs & Friends."

Sku's Recent Eats | recenteats.blogspot.com
> Despite the name, Steve Ury's site is chock-full of thoughtful information about whisky.

Whisky.com | whisky.com
> A voluminous site based in Germany devoted to whisk(e)y of all kinds.

Periodicals

Unfiltered, The Magazine of the Scotch Malt Whisky Society.
> The Scotch Malt Whisky Society, Edinburgh, Scotland.

Whisky Advocate. M. Shanken Communications, New York, New York.

Whisky Magazine. Paragraph Publishing Limited, Norwich, Great Britain.

Glossary of Terms

BARREL: In the context of scotch, usually a standard American ex-bourbon barrel, which holds 53 gallons, or about 200 liters.

BUTT: The standard size for a sherry cask, which holds 132 gallons, or about 500 liters. Sherry butts are usually made of American oak.

CASK: The generic term for a wooden container, typically rounded, with flat ends, that is used to age whisky.

CASK STRENGTH: Literally, the strength of a whisky when it comes out of a cask as measured by the amount of alcohol by volume. Typically, a whisky labeled "cask strength" has been slightly adjusted with water to maintain consistency across a batch. Nevertheless, the term connotes a high alcohol by volume.

CONGENER: The generic term for the parts of a distillate other than water and ethanol, usually present in trace amounts. Spirit stills are used partly to separate out the desirable congeners from the undesirable ones.

DUNNAGE HOUSE: A large, low warehouse, typically with earth floors and stone walls, used to age whisky.

FINISH: After a whisky has been aged, a distiller may choose to "finish" it in a cask that previously held wine, beer, or other spirits to impart some of those liquids' qualities to the whisky.

HOGSHEAD: A cask holding 66 gallons, or 250 liters. Hogsheads are typically rebuilt standard American barrels, with added staves and heads to increase their size.

KILN: A type of furnace used to dry barley after it has begun to germinate. Kilns traditionally used peat for fuel, though today it is usually natural gas.

MALT: Barley that has been allowed to begin germinating, but is then dried over a heat source to stop it from sprouting. The malting process allows a barley seed to produce the enzymes needed to convert the seed's starch into sugar.

MASH: A combination of grain and hot water produced in a mash tun, the result of which is a sugar-rich liquid called wort.

MASH TUN: The vessel in which mash is produced. These days, it is usually made of stainless steel.

PEAT: Semi-decomposed plant matter, which can be cut into bricks and burned for fuel. Peat is found worldwide, but in Scotland it is prized, as it was traditionally used to dry barley that has begun to sprout. Today peat is unnecessary, but still used frequently because it imparts a pungent, smoky aroma and flavor to a whisky.

PIPE: A cask used to age port, it's rounder and squatter than a sherry butt, though they hold the same volume of liquid—132 gallons, or 500 liters.

PROOF: In the United States, proof is an alternative measure of a beverage's alcohol by volume, defined as two times the A.B.V. (A 100-proof whisky is 50 percent alcohol.) In Britain, 100 proof is traditionally defined as the alcohol content necessary to allow gunpowder to burn when it is doused in the liquid—namely, 57 percent. So 100 proof in British terms is equivalent to 114 proof in American terms. These days, though, Britain simply lists the A.B.V. on the bottle.

QUARTER CASK: A barrel that holds 21 gallons, or 80 liters.

RACKHOUSE (OR RICKHOUSE): Uncommon in Scotland, a rackhouse is a multistory facility used to age whisky.

SHERRY: A variety of fortified wines produced in the Jerez region of Spain. Sherries range from dry and crisp to thick and sweet. Sherry was immensely popular in nineteenth-century Britain, and the constant flow of Sherry shipping casks provided whisky distillers with a ready source of containers for aging—though over time sherry casks became especially prized for the influence residual sherry soaked into the wood had on the whisky. As the sherry industry declined, distillers began to "rent" sherry—essentially subsidizing the industry—in order to keep up its supply of sherry casks.

STILL (WASH, SPIRIT): There are two types of stills. A pot still is, essentially, a pot with a conical top, out of which runs a metal pipe. The whisky wort is added in batches and then cooked; the alcohol, some water, and trace amounts of congeners boil off and are collected once they cool down. A continuous still, also known as a Coffey, patent, or column still, is a column with a heat source at the bottom and a metal pipe at the top; as the wort is introduced at the mid-level, it drops to the bottom to be vaporized, and what rises to the top is captured in a manner similar to a pot still. The advantage is that the still can be used constantly, hence the name. Typically, a distillery will have two or three stills per set—the "wash" still, to strip most of the water and unwanted elements off, and one or two "spirit" stills, to refine and fine-tune the spirit.

WASH: Essentially, unhopped beer. Wash is the result of adding yeast to wort; the yeast eat the sugar in the wort, producing alcohol. Once the yeast have died off, the wash can be distilled.

WASHBACK: A vessel, traditionally made of Oregon pine but these days more often made of stainless steel, in which wort and yeast are combined to produce a wash.

WORT: The sugar-rich liquid produced from a mash, to which yeast is added to produce alcohol.

Risen's Top Whiskies

Taste is subjective, and it would be a fool's errand to suggest that one could rank the whiskies in this book with anything approaching objectivity. Still, some whiskies are better than others, and a few truly stand out. Below are my favorites, listed in alphabetical order and broken down into seven somewhat overlapping categories (and the pages where they appear in the guide).

Top Overall Whiskies

Balvenie Aged 30 Years	97
Craigellachie Aged 23 Years	130
Glengoyne Aged 25 Years	67
Glenmorangie Signet	181
Springbank Aged 18 Years	264

Top Value Whiskies

Aberfeldy 12 Years in Oak	62
Deanston Virgin Oak	136
Finlaggan Old Reserve	143
Glen Moray Sherry Cask Finish	184
Speyburn Aged 15 Years	259

Top Peated Whiskies

Bruichladdich Octomore 7.4	118
Lagavulin Aged 16 Years	214
Laphroaig Aged 25 Years	222
Port Askaig 110 Proof	248
Talisker Aged 25 Years	271

Top Gift Whiskies

Top Introductory Scotches

Top Scotch for Scotch Lovers

Top Prestige Whiskies

Single Malt Checklist

This alphabetical listing with page numbers includes all the whiskies covered in this guide. The checklist is by no means a complete accounting of single malt expressions. Feel free to give us your suggestions for what might be included in future editions via email to whisky@scottandnix.com.

☐ Laphroaig Aged 25 Years	222	
☐ Laphroaig Cairdeas 2016	220	
☐ Laphroaig Cask Strength	218	
☐ Laphroaig Lore	221	
☐ Laphroaig QA Cask	217	
☐ Laphroaig Quarter Cask	219	
☐ Laphroaig Select	217	
☐ Laphroaig Triple Wood	219	
☐ Ledaig Aged 10 Years	223	
☐ Ledaig Aged 18 Years	223	
☐ Ledaig Marsala Finish	224	
☐ Lismore	225	
☐ Lismore Aged 15 Years	225	
☐ Lismore Aged 18 Years	226	
☐ Lismore Aged 21 Years	226	
☐ Loch Lomond Aged 12 Years	227	
☐ Loch Lomond Aged 18 Years	228	
☐ Longmorn Aged 16 Years	229	
☐ Longrow Aged 18 Years	230	
☐ Longrow Peated	229	
☐ Macallan 12 Years Old	232	
☐ Macallan 18 Years Old	235	
☐ Macallan Classic Cut	233	
☐ Macallan Double Cask	233	
☐ Macallan Fine Oak 10	232	
☐ Macallan Fine Oak 15	234	
☐ Macallan Fine Oak 17	234	
☐ Macallan Rare Cask	235	
☐ McClelland's Highland	239	
☐ McClelland's Islay	239	
☐ McClelland's Lowland	238	
☐ McClelland's Speyside	240	
☐ Mortlach 18 Years Old	242	
☐ Mortlach 25 Years Old	243	
☐ Mortlach Rare Old	241	
☐ Muirhead's Silver Seal	244	
☐ Oban Aged 14 Years	245	
☐ Oban Aged 18 Years	247	
☐ Oban Distillers Edition	246	
☐ Oban Little Bay	246	
☐ Old Pulteney Aged 12 Years	249	
☐ Old Pulteney Aged 17 Years	250	
☐ Old Pulteney Aged 21 Years	251	
☐ Old Pulteney Aged 35 Years	251	
☐ Old Pulteney Navigator	250	
☐ Port Askaig 110 Proof	248	

☐ Royal Brackla Aged 12 Years	252
☐ Royal Brackla Aged 16 Years	253
☐ Scapa Glansa	255
☐ Scapa Skiren	254
☐ Singleton 12 Years Old	149
☐ Singleton 15 Years Old	150
☐ Singleton 18 Years Old	150
☐ Smokehead	256
☐ Speyburn Aged 10 Years	258
☐ Speyburn Aged 15 Years	259
☐ Speyburn Arranta	258
☐ Speyburn Bradan Orach	257
☐ Speyside Aged 12 Years	260
☐ Springbank Aged 10 Years	262
☐ Springbank Aged 15 Years	263
☐ Springbank Aged 18 Years	264
☐ Springbank Cask Strength	262
☐ Springbank Green	263
☐ Stronachie 10 Years Old	265
☐ Stronachie 18 Years Old	266
☐ Stronachie Aged 12 Years	266
☐ Talisker Aged 10 Years	269
☐ Talisker Aged 18 Years	269
☐ Talisker Aged 25 Years	270
☐ Talisker Aged 30 Years	271
☐ Talisker Distillers Edition	267
☐ Talisker Storm	268
☐ Tamdhu Aged 10 Years	272
☐ Tamdhu Batch Strength	273
☐ Tobermory Aged 10 Years	274
☐ Tobermory Batch Strength	275
☐ Tomatin Aged 12 Years	277
☐ Tomatin Aged 14 Years	277
☐ Tomatin Aged 15 Years	278
☐ Tomatin Aged 18 Years	278
☐ Tomatin Cù Bòcan	279
☐ Tomatin Dualchas	276
☐ Tomintoul Aged 10 Years	280
☐ Tomintoul Aged 12 Years	281
☐ Tomintoul Aged 14 Years	281
☐ Tomintoul Aged 16 Years	282
☐ Tomintoul Old Ballantruan	283
☐ Tomintoul With a Peaty Tang	282
☐ Tormore Aged 12 Years	284
☐ Trader Joe's Highland	285

Index

Colophon

The text and heads of this book are set in *Franklin ITC Pro*, designed in 2007 by David Berlow.

All files for production were prepared on Mac computers.

The paper is 128gsm Kinmari Matt Art.

Production was managed by Michelle Morgan and Graham Green.

It was indexed by Abby Parker.

It was edited by George Scott and Amelia Iuvino.

The cover and endpapers were designed by Spencer Charles and Kelly Thorn of Charles & Thorn.